LOVE AND POWER

Love and Power

THE ROLE OF RELIGION AND MORALITY IN AMERICAN POLITICS

Michael J. Perry

NEW YORK OXFORD
OXFORD UNIVERSITY PRESS

Oxford University Press

Oxford   New York   Toronto
Dehli   Bombay   Calcutta   Madras   Karachi
Kuala Lumpur   Singapore   Hong Kong   Tokyo
Nairobi   Dar es Salaam   Cape Town
Melbourne   Auckland   Madrid

and associated companies in
Berlin   Ibadan

Library of Congress Cataloging-in-Publication Data
Perry, Michael J.
Love and power : the role of religion and morality in
American politics / Michael J. Perry.
p.   cm. Includes index.
ISBN 0-19-506860-2
ISBN 0-19-508355-5 PBK
1. Political ethics—United States.
2. Pluralism (social sciences)—United States.   I. Title.
JK468.E7P47   1991
172'.0973—dc20   90-26259

9 8 7 6 5 4 3 2 1

Printed in the United States of America
on acid-free paper.

On November 16, 1989, in San Salvador, El Salvador,
six Jesuit priests, their cook, and her daughter were slaughtered:

IGNACIO ELLACURÍA
JOAQUÍN LÓPEZ Y LÓPEZ
AMANDO LÓPEZ
IGNACIO MARTÍN-BARO
SEGUNDO MONTES
JUAN RAMÓN MORENO
JULIA ELBA RAMOS
CELINA RAMOS

This book is for them,
and for countless others less known
and honored, who remind us with their lives and
with their deaths what it can mean
to bring religion to bear on politics.

Acknowledgments

I am grateful to several colleagues for their helpful comments on earlier versions of this book: Milner Ball, Lisa Bergeron, Ted Blumoff, James Burtchael, James Childs, Jr., Ruth Colker, Dan Conkle, George Dent, Dan Farber, Tony Fejfar, Fred Gedicks, David Gregory, Emily Fowler Hartigan, Linda Hirshman, Bill LaPiana, Jane Larson, Robin Lovin, Xavier Monasterio, Richard Sherwin, Rod Smith, Steve Smith, David Smolin, Athornia Steele, Nadine Strossen, and Howard Vogel. I am also grateful for helpful discussions of parts of the book in connection with faculty workshops at the University of Minnesota School of Law (November 1989), the University of Colorado School of Law (December 1989), and the New York Law School (February 1990); a lecture at St. John's University, sponsored by the Department of Government and the School of Law (April 1990); the twelfth annual John E. Sullivan Lecture, Capital University School of Law (October 1990); and the third annual Symposium on Law, Religion, and Ethics, Hamline University School of Law (October 1990).

I am especially grateful to Kent Greenawalt, not only for his helpful comments on an earlier version of this book, but also for his own excellent book on religion and politics, *Religious Convictions and Political Choice* (1988), which was a principal occasion of my writing *Love and Power*. I am also very grateful to George Yamin, who served as my research assistant and principal critic during the summer of 1990, when I was completing the book.

I am ever grateful for the richly supportive environment of the

Northwestern University School of Law, where it has been my privilege to teach since 1982. Early work on this book was supported by the Stanford Clinton Sr. Research Professorship.

This book was conceived before Daniel was conceived; it was begun a few months before he was born; and it was finished a few months into his second year. It seems fitting that a book partly about love came to fruition as I was learning so much about love from Daniel—and from his mother, my dear wife, Sarah O'Leary.

Contents

LOVE AND POWER

Politics that does not contain theology within itself, however little considered, may often be shrewd but remains in the end no more than a business.

Theodor W. Adorno and Max Horkheimer, in
Hans Küng, *Does God Exist?*

Politics without prayer or mysticism quickly becomes grim and barbaric; prayer or mysticism without political love quickly becomes sentimental and irrelevant interiority.

Edward Schillebeeckx, *The Schillebeeckx Reader*

Introduction

This book is about the proper relation of morality to politics in a morally pluralistic society like the United States. More precisely, it is about the proper relation of a person's moral beliefs to her political choices and, especially, to her public deliberation about and her public justification of political choices. I am principally concerned here with *religious* morality—with moral beliefs religious in character—because the problem of the proper relation of religious morality to politics poses the issues I want to address about morality and politics in their most controversial and difficult form. The constructive part of my argument (as distinct from the critical part), therefore, is directed mainly at religious-moral beliefs. However, much of what I have to say about the proper relation of religious morality to politics is meant to apply not just to religious morality but to morality generally,[1] including secular morality.

I am principally concerned, too, with the proper relation of morality to politics in *American* society, not only because I live in the United States but, more important, because the problem of the proper relation of morality, especially religious morality, to politics has arisen with a special urgency in American society.[2] In the contemporary United States more, it seems, than in any other advanced industrial society, there has been "a breakdown in understanding how personal and communal beliefs should be related to public life."[3] Much of what I have to say in this book, however, is meant to apply to the problem of morality and politics as it arises in any morally/religiously pluralistic society.

3

This book begins where a previous one ended. In the conclusion to *Morality, Politics, and Law* I wrote:

> One's basic moral/religious convictions are (partly) self-constitutive and are therefore a principal ground—indeed, the principal ground—of political deliberation and choice. To "bracket" such convictions is therefore to bracket—to annihilate—essential aspects of one's very self. To participate in politics and law . . . with such convictions bracketed is not to participate as the self one is but as some one—or, rather, some thing—else.
>
> Because they are the principal ground of political deliberation and choice, one cannot—least of all in a morally pluralistic society like our own—insulate such convictions from challenge. Politics, then, in a morally pluralistic society, is in part about the credibility of competing conceptions of human good. Political theory that fails to address questions of human good—questions of how human beings, individually and collectively, should live their lives—is, finally, vacuous and irrelevant.
>
> . . . [S]uch questions cannot be bracketed, though, of course, they can be ignored or repressed. Questions of human good—and in particular the deep question of what it means to be authentically human—are too fundamental, and the answers one gives to them too determinative of one's politics, to be marginalized or privatized. . . .
>
> If one can participate in politics and law—if one can use or resist power—only as a partisan of particular moral/religious convictions about the human, and if politics is and must be in part about the credibility of such convictions, then we who want to participate, whether as theorists or activists or both, must examine our own convictions self-critically. We must be willing to let our convictions be tested in ecumenical dialogue with others who do not share them. We must let ourselves be tested, in ecumenical dialogue, by convictions we do not share. We must, in short, resist the temptations of infallibilism. . . . If necessary we must revise our convictions until they are credible to ourselves, if not always or even often to our interlocutors. We must be willing to lend credibility to our convictions by being faithful to them in our lives and not merely in our polemics and our posturing. We must bring our convictions to bear as we use or as we resist power. We must resist and seek to transform a politics that represses, by marginalizing or privatizing, questions of human authenticity.[4]

In this book, after commenting critically on some other, prominent approaches to the problem of the proper relation of morality to politics, I elaborate and defend an approach that incorporates, develops, and systematizes much of what I only sketchily suggested in those concluding passages to *Morality, Politics, and Law.*

This is the main question: What is the proper role, if any, of religious-moral discourse in the politics of a religiously and morally pluralistic society like the United States? If religious-moral discourse should not be excluded from "the public square", how should it be included: In particular, how should such discourse be brought to bear in the practice of political justification? The serious challenge, in my view, is to define a middle ground between, on the one side, the position of Kent Greenawalt and others (whose work I discuss in chapter 1) who would largely exclude religious-moral discourse from political-justificatory practice and, on the other side, the position of those who would bring religious-moral discourse to bear in a sectarian, divisive way. Must we conclude that there is, alas, no stable "middle ground"?

Love and Power is, in part, an effort to grapple with what has aptly been called "no small political problem": On the eve of a significant moment in American political history, the election of the first Catholic, John F. Kennedy, to the White House, the American Jesuit John Courtney Murray wrote:

> Pluralism . . . implies disagreement and dissension within the community. But it also implies a community within which there must be agreement and consensus. There is no small political problem here. If society is to be at all a rational process, some set of principles must motivate the participation of all religious groups, despite their dissensions, in the oneness of the community. On the other hand, these common principles must not hinder the maintenance by each group of its own different identity. The problem of pluralism is, of course, practical; as a project, its "working out" is an exercise in civic virtue. But the problem is also theoretical; its solution is an exercise in political intelligence that will lay down, as the basis for the "working out," some sort of doctrine.[5]

In *Love and Power* I "lay down" several principles "as a basis for the 'working out' "—principles to guide religious participation in the politics of a religiously/morally pluralistic society like our own.[6]

Because I use the term "pluralism" (and related terms) in more than one sense in this book, clarity might be served if I sort out the different senses here in the introduction.

- The pluralism that figures most prominently in my discussion is the pluralism to which Murray referred and which is an important feature of American society: moral, including religious-moral, pluralism. A society is morally pluralistic if there are, among the members of the society, competing beliefs or convictions about the good or fitting way for human beings—whether some human beings (for example, the members of the society) or all human beings—to live their lives. (By "conviction" I mean simply a very strong belief. I use the terms "belief" and "conviction" more or less interchangeably throughout this book.)

- Pluralism in a different sense, the pluralism that figures mainly in chapter 2 of this book, is a feature of some conceptions of human nature; indeed, it is a feature of any plausible conception of human nature. A conception of human nature is pluralist if it recognizes that whatever the nature and extent of their commonality, human beings generally differ from one another in important respects—if it recognizes, in particular, that human beings do not all have the same needs and wants—and that therefore the way of life that is good for some of them may well not be good for all of them, and may even be bad for some (others) of them. (Pluralism in a related but different sense recognizes that even for one human being there may be more than one good or fitting way of life. Just as different ways of life can be good, or bad, for different persons, different ways of life can be good for the same person.)

- Pluralism in a still different sense, the pluralism that figures in chapters 6 and 7, describes a positive understanding of moral (including religious-moral) pluralism, an understanding according to which a morally pluralistic context can often be a much more fertile source of deepening moral insight than can a morally monistic context (one in which virtually everyone adheres to more or less the same convictions about human good).

Finally, a word about the title: *Love and Power.* I hope that the point of the title will be clear at least by the end of chapter 5, in which I discuss, among other things, the essentially political nature of religion, including the political character of the Gospel commandment to "love one another". The title occurred to me several years ago, before I began to draft this book, when I read a story about John Noonan in *Newsweek*. (Before becoming a judge of the United States Court of Appeals for the Ninth Circuit, Noonan was a professor of law at the University of California at Berkeley. A prolific scholar with a special interest both in jurisprudence and in legal history, Noonan holds, in addition to a law degree, a Ph.D. in philosophy.) In the story Noonan (whose religious background, like mine, is Catholic) was quoted as saying that "[t]he central problem of the legal enterprise is the relation of love to power."[7] This book is, in part, an extended gloss on Noonan's statement.

1

Neutral Politics

The United States, like many other societies, is morally pluralistic: No one set of beliefs about how it is good or fitting for human beings to live their lives prevails in American society. (The morally pluralistic character of American society, however, unlike that of other societies, is congenital: "As it arose in America, the problem of pluralism was unique in the modern world, chiefly because pluralism was the native condition of American society. It was not, as in Europe and England, the result of a disruption or decay of a previously existent religious unity."[1]) Although some quite general beliefs about human good are widely shared in American society, many beliefs about human good are widely, deeply, and persistently disputed. That state of affairs gives rise to a fundamental inquiry about the proper relation of morality to politics: In American society (or in any similarly pluralistic society) should disputed beliefs about human good play any role in public deliberations about, or in public justifications of, contested political choices? (I develop the distinction between deliberation and justification in chapter 3.) For example, is it ever appropriate, in American society, for a citizen to (seek to) justify to fellow citizens,[2] on the basis of one or more of her beliefs about human good, a political choice she has made or supports, if some to whom she is justifying the choice do not share the beliefs? By the end of this book I will have addressed such questions at length—and with particular reference to religious beliefs about human good. In this chapter, partly to set the stage for what follows, I comment critically on several prominent arguments about the proper relation of morality to politics.[3] The thrust of the arguments, or of most of them, is that disputed beliefs (in the case of one argument, disputed *religious* beliefs) about human good should play no or at most a marginal role in political justification.

I

Bruce Ackerman has recently contended for "neutral" politics,[4] in this sense: A citizen should (seek to) justify a political choice to fellow citizens only on the basis of moral premises shared with all to whom she is justifying the choice. As Ackerman explains, "My principle of conversational restraint does not apply to the questions citizens may ask, but to the answers they may legitimately give to each others' questions: whenever one citizen is confronted by another's question, he cannot suppress the questioner, nor can he respond by appealing to (his understanding of) the moral truth; he must instead be prepared, in principle, to engage in a restrained dialogic effort to locate normative premises both sides find reasonable."[5]

A basic problem with Ackerman's shared-premises restraint on political justification is that in a society as morally pluralistic as the United States, there may often be no relevant normative premises shared among those engaged in political argument. Ackerman is not unmindful of the problem: "I have not . . . tried to establish . . . that the path of conversational restraint will not finally lead liberals to a . . . dead end. As you and I discover that we disagree about more and more things, perhaps we will find that the exercise of conversational restraint leaves us nothing to say to one another about our basic problems of coexistence. . . . This seems especially likely since the typical Western society contains many [different moral communities]."[6] Moreover, even when relevant normative premises are shared, or come to be shared in the course of the argument, the premises, and reasoning therefrom, may often be indeterminate: They may often fall far short of resolving the argument. (Resolution of the controversy would then require one or more other premises not shared.) It seems, then, that Ackerman's version of neutral politics is often impossible.

An even deeper problem infects Ackerman's "path of conversational restraint", a problem that remains even when there are relevant, determinate shared premises. By confining justification in any political conversation to normative premises shared among the participants in the conversation, Ackerman is obviously privileging particular premises or beliefs. Justification on the basis of shared and thereby privileged beliefs is what counts. Justification on the basis of other beliefs—beliefs accepted by some but not by all the participants—is beside the point. Consider what this approach means in practice. If Ackerman and I were participants in a two-party political conversation, I suspect that the proportion of Ackerman's relevant beliefs that I would share would be larger, perhaps much larger, the the proportion of mine he would share. (My relevant beliefs—relevant to most fundamental political-moral issues—include religious convictions about human good. My guess is that Ackerman's do not.[7] I explain in chapter 5 what makes a conviction about human good "religious".) Consequently, the proportion of his relevant beliefs that would be privileged would be larger, perhaps much larger, than the proportion of mine that would be privileged. That state of affairs would leave me at a serious disadvantage. Ackerman might get to rely on all or most of his relevant beliefs, including his most important relevant beliefs, while I would get to rely on only some of my relevant beliefs, *not* including the most important ones: my religious convictions about human good. In that sense Ackerman might get to rely on much of the relevant part of his web of beliefs,[8] while I would get to rely only on strands of my web, strands approved—"shared"—by Ackerman. I fail to see what is "neutral" about such a practice of political justification,[9] even though particular arguments yielded by the practice are neutral in the special sense of presupposing the authority only of shared normative premises. (I've already explained why arguments neutral in that sense are often inconclusive.)

II

Thomas Nagel has contended for a politics—for a practice of political justification—not unlike the politics Ackerman has recommended. But whereas Ackerman's preferred term is "neutral",

Nagel's is "impartial". Nagel's effort to explicate the concept of "impartial" political justification is addressed to "the . . . issue of political legitimacy"; it is an "[attempt] to discover a way of justifying coercively imposed political and social institutions [and policies] to the people who have to live under them, and at the same time to discover what those institutions and policies must be like if such justification is to be possible."[10] Nagel's point of departure, then, is the problem of the legitimacy of political coercion; a condition of such legitimacy, in Nagel's view, is satisfaction of "an especially stringent requirement of objectivity in justification."[11] For Nagel, political justification satisfies this requirement if it is "impartial".

What is Nagel's conception or interpretation of "impartial" political justification?[12] Nagel posits "a highest-order framework of moral reasoning . . . which takes us outside ourselves to a standpoint that is independent of who we are. It cannot derive its basic premises from aspects of our particular and contingent starting points within the world. . . ."[13] "[T]he epistemological standpoint of morality", insofar as political justification is concerned, must be "impersonal".[14] For Nagel, then, "impartial" political justification is "impersonal" justification: justification "from a standpoint that is independent of who we are", "from a more impersonal standpoint".[15] But trading in "impartial" for "impersonal" doesn't get us very far, as Nagel recognizes: "The real difficulty is to make sense of this idea [impartial/impersonal justification]. . . . When can I regard the grounds for a belief as objective in a way that permits me to appeal to it in political argument, and to rely on it even though others do not in fact accept it and even though they may not be unreasonable not to accept it? What kinds of grounds must those be, if I am not to be guilty of appealing simply to my belief, rather than to a common ground of justification?"[16] Nagel's answer is in the form of a specification of the conditions political justification must satisfy if it is to be "impartial" (and, in that sense, "objective"). According to Nagel's specification there are two requirements, two epistemological criteria, that "public justification in a context of actual disagreement" must satisfy. Nagel's first requirement governs one's offer of justificatory reasons, while his second requirement governs one's rejection of such reasons offered by others. The heart of the requirements, taken together, is that in political-justificatory discourse one should neither offer nor reject reasons except on the basis of what Nagel calls "the exercise of a common critical rationality" and of "consideration of evidence that can be shared".[17]

Is the practice of impartial political justification, as Nagel conceives it, truly impartial? What is "evidence that can be shared"? Falsifiable empirical claims? Anything else? One's experience that an activity—drug use, for example—is destructive of the drug user's well-being (not to mention the well-being of others—family members, for example—affected by the drug user's addiction)? Such experience can be personal/direct—I may be or have been a drug user—but it can also be vicarious/indirect—my spouse may be or have been a drug user, or I may have read a novel, or seen a movie, about drug use.[18] Does a community's experience (comprising many individual's experiences, some of which are personal, some of which are vicarious) that an activity—say, homosexual sex—can be constitutive of well-being count as "evidence that can be shared"? The experience of an historically extended community—of a "tradition"—that a particular way of life is truly human? Consider, in that regard, James Burtchaell's comment that "[t]he Catholic tradition embraces a long effort to uncover the truth about human behavior and experience. Our judgments of good and evil focus on whether a certain course of action will make a human being grow and mature and flourish, or whether it will make a person withered, estranged and indifferent. In making our evaluations, we have little to draw on except our own and our forebears' experience, and whatever wisdom we can wring from our debate with others."[19] If it rules out reliance on such experience, Nagel's "evidence that can be shared" requirement is implausibly restrictive. Indeed, Joseph Raz has argued that the requirement "is so stringent that it rules out reliance on common everyday observations of fact, as well as much scientific knowlege. We often rely on sense perception and on memory as important reasons for our beliefs. Similarly we rely on our situation (right next to the accident, in the bright light of day, and so on) as reasons to trust our sense perceptions or our memories."[20]

Let's put aside problems with Nagel's implausibly restrictive "evidence that can be shared" requirement, because more troubling ones await. What does Nagel mean by "the exercise of a common critical rationality"?[21] As I explain in chapter 4, the implicit basic test for determining what beliefs or claims it makes sense for a person to accept or to reject (or neither to accept nor to reject)—what beliefs or claims it is "rational" or "reasonable" for her to accept or reject (or neither)—is coherence with whatever else she happens to believe, coherence with beliefs currently authoritative for her. Confining political justification to "the exercise of a common critical rationality" seems to mean, then, in effect, confining it to reasons or premises that cohere with, that can be supported on the basis of, whatever beliefs are universally or almost universally—"commonly"—accepted, accepted by all or almost all persons in our morally pluralistic society. If, as it certainly seems, that is what Nagel's rationality requirement finally comes to, then, in effect, Nagel has followed Ackerman's strategy of imposing something very like a shared-premises requirement on political justification.[22]

Notice, however, that in Ackerman's hands the shared-premises restraint encounters an insurmountable difficulty it does not encounter in Nagel's hands. Ackerman, unlike Nagel, does not begin with a presumption against political coercion. Nor does he begin with a presumption for it. A decision not to pursue a coercive political strategy must be justified no less than a decision to pursue the strategy.[23] The fact that there may be no neutral justification for pursuing a coercive strategy does not mean that those against the strategy prevail, because there may be no neutral justification for not pursuing the strategy. For Ackerman, then, the fact that there are often no relevant shared premises among interlocutors, or that the shared premises are often indeterminate, entails that there is often no neutral resolution of political conflict. Unlike Ackerman, Nagel begins with a presumption against political coercion. A decision not to pursue a coercive strategy need not be justified. Thus, for Nagel the fact that there may be no relevant shared premises, or that the shared premises may be indeterminate, does not entail irresolution: If there is no impartial justification for pursuing a coercive strategy, those against the strategy prevail.[24]

However, Nagel's point of departure—his presumption against political coercion—is deeply problematic: It is, in effect, a question-begging presumption in favor of the social and economic status quo, where political coercion is a way of reforming the status quo; where political coercion is a way of maintaining the status quo, it is a question-begging presumption against the social and economic status quo. Either way, Nagel's point of departure is not impartial.[25] Ackerman's point of departure, by contrast, is neutral as to political coercion, but because it is neutral, his shared-premises requirement encounters an insurmountable difficulty. Nagel's shared-premises restraint avoids the difficulty, but only because Nagel embraces a presumption, against political coercion, that is clearly not impartial. The politics partly constituted by the presumption is therefore not impartial. If Nagel were to correct his position by letting go his embrace of the presumption, he would then encounter the same difficulty Ackerman encounters: There would often be no impartial resolution of political conflict. Nagel's impartial politics, like Ackerman's neutral politics, would often be impossible.

But there is an even more basic problem with Nagel's approach, a problem that would remain even if Nagel did not embrace the presumption against political coercion, and even when there are relevant, determinate shared premises. It is a problem that, as I indicated earlier, infects Ackerman's approach as well, and my criticism of Ackerman's approach can be adapted to Nagel, whose approach is similar. By confining political justification to "the exercise of a common critical rationality," Nagel is simply privileging particular beliefs: beliefs accepted by all, or almost all, persons in our pluralistic society. Coherence with privileged (shared) beliefs is to be the sole touchstone of rational acceptability, insofar as political justification is concerned. Coherence with other beliefs— beliefs accepted by some but not by all persons in our society—is beside the point. I suspect that the proportion of Nagel's moral (including political-moral) beliefs that are privileged under his approach is much larger than the proportion of mine that are privileged. (For example, whereas I have what Nagel calls "personal religious convictions", apparently Nagel does not.[26] My "personal religious convictions" are not privileged.[27]) That state of affairs leaves me and many others at a serious disadvantage vis-à-vis Nagel and other devoutly secular intellectuals. In many political arguments Nagel might get to rely on all or most of his relevant beliefs, including his most important relevant beliefs, while I would get to rely on only some of my relevant beliefs, *not* including the most important ones: my religious convictions about human good. Nagel might get to rely on much of the relevant part of his web of beliefs, while others of us would get to rely on only strands of our webs, strands that are rationally acceptable in terms of, that cohere with, privileged beliefs. Therefore, just as Ackerman's practice of "neutral" political justification is, in the end, not neutral, Nagel's practice of "impartial" political justification is not impartial,[28] even though particular arguments yielded by the practice are impartial in the special sense of presupposing the authority only of widely accepted beliefs.

The only truly neutral/impartial practice of political justification is one that lets everyone rely on her relevant convictions. (Such a practice, however, does not often yield particular arguments that are neutral/impartial; it yields, instead, arguments that presuppose the authority of disputed convictions.) As my discussion of Ackerman's and Nagel's positions indicates, a practice of political justification that tolerates only neutral/impartial arguments is not itself neutral/impartial. The practice of political justification (and political deliberation) I elaborate and defend later in this book, like the practices defended by Ackerman and Nagel, is not neutral/impartial. As I later explain, a truly neutral/impartial practice of political justification is inappropriate in American society: Not every kind of reliance on every kind of conviction is appropriate in a liberal society as pluralistic as the United States. But unlike Ackerman's and Nagel's practices, the dialogic practice I defend (in chapters 3 and 6) does not exclude all but neutral/impartial arguments. A practice that includes only neutral/impartial arguments is, as Ackerman's and Nagel's practices illustrate, impossibly restrictive (unless, like Nagel's practice, it is wedded to a question-begging presumption against political coercion; even then, Nagel's "evidence that can be shared" requirement is implausibly restrictive). The practice I defend includes some, but not all, arguments that are not neutral/impartial; for example, it excludes arguments that fail the standards of public intelligibility and public accessibility I discuss in chapter 6. (The practice I defend includes any political argument a secular liberal like Ackerman or Nagel would probably want to make, though their practices seem to exclude some arguments I would want to make. The particular way in which

Ackerman's and Nagel's justificatory practices are partial, rather than neutral/impartial, is just what one might have expected, given Nagel's and Ackerman's earnestly skeptical attitudes toward religious sensibilities and convictions.[29]) In particular, the practice I defend makes room for some (but not all) kinds of reliance on some (but not all) kinds of disputed convictions.

III

In *Religious Convictions and Political Choice* Kent Greenawalt challenges what he sees as a principal liberal dogma: the claim that it is illiberal—illegitimate in terms of liberal premises—for citizens (and for the public officials who represent them) to rely on their religious convictions in making political choices. The bulk of Greenawalt's book is devoted to contending that often such reliance— reliance in *making* political choices as distinct from reliance in *justifying* them—is not only not inconsistent with what Greenawalt calls "the [liberal] premises that underlie our political institutions"[30] but even necessary. (As I later explain, Greenawalt's basic position on the crucial issue of political justification has an affinity with Ackerman's and Nagel's positions.) In Greenawalt's view these liberal premises "[include] indirect democratic governance, extensive individual liberty, separation of governmental and religious institutions, nonsponsorship of religion by government, and secular purposes for laws."[31]

Greenawalt's basic argument, which in my view is demonstrative, is twofold. First, he establishes that shared premises and reasoning from shared premises substantially underdetermine resolution of many major political conflicts: for example, conflicts over abortion, environmental protection, and animal rights. Resolution of such conflicts requires premises, and often reasoning from premises, not shared. A citizen can often answer for herself many controversial political questions, if at all, only on the basis of deep personal convictions that are not shared across the society (and that cannot be "proven" on the basis of premises that are shared). Second, Greenawalt argues persuasively that it would not make sense, indeed would be unfair, insofar as making political choices is concerned, to proscribe reliance on personal moral convictions, and on reasoning therefrom, if the convictions are religious in character while permitting reliance if the convictions are secular (nonreligious).[32]

Curiously, Greenawalt's basic argument is addressed to a claim that, because few contemporary liberal theorists advance it, is relatively marginal: the claim that citizens should not rely on convictions of a certain sort or sorts in making political choices. Ackerman, Nagel, and John Rawls (whose position I consider in the next section of this chapter), for example, do not even address the question whether such reliance is legitimate, much less argue that it is not. Their principal concern is not the bases on which citizens may rely in *making* political choices but the bases on which citizens may and should rely in *justifying* political choices. Given that there is often more than one path to a political choice—for example, a path that involves reliance on religious convictions and a path that does not[33]—Ackerman and others do not suggest that it is illegitimate for a citizen to take one or another path. (It is quite natural for a religious citizen to take a religious path, after all, especially if she cannot easily maneuver the available nonreligious path, given the religious convictions she carries.) Though it *is* an implication of Ackerman's and Nagel's positions that no political choice should be made, on a religious or any other basis, that cannot be supported by the requisite neutral/impartial political justification, their principal concern is the justification of political choices, not the making of them. Greenawalt acknowledges that the position that political justification be neutral/impartial, *not* the position "that people purge, or try strenuously to purge, [religious] elements from their own political judgments[,] . . . might be offered . . . as what a sympathetic reading of liberal theorists like Rawls and Ackerman would suggest."[34]

In any event, when Greenawalt finally gets past the relatively marginal issue of reliance on religious premises in making political choices to the central issue of reliance in justifying political choices, the general position he espouses has a substantial affinity with the positions of Ackerman and others—as Greenawalt explicitly acknowledges.[35] Indeed, in arguing that the role of religious-moral convictions in political-justificatory discourse should be more circumscribed than that of secular-moral convictions,[36] Greenawalt, unlike many liberals, declines to put all conceptions of human good, religious as well as secular, on the same par: Unlike Ackerman, Nagel, and Rawls, for example, Greenawalt disfavors religious convictions.[37] Greenawalt's general position on the issue of political justification is that the practice he variously calls "public justifications for political positions",[38] "open public discussion",[39] "fully public political discussion",[40] and "fully public discourse advocating political positions",[41] should not involve reliance on religious premises or on reasoning therefrom. For example:

> When a citizen writes a letter to a newspaper, [he should not] try to persuade on the grounds of religious arguments. . . . The government of a liberal society knows no religious truth and a crucial premise about a liberal society is that citizens of extremely diverse religious views can build principles of political order and social justice that do not depend on particular religious beliefs. The common currency of political discourse is nonreligious argument about human welfare. Public discourse about political issues with those who do not share religious premises should be cast in other than religious terms.[42]

Greenawalt's position is not a strategic one. His point is not the obvious (and obviously correct) one that making religious arguments in public can often be ineffective, even counterproductive and perhaps divisive. (If strategy is the issue, in deciding whether to make a religious argument one must be sensitive to all contextual/ situational particularities. What might work in Lynchburg, Virginia, after all, may well backfire in Cambridge, Massachusetts.) Greenawalt's position is normative in character. (The position is contextual, not universalist: a position for contemporary American society and, implicitly, for any similarly pluralistic society.) His basic point is that (questions of strategy aside) making religious arguments, invoking religious premises, in the course of articulating "public justifications for political positions" is generally inappropriate: "The liberal ground rules for public political dialogue are more constraining than the principles relevant to how private citizens make political choices, and religious convictions should figure much less prominently in public justifications for political positions than they may in the development of the positions themselves."[43]

I am skeptical that there are such "liberal ground rules". But even if there are, why should we abide them? Why should we take them seriously?[44] As Greenawalt asks: "Why should it matter [for purposes of political justification] if religious premises are shared?"[45] Greenawalt's answer is that resort to religious premises in political justification "promotes a sense of separation between the speaker and those who do not share his religious convictions and is likely to produce both religious and political divisiveness."[46] That answer may well explain a strategic decision to forsake religious argument, or some types of religious argument, in some contexts, but it hardly bears the weight of Greenawalt's general normative position. After all, preventing "a sense of separation between the speaker and those who do not share his religious convictions" is not invariably the only or supreme value to be secured. More fundamentally, although some kinds of public resort to some kinds of religious premises are certainly problematic in a morally and religiously pluralistic society like the United States, not every kind of public resort to every kind of religious premise has the alienating effect Greenawalt fears, much less produces either religious or political divisiveness. Later in this book I address the important question what kinds of public resort to what kinds of religious premises are appropriate to political-justificatory discourse in American society.

I now want to raise four questions (or sets of questions) about Greenawalt's position on political justification and thereby suggest four difficulties with the position.

First. How is the distinction between personal moral convictions that are secular in character and those that are religious to be administered if, as I later suggest, the relevant "religious" convictions—religious beliefs about human good—are, like many "secular" convictions, fundamentally about what it means to be "truly, fully human",[47] and if such religious convictions are not even necessarily theistic in character?[48] Buddhism is, in the main, nontheistic. Are Buddhist convictions "religious" or "secular"?

Second. Greenawalt spends the better part of his book trying to persuade us—and, in my view, succeeding in the effort—that many fundamental political controversies cannot be resolved on the basis either of shared premises or of reasoning from shared premises. "[S]hared principles of justice, shared methods of assessing values, and shared ways of determining facts", writes Greenawalt in a recent essay, "will often prove inconclusive."[49] In the same essay Greenawalt comes close to suggesting that when "shared principles of justice" and so forth *do* prove inconclusive, we simply forgo "public justifications for political positions". I say "comes close to suggesting". What he actually suggests is that "public advocacy be conducted in the nonreligious language of shared premises and modes of reasoning."[50] But that suggestion is the functional equivalent of the suggestion that we forgo "public advocacy" of our positions on matters like abortion: Greenawalt had just finished telling us, with respect to political controversies over matters like abortion, that "shared premises and modes of reasoning" are often inconclusive; why, then, should we accept something that seems implicit in, if not presupposed by, Greenawalt's suggestion that "public advocacy be conducted in the nonreligious language of shared premises and modes of reasoning", namely, that such premises/reasoning can invariably be adequate for purposes of "public advocacy"? Let us assume that Greenawalt, were he to recur to his own earlier point that such premises/reasoning "will often prove inconclusive", would acknowledge that "shared premises and modes of reasoning" cannot invariably be adequate for purposes of public adequacy. Let us assume further, then, that Greenawalt would amend his suggestion to say, as in his book he certainly seems to say, that "public justifications of political positions"—"public advocacy"—may sometimes be based on something in addition to shared premises and modes of reasoning, namely, moral premises (and reasoning based on moral premises) that are not shared—that are, in that sense, controversial—*but only if the (controversial) moral premises are secular rather than religious in character.* That suggestion, too, is deeply problematic: What if no secular justification is available to a person; for example, what if the only justification available to her, given the position she wants to defend, is based partly on moral premises religious in character; or, what if the only authentic justification available to her, the only justification that she herself really accepts, given her particular constellation of secular and religious beliefs, is based partly on (her) religious convictions? Why should one person be asked to forgo "public advocacy" of her position on the ground that her advocacy would appeal to controversial *religious* premises about human good, when another person is invited to engage in public advocacy of his position because his advocacy appeals merely to controversial *secular* premises about human good?

Third. Greenawalt argues persuasively that, the fears of some liberals to the contrary notwithstanding, there is good reason to conclude that in making political choices reliance on religious convictions is not especially divisive or otherwise problematic (for example, sectarian or dogmatic) as compared with reliance on secular convictions, even in a society as religiously pluralistic as ours.[51] He writes, for example: "Unless a society was actually hostile to religion or riven by religious strife, how could it be thought preferable for people to rely on nonreligious personal judgments rather than upon religious convictions? . . . [I]f the worry is openmindedness and sensitivity to publicly accessible reasons, drawing a sharp distinction between religious convictions and [nonreligious] personal bases [of judgment] would be an extremely crude tool."[52] Greenawalt's argument seems quite sound: Religious convictions about human good need not be defended in a publicly inaccessible way, nor are religious persons necessarily less openminded, even when their religious convictions are in question, than nonreligious persons. (I develop both points in chapter 6.) But then, doesn't Greenawalt's case in that regard lend at least some support to the claim that in *justifying* political choices, too, resort to religious convictions is not especially problematic?[53]

Fourth. Greenawalt qualifies his general position on political justification in several ways:

1. Informing or reporting to the public about a religious perspective on a political controversy is not inappropriate.[54]
2. Religiously based political advocacy by "religious leaders" is not inappropriate.[55] Indeed, "conceivably the second exception should be expanded to embrace all those who seriously conceive of themselves as having a special expertness or vocation in religious matters, whether or not they are recognized leaders among their fellows."[56]
3. Religiously based political advocacy in general circulation periodicals as an effective way of reaching an audience that shares the underlying religious premises is not inappropriate.[57]
4. Efforts to proselytize nonbelievers by developing "connections between religious premises and [appealing] political conclusions" are not inappropriate.[58]

5. Reliance on general religious premises "widely shared"—
   "premises like 'God loves us all' or 'Social justice is a duty to
   God as well as to other humans' "—is not inappropriate
   (though it may be impolitic in some contexts).[59]
6. "[R]eferences to imagery that derives from our religious heritage" are not inappropriate. "Ethical notions like the Golden
   Rule, stories from the Bible, and personal exemplars like St.
   Francis of Assisi are part of our general cultural heritage.
   These sources of understanding and appeal should not be
   extirpated from public discourse, especially since, as John
   Coleman insists, this religious tradition may provide the rich-
   est source of cultural symbols for the perspective that people
   should care deeply about each other and for the common
   welfare."[60]

Later in this book I elaborate and defend a conception of political dialogue in which reliance (of certain kinds) on religious premises (of certain kinds) can be a fitting mode of political justification (and of political deliberation) even in a society as religiously
and morally pluralistic as ours. Those chapters constitute my constructive response to Kent Greenawalt's unqualified, general position, and similar positions, on the issue of political justification
(just as this chapter constitutes my critical response). But given
the many exceptions Greenawalt allows, some of which are quite
substantial, we might fairly ask what remains of his general position. Hasn't it been "qualified" away, or at least qualified to the
point that many of us who believe that religious premises may
and even should play a role in political-justificatory discourse
have little left to quarrel with? In terms of his unqualified position on political justification, Greenawalt's position, as I said and
as Greenawalt acknowledges, has an affinity with Ackerman's
and Nagel's positions, at least to the extent of ruling out a role for
religious (though not secular) moral convictions. Greenawalt's
qualified position, however, seems a substantially different matter. The position on the proper relation of religious moralities to
political justification (and to political deliberation) for which I
contend in this book is congruent with basic features of Greenawalt's qualified position.

IV

I now want to consider relevant aspects of John Rawls' position on the central issue of political justification, which, while more promising, in my view, than the positions of Ackerman, Nagel, and Greenawalt, is still not satisfactory. Rawls' early efforts were, or at least seemed to be,[61] aimed at justifying his principles of justice in a way that did not privilege—that did not presuppose the superiority of—any conception of human good relative to any other conception. In that sense, Rawls' efforts were aimed at achieving a "Right-prior-to-Good" (RpG) justification of his principles of justice. The principles could then serve as the neutral basis for the justification/legitimation, or for the critique, of political institutions, practices, and policies. In that way political arguments could be appropriately neutral/impartial among all competing conceptions of human good.[62] The problem with Rawls' early strategy is that there are no such principles of justice, no principles that can be justified in a RpG way. At least, as I have explained in detail elsewhere, Rawls did not provide such a justification, and it is difficult to imagine a RpG justification of principles of justice.[63] Significantly, as Rawls' recent efforts illustrate, not even Rawls now thinks, if he ever did, that principles of justice can be justified in a way that does not privilege one or more conceptions of human good. That strategy for achieving a neutral politics has been discredited and abandoned.

Rawls' recent efforts differ in a crucial respect from his earlier efforts. Whereas his early efforts were aimed at achieving a RpG justification of his principles of justice, his recent efforts are aimed at explicating and achieving a justification of a different sort: in effect, a "Good-prior-to-Right" (GpR) justification, in the sense of a justification that presupposes the authority either of a certain conception or of a certain range of conceptions of human good.[64] As Joseph Raz, comparing the two kinds of justification, has explained, in a GpR justification "different ideals of the good, far from being excluded from the argument for the doctrine of justice, will form the starting points of this argument. . . . [A]s a result, supporters of different conceptions of the good will follow differ-

ent routes in arguing for the doctrine of justice. There will be a
unanimity in the conclusion but (given the different starting points)
no unanimity on the route to it."[65] Although Rawls' original justification of his "theory of justice"[66] had commonly been understood
to be of the RpG sort, in an essay published in 1985 Rawls makes a
number of statements indicating, in effect, that the justification at
which he now aims is of the GpR sort. For example: "We hope that
this political conception of justice may at least be supported by
what we may call an 'overlapping consensus,' that is, by a consensus that includes all the opposing philosophical and religious doctrines likely to persist and to gain adherents in a more or less just
constitutional democratic society."[67] For Rawls, the relevant range
of opposing doctrines—the range privileged by, the range the authority of which is presupposed by, his (GpR) justification—is
conceptions included in the "overlapping consensus".

As of 1985 Rawls allows that for anyone who adheres to a comprehensive philosophical, religious, or moral doctrine—in effect,
to a conception of human good[68]—included in the overlapping
consensus, her acceptance of Rawls' principles of justice, of his
"political conception of justice" (if she does accept it), depends on,
is "supported by", the doctrine or conception of human good to
which she adheres. In that sense, her conception of human good
plays an essential, justificatory role in her acceptance of the principles of justice: "[I]n such a consensus each of the comprehensive
philosophical, religious, and moral doctrines accepts justice as fairness in its own way; that is, each comprehensive doctrine, from
within its own point of view, is led to accept the public reasons of
justice specified by justice as fairness. We might say that they
recognize its concepts, principles, and virtues as theorems, as it
were, at which their several views coincide. . . . [I]n general, these
concepts, principles, and virtues are accepted by each as belonging
to a more comprehensive philosophical, religious, or moral doctrine."[69] In a 1987 essay, "The Idea of an Overlapping Consensus",
Rawls amplifies the point: "[D]espite the fact that there are opposing [conceptions of human good] affirmed in society, there is no
difficulty as to how an overlapping consensus may exist. Since
different premises may lead to the same conclusions, we may simply suppose that the essential elements of the political conception
[of justice], its principles, standards and ideals, are theorems, as it

were, at which the [conceptions of human good] in the consensus intersect or converge."[70]

I have said that by 1985 Rawls' efforts have been aimed at explicating and achieving a justification of the GpR sort. Yet, in 1988 Rawls published an essay contending for "the priority of right": "The idea of the priority of right is an essential element in what I have called political liberalism, and it has a central role in justice as fairness [that is, in Rawls' theory of justice] as a form of that view."[71] The apparent thrust of this passage, and of the essay in which it appears, to the contrary notwithstanding, Rawls did not change course (again) in 1988. The priority of right Rawls defends in his 1988 essay, if a priority at all, is an innocuously weak version of it, indeed, a version so weak as not to be inconsistent with the priority of good. Recall the strong version of the priority of right: A justification is of the Right-prior-to-Good sort if it does not privilege any conception or range of conceptions of human good. Compare Rawls' weak version of the priority of right:

> I begin by stating a distinction basic for my discussion—namely, the distinction between a political conception of justice and a comprehensive religious, philosophical, or moral doctrine [that is, a "conception of the good"]. The distinguishing features of a political conception of justice are . . . [inter alia] that accepting the political conception does not presuppose accepting any particular comprehensive religious, philosophical, or moral doctrine. . . .
>
> [A] political conception *must* draw upon various ideas of the good. The question is: subject to what restriction may political liberalism do so? The main restriction would seem to be this: the ideas included must be political ideas. That is, they must belong to a reasonable political conception of justice so that we may assume [inter alia] . . . that they do not presuppose any particularly fully (or partially) comprehensive doctrine.[72]

Rawls' weak version of "the priority of right" is not inconsistent with the priority of good, because to say that "accepting the political conception does not presuppose accepting any particular comprehensive religious, philosophical, or moral doctrine" is *not* to say that accepting the political conception does not presuppose the authority of a particular range of such doctrines. Clearly, the sort of justification Rawls began explicating in 1985 *does* privilege a particular range of such "comprehensive" doctrines, namely, the

doctrines included in Rawls' "overlapping consensus". The justification Rawls now wants to achieve for his own political conception
of justice is, therefore, a justification of the Good-prior-to-Right
sort—even though Rawls insists that "the priority of right is an
essential element in . . . political liberalism, and it has a central
role in justice as fairness as a form of that view." In particular, it is
a justification that privileges a certain range of conceptions of
human good.[73]

I said that Rawls' position on the central issue of political justification is more promising than the positions of Ackerman, Nagel,
and Greenawalt. Unlike Ackerman and Nagel, Rawls does not
impose on the practice of political justification any impossibly restrictive conditions. Unlike Greenawalt, Rawls does not distinguish between "religious" convictions and "secular" convictions—
a distinction that can be quite difficult to administer—and then
take the problematic step of disfavoring the former relative to the
latter.

Nonetheless, Rawls' position on political justification, as I
said, is not satisfactory. Our politics—our practice of political
justification—will somehow have to proceed without benefit of a
political conception of justice supported by an overlapping consensus. As Rawls himself acknowledges, "[A]n overlapping consensus
is [not] always possible, given the doctrines currently existing in
any democratic society. It is often obvious that it is not, not at least
until firmly held beliefs change in fundamental ways."[74] It is doubt-
ful that a political conception of justice supported by an overlapping consensus, whether Rawls' own conception ("justice as fairness") or some other, will ever emerge in a society as morally
pluralistic as the United States. (Rawls acknowledges the "likel[i-
hood] that more than one political conception may be worked up
from the fund of shared political ideas; indeed, this is desirable, as
these rival conceptions will then compete for citizens' allegiance
and be gradually modified and deepened by the contest between
them."[75]) As Joseph Raz suggests, "Rawls' route seems barren in
pluralistic societies, like ours. The degree of existing diversity is
just too great."[76] (Raz continues: "Furthermore, . . . there seems
to be little reason to reject valid or true principles, the implementa-
tion of which may actually be of benefit to all, just because a small
sector of the population cannot be convinced of this fact."[77]) Even

if a political conception of justice supported by an overlapping consensus is possible in American society, there is at present no such conception in the United States.

Are there at least some political-moral premises supported by an overlapping consensus, even if the premises are not sufficiently integrated to constitute a systematic political conception of justice? Some constitutional norms are political-moral premises. Do such norms, or some of them, enjoy the support of an overlapping consensus? (Which ones? Norms pertaining to religious liberty? To racial discrimination?) To the extent some political-moral premises enjoy consensual support, given our pluralism they are likely to be rather abstract or general premises and thus rather indeterminate with respect to the actual political conflicts that beset us. To the extent some concrete or particular and therefore relatively determinate political-moral premises enjoy some support in our society, given our pluralism the support is likely to be narrow rather than broad (and therefore hardly consensual). The conception of the proper role of beliefs, including religious beliefs, about human good in political deliberation and justification for which I contend in this book has some affinity with a Rawlsian strategy of identifying normative materials, concerning political morality, supported by a wide consensus. (I address the problem of indeterminacy in chapter 6.) But the hope that there is on the horizon a full-blown political conception of justice that, when it arrives, will enjoy the support of an overlapping consensus, seems wistful. For the foreseeable future, at least, it seems that our pluralistic politics must proceed without benefit of such a conception.

V

But proceed how? As I've explained, Rawls has given up the quest for a neutral politics in the sense of a politics in which the principles of justice that are to serve as the basis of political justification are themselves justified in a RpG way. Is there some other conception, some *realizable* conception, of a politics—of a practice of political justification—neutral/impartial in a strong sense?[78] Will some theorist succeed where Ackerman and Nagel, among others, have so far failed? As Ackerman has himself forthrightly acknowledged, "The history of liberal thought gives substance to [skepticism about the possibility of a practice of neutral political justification]. Although many have sought to blaze a path to neutrality, the goal has proven disturbingly elusive."[79] If Ackerman, Nagel, or others want to persist in the quest for a neutral/impartial politics, so be it. Understandably, others of us believe that the quest for the Holy Grail of neutral/impartial political justification is spent and that it is past time to take a different, more promising path.

2

Politics and the Question of the "Truly, Fully" Human

At the beginning of the preceding chapter I asked whether disputed beliefs about human good should play any role in public deliberations about, or public justifications of, contested political choices. Arguments like those developed by Bruce Ackerman and Thomas Nagel are largely to the effect that disputed beliefs about human good should play no or at most a marginal role in political justification. The basic problem with that position, as I indicated in my comments on Ackerman's and Nagel's arguments, is that a politics—a practice of political justification—from which disputed beliefs about human good are excluded (because, as in Ackerman's argument, they are not shared or because, as in Nagel's, they fail certain epistemological criteria) is impossibly restrictive: Such a politics is bereft of the normative resources required for addressing, much less resolving, the most fundamental political-moral issues that engage and divide us. Only a politics in which beliefs about human good, including disputed beliefs, have a central place is capable of addressing our most basic political questions. In this chapter I illustrate the point, which is important and merits separate treatment. Specifically, I argue that a politics from which disputed beliefs about human good are excluded cannot address a political-moral question that, at the close of the twentieth century, is indisputably and appropriately at the very heart of domestic and international politics: Are there human rights and, if so, what are they?[1]

The claim that a right exists—*any* right, whether a moral right or
a legal right, a human right or some other kind of right—may be
either descriptive or prescriptive in character (or both). The descriptive claim that a right exists is the claim that the right is conferred by some specified entity or entities (such as a person, a
family, a church, a state). The prescriptive claim that a right exists
is the claim that the right *ought* to be conferred by some specified
entity (or entities).[2] There are different kinds of prescriptive
rights-claims, for example, prescriptive legal-rights-claims: claims
that, given certain authoritative legal norms, such-and-such a (legal) right ought to be conferred (by the courts on behalf of the
state, for example). I'm interested here in prescriptive moral-
rights-claims: claims that, given certain authoritative moral norms,
such-and-such a (moral) right ought to be conferred. In particular,
I'm interested in prescriptive moral-rights-claims of a certain sort:
claims that such-and-such a (moral) right ought to be conferred on
all (or virtually all) human beings. I shall call claims of that sort
"human-rights-claims".[3] How can such claims—claims that some
specified entity (or entities) ought, as a moral matter, to confer
such-and-such a right on (virtually) all human beings, that conferral of the right is morally required—be justified, if at all? Can
such claims be justified without reliance on further claims, sometimes disputed, about human good?[4]

I

A claim that a state of affairs is generally good or bad, not just for
some human beings for whom the state holds but for (virtually)
any human being for whom it holds, presupposes that human beings are all alike in some respect or respects. Human-rights-claims
are a prominent example: A human-rights-claim is to the effect
that such-and-such a right ought to be conferred on (virtually) all
and not just on some human beings because conferral of the right
on any human being is, as a general matter, conducive to, perhaps
even constitutive of, his authentic good no matter who he is. The
presupposition that human beings are all alike in some significant
respects is not inconsistent with the pluralist view that human beings are also different from one another in many respects, that

human beings have many different needs and wants, even different biological needs. The universalist presupposition, however, is that whatever the significant differences among them, human beings have many of the same needs; that some needs are common to all human beings; that, therefore, some things are of value to every human being; that what satisfies a common human need is, at least in normal circumstances, good for any human being; that there are some things that any human being must have or do if he is to live a good or fitting life.[5]

Any plausible conception of human good—of human well-being, of human nature—must be pluralist.[6] Human beings differ from one another across time, of course. But they also differ from one another across space. They differ from one another interculturally. They even differ from one another intraculturally.[7] A conception of human good, however, can be universalist as well as pluralist: It can acknowledge sameness as well as difference, commonality as well as variety.[8] Inevitably there are differences as to how universalist and how pluralist a conception of good should be.[9] Such differences—competing conceptions or interpretations of common human needs—are often reasonable, given the inconclusive state of moral anthropology. But is a radically anti-universalist position reasonable?

A curious challenge to an ideal of politics in which questions about what is good for all human beings, including questions about human rights, are a fundamental concern, is a kind of anthropological view according to which nothing is good for all human beings because, beyond some biological needs, there are no significant needs common to all human beings; no needs, therefore, such that what satisfies them is good, not just for this person or that, or for this group or that, but for any and every person, *for human beings generally*. Is it plausible to insist that human beings do not have significant needs in common, that is, significant *social* needs, needs beyond the merely biological needs all human beings obviously share? Is it plausible to deny that there are needs common to all human beings, needs such that what satisfies them is good for every human being? Such a view, which Richard Rorty, among others, seems to advance,[10] is not pluralist ("although some things are good for all humans, other things are good only for some humans") but nihilist ("nothing is good for all humans").

Why would anyone doubt that there are significant needs common to all human beings? After all, some significant appetites and senses—social appetites and senses no less than biological—certainly seem to be shared across the human species. Of course, shared appetites and senses can be and often are shaped in different ways by different cultures *and* by different individual histories within a single culture. Not all differences are due merely to differences in how common appetites and senses have been shaped: Some significant appetites and senses are not shared across the human species. Nonetheless, some appetites and senses *are* shared. Therefore, some significant (social) needs are shared across the human species: the needs that are the correlates of the shared appetites and senses. Some needs are universal and not merely local in character. Philippa Foot has put these points succinctly but eloquently:

> Granted that it is wrong to assume an identity of aim between peoples of different cultures; nevertheless there is a great deal that all men have in common. All need affection, the cooperation of others, a place in a community, and help in trouble. It isn't true to suppose that human beings can flourish without these things—being isolated, despised or embattled, or without courage or hope. We are not, therefore, simply expressing values that we happen to have if we think of some moral systems as good moral systems and others as bad. Communities as well as individuals can live wisely or unwisely, and this is largely the result of their values and the codes of behavior that they teach. Looking at these societies, and critically also at our own, we surely have some idea of how things work out and why they work out as they do. We do not have to suppose it is just as good to promote pride of place and the desire to get an advantage over other men as it is to have an ideal of affection and respect. These things have different harvests, and unmistakably different connections with human good.[11]

Given the seeming obviousness of these allied premises—that there are significant needs common to all human beings, that therefore some things (whatever satisfies a common human need) are of value to every human being, that there is, in that sense, a good common to every human being, a *human* and not merely local good—what might lead one to doubt or even deny all this? (The denial extends to the morally fundamental, "religious" claim, discussed in the next section of this chapter, that an essential part of what it means to be human—truly human, fully human—and thus what anyone needs to do who would be human, is to accept responsibility for the basic well-being of the Other. Of course, to reject the denial that there are significant needs common to all human beings is not necessarily to agree that what anyone needs to do who would be truly, fully human is to accept responsibility for the well-being of the Other.) Why would anyone deny what according to Rorty "historicist thinkers [ever since Hegel] have denied[:] that there is such a thing as 'human nature' or the 'deepest level of the self.' Their strategy has been to insist that socialization, and thus historical circumstance, goes all the way down, that there is nothing 'beneath' socialization or prior to history which is definatory of the human. Such writers tell us that the question 'What is it to be a human being?' should be replaced by questions like 'What is it to inhabit a rich twentieth-century democratic society?' . . ."[12]

This "historicist" (or "postmodern") insistence that it's socialization all the way down is not merely some innocuous if implausible (silly?) position in a far corner of academic philosophy. As Rorty's statement about "historicist thinkers since Hegel" suggests, the denial of *human* good or well-being, of *human* needs—the denial, in that sense, of "the human", of "human nature", in the sense of the social as distinct from merely biological dimension of human being—is not uncommon among contemporary thinkers.[13] More important, the denial is clearly subversive of human-rights-claims:

> A vision of future social order is . . . based on a concept of human nature. If in fact man is an indefinitely malleable, completely plastic being, with no innate structures of mind and no intrinsic needs of a cultural or social character, then he is a fit subject for the "shaping behavior" by the state authority, the corporate manager, the technocrat, or the central committee. Those with some confidence in the human species . . . will try to determine the intrinsic human characteristics that provide the framework for intellectual development, the growth of moral consciousness, cultural achievement, and participation in a free community.[14]

The question is all the more urgent, therefore: What might lead to, what might explain, a denial of the human? What might lead to or explain nihilism (as distinct from pluralism) about human good?

I don't have a confident answer. Perhaps a partial explanation is that some such denials confuse conceptions of human nature with human nature itself. It is one thing to insist that conceptions of human nature are irreducibly contingent, that they—like the languages, the vocabularies, constitutive of the conceptions—bear the traces (and perhaps nothing but the traces) of particular times and places, of particular histories and cultures. It is another thing altogether to insist that there is no such thing as human nature. It is one thing to insist that conceptions of human nature are socially constructed and that there are good reasons to be wary about any such conception. It is another thing altogether to insist that we can get along quite nicely, thank you, without any conception of human nature, or to insist that putative human nature itself is socially constructed ("there's no *there* there, it's socialization all the way down").[15] A recent comment by feminist legal theorist Robin West, though directed specifically to other feminist theorists, is relevant here:

> What is of value in critical social theory for feminists? My suspicion is that what attracts many feminists to critical social theory is not its anti-essentialism, but more simply its skepticism: its refusal to accept any particular account of truth or morality as the essential true, moral or human viewpoint. This skepticism is entirely healthy and something we should treasure. The anti-essentialism of the critical theorist's vision, by contrast, is something we should reject. Surely we can have this both ways. Skepticism toward particular claims of objective truth, a particular account of the self, and any particular account of gender, sexuality, biology or what is or is not natural, is absolutely necessary to a healthy and modern feminism. But that skepticism need not require an unwillingness to entertain descriptions of subjective and intersubjective authenticity. . . .[16]

As Philippa Foot, Martha Nussbaum, and Robin West understand,[17] but as Richard Rorty and other "historicists" apparently do not, questions about *human* good—about what is good for human beings generally—including questions about *human* rights, are not misconceived. Contra Rorty, the question "What is it to be a human being?" should not be replaced by other questions. This is not to deny that there are other important, and sometimes complementary, questions, such as "What is it to inhabit a rich twentieth-century democratic society?" Nor is it to deny "the very poignant sense in which we may be unable to choose between cultures" or between ways of life within a single culture: "We may indeed be able to understand the transition [from one culture or way of life to another] in terms of gain and loss, but there may be some of both, and an overall judgement may be hard to make."[18] It bears emphasis, however, that this inability to adjudicate between or among cultures or ways of life, as Charles Taylor explains,

> presupposes that we can, in principle, understand and recognize the goods of another society [or of another way of life] as goods-for-everyone (and hence for ourselves). That these are not combinable with our own home-grown goods-for-everyone may indeed be tragic but is no different in principle from any of the other dilemmas we may be in through facing incombinable goods, even within our own way of life. There is no guarantee that universally valid goods should be perfectly combinable, and certainly not in all situations.
>
> . . . It may be that our contact with certain cultures will force us to recognize incommensurability, as against simply a balance of goods- and bads-for-everyone that we cannot definitively weigh up. But we certainly shouldn't assume this is so a priori.
>
> Until we meet this limit, there is no reason not to think of the goods we are trying to define and criticize as universal, provided we afford the same status to those of other societies we are trying to understand. This does *not* mean of course that all our, or all their, supposed goods will turn out at the end of the day to be defensible as such; just that we don't start with a preshrunk moral universe in which we take as given that their goods have nothing to say to us or perhaps ours to them.[19]

II

The serious challenge to any and all human-rights-claims, then—claims about what rights ought to be conferred on *all* human beings—is not the nihilist position. The serious, and fundamental, challenge is this:

> Why should we [those who, according to the claim, ought to confer the right in question] take seriously the project of protecting the well-being of all human beings; in particular, why should we care about protecting such well-being to the degree it would be protected

were we to confer the right in question? Why, indeed, should we give a damn about the well-being of *all* human beings, as distinct from the well-being of some human beings, for example, the members of our family/tribe/race/religion/and so on?

I want to consider four distinct responses to that challenge.

a

One response to the challenge is, in effect, little more than a definitional stratagem, according to which giving a damn about the well-being of all human beings is what it means to be "moral". Indeed, according to a common version of the stratagem, being concerned about the well-being of all human beings no less than one is concerned about one's own well-being ("equal concern"), respecting the well-being of all human beings no less than one respects one's own ("equal respect"), is what it means to be "moral". To be "moral" is to be "impartial" in that sense. "The moral point of view" is "the impartial (or universal) point of view". One ought to give a damn about the well-being of all human beings because it's the "moral" thing to do.[20] That response is unavailing because it avoids the real challenge, which can be expressed this way in response to the definitional stratagem:

> You claim that morally we ought to do X. We ask why we ought to do X. You say that doing X is what it means to act morally. That response is a wasted gambit. For the sake of argument we'll stipulate to your definition of "moral". Our challenge remains: Why ought we to be "moral" in the stipulated sense? Why ought we to give a damn about being "moral" or doing the "moral" thing? As a practical matter we're back where we started: Why ought we to do X? What reasons—what real-world, flesh-and-blood reasons—can you give us for doing X? (Your definitional reason is hardly such a reason.)

The fundamental challenge to human-rights-claims is a demand for reasons. James Nickel has distinguished between two different interpretations of the demand: one according to which it is "a demand for prudential reasons" and another according to which it is "a request for moral [as distinct from merely "prudential"] reasons".[21] (The distinction between "prudential" and "moral" is deeply problematic, at least for anyone with an Aristotelian understanding of morality.[22] But let's move on.) The second interpretation, Nickel suggests, "assumes that one's audience has transcended egoism and is prepared to accept arguments that appeal directly to what is reasonable from the moral point of view, whether or not it can be shown that adopting this perspective is likely to promote the long-term interests of the individual."[23] But the problem is larger, much larger, than "egoism": One may favor, not oneself, or even one's family, but one's tribe, or race, or religion, or country. The assumption that those to whom human-rights-claims are addressed have "transcended" such favoritism is wildly implausible. The fundamental challenge to human-rights-claims is a real-world challenge: Many to whom such claims are addressed have conspicuously not adopted anything like "the moral (impartial, universal) point of view". "The moral point of view" is not a justificatory basis for human-rights-claims, at least, not a fundamental basis. "The moral point of view" is itself in dire need of justification, especially in a world, *our* world, the *real* world, that is often fiercely partial/local rather than impartial/universal.

The question remains: What reasons can be given to the addressees of human-rights-claims for giving a damn about the well-being of all human beings (and thus for adopting the moral point of view, in the stipulated sense of "moral")? Charles Taylor, commenting critically on moral theories that are variations on the definitional stratagem, in particular theories that exclude discourse about human good, has put the point this way:

> [Such theories] leave us with nothing to say to someone who asks why he should be moral. . . . But this could be misleading, if we seemed to be asking how we could convince someone who saw none of the point of our moral beliefs. There is nothing we can do to "prove" we are right to such a person. But imagine him to be asking another question: he could be asking us to make plain the point of our moral code, in articulating what's uniquely valuable in cleaving to these injunctions [for example, act "impartially"]. Then the implication of these theories is that we have nothing to say which can impart insight. We can wax rhetorical and propagandize, but we can't say what's good or valuable about [the injunctions], or why they command assent.[24]

b

A second response to the challenge relies on an approach to the
justification of rights according to which a person, *P*, cannot "rationally" reject the conferral—on at least some, if not all, human
beings—of rights the conferral (and respect) of which somehow
satisfies (maximizes satisfaction of) preferences *P* has. The problem with that approach is that given a realistic view of the preferences many persons have, the approach may succeed in justifying
(conferral of) only a few rights constituting in effect "a mere nonag-
gression treaty".[25] Further, it may succeed in justifying such rights
not as *human* rights—rights possessed by (virtually) all human
beings—but only as rights possessed by persons who are in, or who
realistically may arrive at, a position to do one another harm.[26]
Given the preferences many persons have, it is difficult to see how
the approach could begin to justify—or could begin to justify as
human rights—the range of rights that in the period since the end
of World War II many have urged be established as human rights in
international law, or even the range of rights that have actually
been established as human rights in international law in the post-
war period: rights concerning, inter alia, (a) religious and political
freedom, (b) nondiscrimination based on race and sex, (c) fairness
in the enforcement of criminal laws, and (d) material ("economic")
well-being.[27] It is even difficult to see how the approach in question
could justify the range of rights established as human rights in our
own domestic legal system, in particular the human rights established under the Constitution. (Many constitutional rights are human rights: the rights, not merely of citizens, but of all persons.[28])
The justification of human-rights-claims of the sort with which we
are familiar in the world today, and the evaluation of such claims,
clearly require more substantial grounding—and, alas, more controversial grounding—than premises about what no person can
"rationally" reject.

c

A third response relies on a practice of (putatively) "neutral" political justification like the practices recommended by political theo-

rists such as Ackerman and Nagel. The relevant problem with that response, however—a problem I highlighted in the preceding chapter—is that such a practice is impossibly restrictive: The justifications yielded by such a practice often underdetermine resolution of political arguments, including arguments about human-rights-claims. The approach to the justification of rights discussed in the preceding paragraph can be understood as a variation on "neutral" political justification because it is a justification to a person based on nothing more controversial than the good of maximizing satisfaction of his own preferences. But, like "neutral" political justification generally, and as I noted in the preceding paragraph, such an approach cannot begin to justify a significant range of rights, much less justify them as *human* rights.

d

A fourth response to the fundamental challenge relies squarely on convictions about human good by arguing that giving a damn about the well-being of all human beings is a sensibility and a practice partly constitutive of the good life for everyone. According to a response of this sort, the life that is profoundly good or fitting for everyone to live, the meaningful life for each and every human being, the life that is, in that sense, "truly, fully" human,[29] includes concern and respect for the well-being of all human beings and not just for the well-being of oneself or one's family or tribe or race or religion. Consider, for example, the moral image central to what Hilary Putnam has called "[t]he Jerusalem-based religions": an image that "[stresses] equality and also fraternity, as in the metaphor of the whole human race as One Family, of all women and men as sisters and brothers."[30] For Christians the basic shape of the good life is indicated by the instruction given by Jesus at a Passover seder on the eve of his execution: "I give you a new commandment: love one another; you must love one another just as I have loved you."[31] Such a sensibility is not confined to the semitic spiritualities; it is an aspect of Indic spiritualities, too. For Buddhists, for example, the good life centrally involves compassion for all sentient creatures and therefore for all human beings.

Why should we "love one another just as I have loved you"? The answer, in the vision of the Jerusalem-based religions—a vision rooted in the lived experience of the Jerusalem-based religious communities—is that the Other, too, including the outsider, the stranger, the alien, is a "child" of the one, creator God[32] and therefore "sister" or "brother"; the Other, too, no less than oneself, is therefore of intrinsic and inestimable worth. As it has been put in the introduction to a recent selection of writings from the Talmud:

> From this conception of man's place in the universe comes the sense of the supreme sanctity of all human life. "He who destroys one person has dealt a blow at the entire universe, and he who sustains or saves one person has sustained the whole world." . . .
>
> The sanctity of life is not a function of national origin, religious affiliation, or social status. In the sight of God, the humble citizen is the equal of the person who occupies the highest office. As one talmudist put it: "Heaven and earth I call to witness, whether it be an Israelite or pagan, man or woman, slave or maidservant, according to the work of every human being doth the Holy Spirit rest upon him." . . . As the rabbis put it: "We are obligated to feed non-Jews residing among us even as we feed Jews; we are obligated to visit their sick even as we visit the Jewish sick; we are obligated to attend to the burial of their dead even as we attend to the burial of the Jewish dead."[33]

Such a response to the fundamental challenge to human-rights-claims consists mainly of a conception of human good, in particular of convictions about what it means to be (truly, fully) human, about what is of real and ultimate value in life, about what makes a life most deeply meaningful. ("[T]o find out what our nature is seems to be one and the same thing as to find out what we deeply believe to be most important and indispensable [in a human life]."[34]) It is far from clear that there is any response to the challenge not rooted, finally, in such convictions, convictions "religious" in the sense I elaborate in chapter 5.[35]

The obvious and great problem with any response that appeals to particular convictions about human good, especially religious convictions about the meaningfulness of life, is that in a pluralistic society like our own, and even more so in our pluralistic world, there are competing convictions, both secular and religious, about human good. It is difficult to see how grounding human-rights-claims on premises about the good or fitting or meaningful way for human beings to live their lives can serve to justify the claims to those for whom the premises are not authoritative.[36]

But, as I contend in chapter 6, in the course of arguing for the possibility of ecumenical politics in our religiously and morally pluralistic domestic context, there is good reason to believe that significant premises about human good, significant standards of political-moral judgment, are authoritative for many (though not for all) persons and groups in American society. Indeed, basic premises about human good are widely authoritative not just in American society (for example) but internationally. Consider the post–World War II phenomenon of international discourse about human rights, which has grown larger (including more and more participants)[37] and more vigorous with the passage of time. The existence and indeed vitality of this international human-rights discourse is not surprising: The great religious traditions, Indic as well as semitic, are principal participants in the discourse, and they are tending to converge with one another, and with Marxism, in affirming that an essential part of what it means to be fully human, an essential requirement of the meaningful life for everyone, is to accept responsibility—*some* responsibility—for the basic aspects of the well-being of the Other (the outsider, the stranger, the alien). A growing literature documents and discusses that emergent convergence.[38] Just as religious pluralism has not been an impediment to but, rather, an occasion of, a stimulus to, the emergence of ecumenical theology,[39] religious and moral pluralism need not be an impediment to but, instead, may be an occasion of the emergence of ecumenical politics. International discourse about human rights, which illustrates the possibility of ecumenical politics even in an international context, certainly suggests the possibility of ecumenical politics in a religiously/morally pluralistic domestic context like our own. If ecumenical political discourse is possible internationally, then it is surely possible domestically.

III

It is not surprising that in many societies, especially modern societies, conceptions of human authenticity—of what it means to be "truly, fully" human—and interpretations of human needs are

disputed. Nor is it surprising that such disputes are often contested, sometimes obliquely, in politics. Nor, finally, is it surprising
that in some societies, especially pre-modern societies, a particular
conception/interpretation of the human—a particular "ideology"
of the human—has sometimes achieved a hegemonic status, with
the consequence that contests over the human have become repressed. What *is* surprising is the effort to imagine a politics—
neutral politics—from which such contests are to be excluded or,
at least, in which they are to be marginalized. Contests over human good have been and remain central to politics, not marginal
(however repressed such contests may sometimes be). Moreover,
the questions at issue in such contests—questions about human
good, including the question of what it means to live a truly, fully
human life—include questions that are indisputably political: questions about the authentically human way to live the collective life,
the life in common. It seems fanciful to suppose that contests over
human good could ever be anything but central to politics.

The point I want to emphasize, however—the point I have illustrated in this chapter—is that a practice of political justification
from which disputed beliefs about human good are excluded lacks
the normative resources required for addressing our most fundamental political-moral questions, like questions about human
rights. Only a politics in which beliefs about human good, including disputed beliefs, have a central place is capable of addressing
such questions. I begin, in the next chapter, to elaborate and defend such a politics.

3

Ecumenical Politics

In chapter 1, when criticizing Ackerman's and Nagel's respective positions, I explained that a practice of political justification that tolerates only neutral or impartial arguments is not itself neutral or impartial.[1] More troubling, however, is the fact that, as I explained in chapter 1 and illustrated in chapter 2, a practice of political justification, like Ackerman's and Nagel's practices, that excludes or marginalizes disputed beliefs about human good is bereft of the normative resources required for addressing, in more than a superficial way, much less resolving, the most fundamental political-moral questions that engage and divide us, like questions about human rights. An ideal of politics (political justification) that, like Ackerman's or Nagel's ideal, requires us to stand mute before such profound and profoundly difficult questions could scarcely be less adequate to the reality of political conflict and crisis in the modern world. The ideal of politics I begin elaborating and defending in this chapter is one in which beliefs about human good, including disputed beliefs, are central. I call this ideal "ecumenical" politics. In ecumenical politics beliefs about human good play a basic role in public deliberations about, and public justifications of, contested political choices.

The practice of ecumenical political deliberation and justification I defend here is like the justificatory practices defended by Ackerman and Nagel in this respect: It is not a neutral/impartial practice. A truly neutral/impartial justificatory practice, one that lets everyone rely on her relevant convictions, is inappropriate in

American society: As I later explain, not every kind of reliance on every kind of conviction is appropriate in a modern liberal society, least of all in one as religiously/morally pluralistic as the United States. But unlike Ackerman's and Nagel's practices, the practice I defend does not exclude all but neutral/impartial arguments. A practice that includes only neutral/impartial arguments is, as Ackerman's and Nagel's practices illustrate, impossibly restrictive. The practice I defend makes room for some (but not all) kinds of reliance on some (but not all) kinds of disputed convictions.

In this chapter my principal aims are, first, to introduce the ideal of ecumenical politics, in particular, to introduce the practice of ecumenical political dialogue, which is a principal constituent of ecumenical politics; and, second, to specify several reasons for taking ecumenical politics seriously and, in particular, for taking seriously ecumenical political dialogue.

I

The *Oxford English Dictionary* defines "ecumenical", in relevant part, as "Belonging to the whole world; universal, general, worldwide."[2] The adjective is often used to modify "religion" or "theology". "Ecumenical" theology aspires to discern or achieve, in a theologically pluralistic context, a common ("universal") theological ground, mainly through a dialogic or dialectical transcending of "local" or "sectarian" differences. (Dialogue is thus a principal constituent of ecumenical theology.) The effort to achieve a common ground does not presuppose that all theological differences can be overcome, or even that overcoming all such differences would be a good thing. Ecumenical theology values theological pluralism; indeed, contemporary ecumenical-theological projects are typically and enthusiastically pluralist, in this sense: Those who engage in such projects understand that being challenged by (as well as respectfully challenging) a theology or theologies different, perhaps very different, from one's own can be an exceptionally fruitful way to achieve a deeper understanding of theological truth.[3] By analogy, "ecumenical" politics aspires to discern or achieve, in a religiously and morally pluralistic context, a common political ground. Moreover, as I later explain, ecumenical politics, like ecumenical theology, is pluralist: It values moral (including religious-moral) pluralism.

The principal constituents of ecumenical politics are two practices: first, a certain kind of dialogue; second, a certain kind of tolerance. Here and in chapter 6, I focus on ecumenical political dialogue. In chapter 7, I address the matter of ecumenical political tolerance. Ecumenical politics is, above all, both dialogic and communitarian: It is (as I explain in chapter 6) a politics in which, notwithstanding our religious/moral pluralism, we continually cultivate the bonds of political community—and in which we sometimes succeed in strengthening those bonds, even, occasionally, in forging new bonds—through dialogue of a certain kind. Ecumenical politics institutionalizes a particular conception of "the place of religion in American life" and of "how we should contend with each other's deepest differences in the public sphere."[4] The aim of ecumenical politics is, in words borrowed from *The Williamsburg Charter,* "neither a naked public square where all religion is excluded, nor a sacred public square with any religion established or semi-established." The aim, rather, "is a civil public square in which citizens of all religious faiths, or none, engage one another in continuing democratic discourse."[5]

The general purposes for which citizens speak in the public square, for which they "engage one another in continuing democratic discourse", are several. A citizen might speak in the public square, and, in the course of speaking, engage in dialogue, for one or more of the following general purposes:

1. to *declare* (report, announce) some or all of the reasons that she supports the political choice she does;
2. to *persuade* others to support the political choice, whether for the same reasons she supports it or for different reasons;
3. to *justify* the political choice to others, in the sense of arguing that the choice is at least permitted, perhaps even required, by relevant authoritative criteria (for example, criteria derived from the United States Constitution);
4. to *deliberate* about, to inquire dialogically (rather than monologically), what political choice she and others should support.[6]

Though the four kinds of political talk—declaratory, persuasive, justificatory, and deliberative—are different, they can be, in many situations, complementary (rather than competitive). In addition to declaring her reasons, a citizen can aim, minimally, to justify her choice and, maximally, to persuade others to support the same choice (whether for the same or different reasons), all the while remaining willing to deliberate further (if she is not dogmatic about her choice). Actual instances of political talk often involve, in addition to, or even instead of,[7] declaration, elements of persuasion, justification, and deliberation. Indeed, talk consisting only of declaration, even if the talk is embedded in a dialogic mode, would scarcely count as dialogue in anything but a weak sense. (Of course, talk that is solely declaratory and thus is, at best, dialogue only in a weak sense can precipitate conversation that is dialogue in a much stronger sense.)

The distinction between persuasion and justification is important. To try to persuade someone to support a particular political choice is to try to convince her that *her own premises,* including, perhaps, premises about her self-interest, support or even require the choice.[8] One way to try to justify a political choice to a person is to try to persuade her that her own premises support or require the choice. But to justify a choice to a person is not necessarily to persuade her that her own premises support or require the choice. (Perhaps her own premises do not support, much less require, the choice.) Trying to justify a political choice to a person, when persuasion is not possible, typically involves trying to establish that relevant authoritative premises—premises that, for one reason or another, have authority in the dialogic context—permit, support, or require the choice. The practice of justification presupposes that a premise can have (political-moral) authority in a dialogic context even if one or more persons in the context do not accept the premise, in the way a constitutional norm regarding racial discrimination, for example, has (legal) authority in the context of a court case even if a party to the case rejects the norm.[9] I return to the point in chapter 6.

As between persuasion and justification, I am concerned mainly with justification (although, as I said, one way to try to justify is to try to persuade). Persuasion may or may not be possible in a particular dialogic setting, depending on what premises the interlocutors happen to share. I am interested in the practice of justification in the pluralistic setting of contemporary American politics (and in any similarly pluralistic setting). For reasons I later develop, I am also concerned with deliberation. (Focusing exclusively on justificatory political dialogue is myopic. Among other things, deliberative dialogue is a powerful instrument of self-critical rationality.) I am interested in the practice of deliberation in a pluralistic political setting like our own. The kinds of political dialogue with which I am principally concerned, therefore, are those that substantially involve, in addition to or even instead of declaration, either justification or deliberation or both.

Ecumenical political dialogue, whether justificatory or deliberative or both, aspires to discern or achieve, in a religiously/morally pluralistic context, a common ground that transcends "local" or "sectarian" differences. To the extent such dialogue is genuinely deliberative, "what is at issue . . . is not 'what should I do?' or 'how should I conduct myself?' but: 'how are we to "be" together, and what is to be the institutional setting for that being-together?' . . . It is not self-deliberation about my life, but mutual deliberation conducted between agents implicated in a common life."[10] However, ecumenical political dialogue does not always or even often lead to agreement. Not all the important religious or moral differences "between [or among] agents implicated in a common life" can be overcome. Indeed, as I explain in chapter 6, ecumenical political dialogue should not always lead to agreement, not all the important differences should be overcome; agreement is not the true test or measure of the success of such dialogue. Ecumenical political dialogue is pluralist in the sense that it presupposes the value of religious/moral pluralism: Valuing such pluralism is a prerequisite to such dialogue. (More about that in chapter 6.) Because common ground cannot always be achieved, another aspiration of ecumenical political dialogue is to achieve a position on a political issue that is within the range of reasonable positions on the issue, given the relevant authoritative premises.

II

I continue elaborating, in chapter 6, the practice of ecumenical political dialogue. In the remainder of this chapter I want to begin defending the practice and, inferentially, the kind of politics the practice (in conjunction with the practice of ecumenical political tolerance) constitutes. Why should we take ecumenical political dialogue seriously? Why should we take seriously the kind of politics of which such dialogue is a principal constituent? Why should we care about such dialogue and politics? For example, why should a member of a religious community—an evangelical Baptist, say—take seriously ecumenical political dialogue, especially of a deliberative kind: "external" dialogue, dialogue with persons who are not members of her religious community and who may not share her basic religious convictions? Why shouldn't she be content with "internal" dialogue, dialogue with persons who are members of her community or at least share her basic convictions?

There are several reasons for taking ecumenical political dialogue seriously. A principal such reason: political community of a certain kind, which ecumenical political dialogue helps both to make possible and to strengthen. I articulate that reason principally in chapter 6. In this chapter I identify some other reasons for taking ecumenical political dialogue seriously. One such reason is practical and concerns both the justificatory and the deliberative aspects of dialogue. The reason can be cast as a (rhetorical?) question: In our religiously/morally pluralistic society, where we members of different religious and moral communities, we citizens with different basic religious and moral convictions, must make political choices about our life in common, what are the alternatives to ecumenical political dialogue? "Neutral" political dialogue is impossibly restrictive (as I explained in chapter 1). Political violence, or the threat of such violence, is an alternative to political dialogue, but in our culture it is virtually axiomatic that dialogue is preferable to violence and that resort to violence, if any, should be last, not first. "We cannot hope to . . . [achieve] a unanimous consensus [in American society, given its religious pluralism]. But we could at least do two things. We could limit the warfare, and we could enlarge the dialogue. We could lay down our arms (at least the more barbarous kind of arms!), and we could take up argument."[11] In chapter 7, I address an issue closely related to the problem of violence: coercive political strategies, which are backed by the threat of (state) violence.

A second reason is grounded in the ideal of self-critical

rationality—I discuss that ideal in the next chapter—and concerns mainly the deliberative aspect of dialogue: We come to the *truest* knowledge of ourselves—of who we truly are, both as individuals and as members of communities, and of how we should therefore live our lives, of what choices we should make—dialogically, not monologically. The practice of internal dialogue—within a community, among its members; or among those who share the same basic religious or moral convictions—can be an important self-critical reflective practice. But not even robust internal dialogue displaces the need for vigorous external dialogue as well. The following observation, though made in the context of ecumenical religious dialogue, is relevant to dialogue generally, including ecumenical political dialogue:

> All that I [as a Christian] need to believe, for genuine [ecumenical] dialogue [with, for example, a Buddhist] to begin, is that Buddhists are not out of touch with reality. Once the fundamental sanity of Buddhists is granted, it follows that there is some point to dialogue, to understanding how the world looks through Buddhist eyes. . . . [T]he Buddhist critique of theism will inevitably cause me to examine and reexamine my own theistic assumptions. As a result of coming to understand reality as seen by Buddhists, my own doctrine of God will be transformed.[12]

I return to this point, about the need for external dialogue, in chapter 6.

A third reason, closely related to the second, emphasizes our nature as *social* beings:[13] We are *essentially* embedded in a complex network of interdependent human relationships; each of us therefore comes to the *fullest* knowledge of ourself as thus embedded— of who I am in relation to others, of what I need or desire from others, of what is being asked or demanded of me by others, of what I have to offer others, and so on—dialogically, not monologically.[14] Ronald Beiner hints at both the second and third reasons (that dialogue is a matrix both of truer and of fuller self-knowledge), though without distinguishing them, in this suggestive passage:

> Human subjects have no privileged access to their own identity and purposes. It is through rational dialogue, and especially through political dialogue, that we clarify, even to ourselves, who we are and

what we want. It is mistaken to assume that we necessarily enter
into dialogue with an already consolidated view of where we stand
and what we are after, conceiving of speech merely as a means to be
used for winning over others, rather than as an end to be pursued
for its own sake. On the contrary, communication between subjects
joined in a community of rational dialogue may entail a process of
moral self-discovery that will lead us to a better insight into our own
ends and a firmer grasp upon our own subjectivity. Here politics
functions as a normative concept, describing what collective agency
should be like, rather than abiding by its present devalued meaning. . . . [I]t is through speech and deliberation that man finds the
location of his proper humanity, between beast and god, in the life
of the citizen.[15]

A fourth reason, which, like the second and third reasons, concerns mainly the deliberative aspect of dialogue, is grounded in a
value absolutely fundamental for many religious communities in
American society, and for many persons who identify with no religious community: *agape*, or love of neighbor.[16] David Lochhead, a
Protestant theologian who has written extensively about interfaith
dialogue, counsels that "[t]he Christian commandment to love
one's neighbor as Christ has loved us translates for the Christian
into the dialogic imperative, the imperative to seek dialogue and to
be open to dialogue whenever and from whomever it is offered."[17]
Any community or person for which or whom love of neighbor is a
constitutive ideal should understand that openness to the Other—
to the stranger, the outsider—in deliberative dialogue facilitates as
well as expresses such love: I can hardly love the Other—the *real*
other, in all her particularity—unless I listen to her and, in listening, gain in knowledge of her, of who she truly is and what she
needs or desires; and unless, having listened, I then respond to
her. (To respond is not necessarily to agree; it may be to question,
even to disagree.)

In genuine human relations, [Hans-Georg] Gadamer notes, the
important point is "to experience the 'Thou' truly as a 'Thou,' that
means, not to ignore his claim and to listen to what he has to
say"—an attitude which requires complete existential "openness"
and availability. Since openness implies readiness to interrogate
and listen to one another, genuine encounter can be said to have
the character of a conversation . . . —a conversation which, far

from being a series of monologues, is governed by the "dialectic of question and answer" and whose distant ancestor is the Platonic dialogue.[18]

I discuss, in chapter 6, the kind of "listening" and "responsiveness" that "existential openness and availability" make possible and that *agape* requires.

III

Ecumenical political dialogue is a practice—a practice that, as I said earlier in this chapter, is a principal constituent of a certain kind of politics. Like the (ecumenical) politics it constitutes, ecumenical political dialogue is also an ideal. To argue, as I just have, that there are good reasons to take seriously the practice of ecumenical political dialogue, and to take seriously, too, the kind of politics, and of political community, such dialogue makes possible, is not to claim that the ideal of ecumenical political dialogue can actually be achieved in each and every situation or context. To what extent, if any, is the ideal achievable in our religiously/morally pluralistic context? What are the situational or contextual prerequisites to such dialogue? What are the existential prerequisites: the habits of character and mind?

I return, in chapter 6, to those and related questions. Clarity will be served, however, if I first address two basic, prior issues: (1) the problem of "rationality" (chapter 4), and (2) the meaning of "religion"—in particular, what it means to say that a moral belief is "religious" in character (chapter 5).

4

Rationality, Truth, and Critique

My elaboration and defense, later in this book, of ecumenical political dialogue presuppose a particular conception—the "coherentist" conception—of rationality. It makes much more sense to address the issue of rationality directly than to presuppose an unarticulated and unexamined position on the issue. I therefore devote this chapter to a discussion both of rationality and of related issues. There is, in any event, a more general reason to pause to address the issue of rationality. In discussions of morality and religion, including (especially?) discussions of the proper relation of religion and morality to politics, the issue of rationality, even when not addressed systematically, often looms large:[1] Are moral convictions rational? Less rational than scientific convictions? Are moral convictions religious in character less rational than secular moral convictions? Is it possible to adjudicate between or among, or at least to discuss, competing moral or religious convictions rationally? Must a politics that would be rational exclude justificatory reliance on moral, or at least on religious-moral, convictions? What is rationality anyway? What does it mean to say that a belief is rational? What are the criteria of the rationality of a belief? And so on. My discussion here of rationality is meant to serve as epistemological background to—and, to some extent, as epistemological grounding for—my elaboration and defense, in later chapters, of ecumenical politics.

I

A conception of rationality is best understood as a criterion or set of criteria for determining what beliefs or claims (propositions and so on) it makes sense to accept (or to reject or neither to accept nor to reject), what beliefs it is "rational" or "reasonable" to accept (or to reject).[2] According to the coherentist conception of rationality that has come to dominate contemporary epistemology, the basic test or measure for determining what beliefs it is rational for a person to accept is coherence with whatever else he happens to believe: coherence with beliefs that are presently authorititative for him.[3] But the coherentist conception does not entail that old beliefs invariably trump new ones. Beliefs that were previously, and long, authoritative for him may not now be: One or more beliefs a person has long accepted may now be in question for him because of the failure of the belief or beliefs to cohere, or to cohere easily, with a new belief that, for whatever reason, now grips him.[4]

Nor does the conception entail that every belief a person accepts is coherent with every other belief he accepts. Not every belief a person accepts is coherent with every other belief he accepts. Some of the incoherences a person may be unaware of, while others he just lives with, at least for now. Although "[t]he identification of incoherence within established belief will always provide a reason for enquiring further," it is "not itself a conclusive reason for rejecting established belief, until something more adequate because less incoherent has been discovered."[5] Moreover, coherence is a matter of degree. At the one extreme, some beliefs are entailed by other beliefs. At the other, some beliefs are merely not inconsistent with other beliefs. Nonetheless, whether it makes sense for a person to believe something—whether the belief is "rational"— depends on what else he believes. A belief quite rational for one person might be quite irrational for another. Similarly, a belief rational for one community, given the other beliefs shared by the members of the community, or by most of them, might be irrational for another community.

As the possibility of a person's or community's having beliefs that do not all cohere among themselves suggests, one or more of a person's or community's beliefs can be irrational for him or it, given his or its other, stronger beliefs.[6] Moreover, as the possibility of "stronger" (and "weaker") beliefs suggests, the rational acceptability *vel non* of a belief is not all-or-nothing; it is, rather, a matter of degree.[7] Just as some beliefs are more fundamental than others for a person, some beliefs are stronger than others for him— though, of course, some less fundamental ones may be stronger than some more fundamental ones.

The coherentist (or, as it is sometimes called, "holist") model of rationality has replaced what Bernard Williams has called "the linear model", which, as Williams explains, "is wrong. No process of reason-giving fits this picture, in the sciences or elsewhere. . . . [T]he foundationalist [epistemological] enterprise, of resting the structure of knowledge on some favored class of statements, has now generally been displaced in favor of a holistic type of model, in which some beliefs can be questioned, justified, or adjusted while others are kept constant, but there is no process by which they can all be questioned at once, or all justified in terms of (almost) nothing. In von Neurath's famous image, we repair the ship while we are on the sea."[8] What is true of reasoning generally, including scientific reasoning, is true of moral reasoning in particular, including religious-moral reasoning: "For the holist . . . the justification of moral knowledge neither depends upon independently known foundations nor is called into question by the impossibility of placing any given moral judgment beyond doubt. Practical justification is a dialectical affair, intelligible only in relation to the simultaneously social and intellectual setting of a particular time and place."[9]

The coherentist conception of rationality does not entail that there are no beliefs common to all persons—or, therefore, to all communities. "[O]ne can maintain that truth is framework-relative while conceding for a large range of propositions nearly all frameworks coincide."[10] There is no reason to doubt that there are common beliefs. After all, we human beings are all members of the same species and we all inhabit the same planetary environment.[11] Indeed, as Richard Rorty has sensibly observed, "everything which we can identify as a human being or as a culture will be something which shares an enormous number of beliefs with us. (If it did not, we would simply not be able to recognize that it was speaking a language, and thus that it had any beliefs at all.)"[12] Nor does the coherentist conception deny that some beliefs are not merely common but "foundational" (epistemically privileged) in one or another sense.[13]

But to say that there are some beliefs common to all persons—and, therefore, to all communities—some of which are foundational beliefs, is not to deny that

- Common (including foundational) beliefs, whatever they are, obviously and radically underdetermine answers to many of the most fundamental questions, especially moral questions, that engage human beings, whether as individuals or as members of a community—and therefore underdetermine as well resolution of many moral conflicts that, often violently, engulf our species. What Alasdair MacIntyre has said of historically extended communities, which he calls "traditions", we may say of moral communities in particular, including historically extended moral communities: "It is not then that competing traditions do not share some standards. All the traditions with which we have been concerned agree in according a certain authority to logic both in their theory and in their practice. Were it not so, their adherents would be unable to disagree in the way in which they do. But that upon which they agree is insufficient to resolve those disagreements."[14]

- The (personal and communal) webs of beliefs in which common beliefs are embedded vary enormously across the human species, because every such web comprises many beliefs not common.[15] Many beliefs are not common to all persons—for example, many beliefs implicated in many fundamental moral, including political, conflicts—but, instead, are historically and culturally various: beliefs born in and nurtured by the experience of particular times and places (and sometimes challenged and transformed by encounter with different times or places).

- Many moral beliefs (for example) that are rational in relation to one web of beliefs (or to one set of beliefs a part of one web), beliefs that cohere with or nest comfortably in one web, are not rational, or even irrational, in relation to another web (or to another set a part of a different web).

II

Every conception of rationality is a theory of truth in the weak sense that every conception of rationality specifies a criterion or criteria for determining what beliefs it makes sense to accept *as true* (or to reject *as false,* or neither to accept nor to reject). Therefore, some theories of truth are conceptions of rationality. However, as I explain in a moment, a theory of truth is not necessarily a conception of rationality. Understood as a theory of truth *that purports to be, as well, a conception of rationality,* the "correspondence" or "copy" theory is unacceptable.

Mortimer Adler has sketched the correspondence theory, which is very likely the man-in-the-street's theory and which, were it sound, would constitute a serious alternative to the coherentist conception. According to Adler, the criterion of the truth of a belief is not (coherence with) further beliefs but (correspondence with) reality-as-it-is-in-itself—"Reality"—independent of whatever anyone may believe about it. Adler writes: "[Truth is— consists in—] a relationship of agreement or correspondence . . . between what a person thinks, believes, opines, or says to himself and what actually exists or does not exist in reality. . . . [T]he truth of thought consists in the agreement or correspondence between what one thinks, believes, or opines and what actually exists or does not exist in the reality that is independent of our minds and of our thinking one thing or another."[16]

The fatal problem with the correspondence theory—again, construed as (also) a conception of rationality—is that we lack access to Reality. Reality is unmediated reality: nonlinguistic, nonconceptual reality. The notion of our words and thoughts corresponding to nonlinguistic, nonconceptual reality is incoherent. The only reality to which we have access, and to which words and thoughts of ours could possibly correspond, is mediated reality: the word- and thought-systems we construct and deploy (and revise and even discard) in trying to deal with, in trying to understand, predict, and control, our perceptions, systems that are determined by and also determine our perceptions in ways we do not (yet) fully understand.[17] In any event, as a criterion of rational acceptability Reality is useless: We would never be able to know whether a belief or theory was rational because Reality is, through and through, an inaccessible criterion.[18] (Moreover, even if Reality were an accessible criterion, it is difficult to discern what the point would be of testing our beliefs for correspondence to Reality: "[I]f we already grasp [unmediated] reality there is no need to test beliefs."[19]) Thus, Adler (and the man in the street) is wrong in imagining that Reality is the criterion of the truth (in the sense of rational acceptability) of beliefs.[20]

I said that, and have now explained why, the correspondence theory of truth, understood as a conception of rationality, is unacceptable. But perhaps I have misconstrued Adler's point. Not every theory of truth purports to be a conception of rationality.[21] Understood merely as an account of what it means to say that a belief is "true"—or, from a different angle, an account of what makes a belief true—whether or not it is now, or would ever be, rational to accept the belief as true, the correspondence theory seems harmless enough. Some even count it as a virtue that, thus understood, the correspondence account "allows us to make assertions such as the following: A theory may be true even though nobody believes it, and even though we have no reason for accepting it, or for believing that it is true; and another theory may be false, although we have comparatively good reasons for accepting it."[22] Unfortunately, the correspondence account also allows us to make assertions such as "A belief may be true even though there is no reason why any human being—past, present, or future—should accept it, and a belief may be false even though there is no reason why any human being—past, present, or future—should reject it." I am in the dark as to what the practical point of making such assertions is.

Moreover, even understood only as an account of what it means to say that a belief is "true"—or of what makes a belief true—as distinct from merely rationally acceptable, the correspondence theory is incoherent. The notion of our beliefs being "true" (though not necessarily rationally acceptable) in the sense of corresponding to unmediated reality—the notion of our words and thoughts corresponding to nonlinguistic, nonconceptual reality—simply makes no sense, even if the relation of "correspondence to" is to be the test merely of truth and not of rational acceptability. "[T]he notion of a transcendental match between our representation and the world itself is nonsense."[23]

The correspondence account of "truth" presupposes what Hilary

Putnam has called an "externalist" perspective. He proposes in its stead an "internalist" perspective and, relatedly, a different—and, in my view, superior—account of the meaning of "truth". It is an account that, as Putnam emphasizes, does not equate truth with rational acceptability. Thus, Putnam, unlike Richard Rorty,[24] sensibly maintains the distinction between a theory of truth and a conception of rationality (though, as I said, there is a weak sense in which every conception of rationality is also a theory of truth):

> To reject the idea that there is a coherent "external" perspective, a theory which is simply true "in itself", apart from all possible observers, is not to *identify* truth with rational acceptability. Truth cannot simply be rational acceptability for one fundamental reason; truth is supposed to be a property of a statement that cannot be lost, whereas justification can be lost. The statement "The earth is flat" was, very likely, rationally acceptable 3,000 years ago; but it is not rationally acceptable today. Yet it would be wrong to say that "the earth is flat" was *true* 3,000 years ago; for that would mean that the earth has changed its shape. In fact, rational acceptability is both tensed and relative to a person. In addition, rational acceptability is a matter of degree. . . . [T]ruth is an idealization of rational acceptability. We speak as if there were such things as epistemically ideal conditions, and we call a statement "true" if it would be justified under such conditions. "Epistemically ideal conditions", of course, are like "frictionless planes": we cannot really attain epistemically ideal conditions, or even be absolutely certain that we have come sufficiently close to them. But frictionless planes cannot really be attained either, and yet talk of frictionless planes has "cash value" because we can approximate them to a very high degree of approximation. . . . [T]he two key ideas of the idealization theory of truth are (1) that truth is independent of justification here and now, but not independent of *all* justification. To claim a statement is true is to claim it could be justified. (2) truth is expected to be stable or "convergent"; if both a statement and its negation could be "justified", even if conditions were as ideal as one could hope to make them, there is no sense in thinking of the statement as *having* a truth-value.[25]

It bears emphasis that rejection of the correspondence theory as a conception of rationality—indeed, rejection of the correspondence theory even as (solely) an account of "truth"—and acceptance of the coherentist conception does not entail denial of "something we have never had any reason to doubt", namely, that "[m]ost of the world is as it is whatever we think about it".[26] (Nor does it entail denial "that the world may cause us to be justified in believing a sentence true".[27] "We are perfectly free", writes Jeffrey Stout, "to use 'reality' to signify '. . . the ineffable cause of sense and goal of the intellect' ".[28]) "To say that the world is out there, that it is not our creation, is to say, with common sense, that most things in space and time are the effects of causes which do not include human mental states."[29]

Given that "the world is as it is whatever we think about it", and given, too, that we live in and have to make our way in the world, some theories about how the world hangs together and some languages for representing the world are going to be more conducive both to our well-being and to our projects than other theories and other languages. This is not to deny that theories and languages are human artifacts and, in that sense, "contingent".[30] Tools are human artifacts, too. But that doesn't mean that we can make just any kind of tool out of a given material. Materials constrain. So, too, do the purposes for which the tools are made (even if tools sometimes have unforeseen uses). Just as materials and purposes constrain our toolmaking, the world ("as it is whatever we think about it"), in conjunction both with our interests (including our "human" interests: the interests we human beings have in common with each other as members of the same species[31]) and with our projects (especially our communal projects, for example, space exploration), is a constraint on our theory-making and language-making.[32] The coherentist conception of rationality neither entails nor presupposes to the contrary. Hilary Putnam, whose views on rationality (which are coherentist) and on truth (which are internalist), as on other matters,[33] I find largely sensible and persuasive, has written that "my view is not a view in which the mind *makes up* the world. . . . If one must use metaphorical language, then let the metaphor be this: the mind and the world jointly make up the mind and the world."[34]

III

That our theory-making and our language-making are constrained by the world (in conjunction with our interests and our projects) is crucial. Just as our beliefs can be inadequate to our interests and our projects—for example, the belief that I can, unaided, "leap tall buildings in a single bound" is inadequate to my interest in avoiding physical injury—our beliefs can be inadequate to the world. But this is not to make the point that some of our beliefs can fail to correspond to the world. That point, in implying that our beliefs can succeed in corresponding to the world, presupposes the correspondence theory. The statement that our beliefs can be inadequate to the world must not be confused with the correspondence theory. "We may say of a false judgment that things are not as the judgment declares them to be, or of a true judgment that he or she who utters it says that what it is is and what it is not is not. But there are not two distinguishable items, a judgment on the one hand and that portrayed in the judgment on the other, between which a relation of correspondence can hold or fail to hold."[35]

What, then, does it mean to say that our beliefs can be inadequate to the world? To say that a belief *is* inadequate to the world might be just a way of saying that the belief is inadequate to one or more of our interests or projects: For example, the world is not such that we human beings can, unaided, leap tall buildings in a single bound. But, the fact that a belief is not now seen to be inadequate to any of our interests or present projects—indeed, the fact that the belief is, so far as we can now tell, eminently adequate to our various interests and projects—does not entail that it is adequate to the world. History is replete with examples of beliefs—for example, some of the beliefs comprised by Newtonian physics—that, on the one hand, led people to do things that worked for them (or seemed to, at least) but that, on the other, eventually came to be seen as rationally unacceptable.

To say that a belief can be inadequate to the world is a way of saying that the belief might eventually come to be seen as rationally unacceptable—that, in that sense, the belief might be false, that it might not get it right, even if, so far as we can now tell, the belief is fully adequate to our interests and projects. It is a way of saying that a different, competitor belief might eventually come to be seen as better: more adequate to our interests and projects.[36] In that sense, the notion of the possibility of one or more of our present beliefs being inadequate to the world is a regulative ideal that challenges intellectual complacency about what we believe and supports development of a practice surely as salutary in morality as in science: self-critical rationality. Because it leaves room for the possibility that our beliefs can be inadequate to the world, the coherentist conception of rationality is in no way inhospitable to self-critical rationality.[37]

In leaving room for the possibility that beliefs can be inadequate to the world, the coherentist conception leaves room for the possibility that some beliefs about a matter can be more adequate to the world than other beliefs about the matter, in particular, that our future beliefs about a matter can be more adequate to the world than our present beliefs. The notion of such a possibility can be understood as an ideal "of final truth, . . . a relationship of the mind to its objects which would be wholly adequate in respect of the capacities of that mind."[38] Putnam's "internalist" account of "truth" as "idealized rational acceptability" is an ideal of final truth. Although it makes no sense—is not "rational"—to reject beliefs not only justified but as well justified as any beliefs of the sort can be, it is nonetheless possible that the beliefs are not adequate to the world, that, in that sense, they are not true.[39]

However, the regulative ideal of final truth—the notion of the possibility of one or more of our beliefs being inadequate to the world—precludes "any conception of that state [the "wholly adequate relationship of the mind to its objects"] as one in which the mind could by its own powers know itself as thus adequately informed . . . ; the Absolute Knowledge of the Hegelian system is from [the coherentist] standpoint a chimaera."[40] We can never know if one or more of our present beliefs about a matter are the final truth about the matter. "No one at any stage can rule out the future possibility of their present beliefs and judgments being shown to be inadequate in a variety of ways."[41]

But that we can never know if a present belief is (a part of) the final truth does not mean that the ideal of such a truth is inconsequential. To the contrary, it is precisely that ideal that cautions us against confusing our present beliefs, whatever they are, with final truth. As Thomas McCarthy has explained, the regulative ideal of final truth "is a driving force behind our critical-reflective practices. This is not to say that we have a substantive conception of 'the Truth' or even an explanatory theory of truth. But we do have an understanding-in-use of 'true' which enables, sometimes even requires, us to call into question accepted beliefs and practices. This is not a metaphysical point. As Wittgenstein might say, it is what we do: we treat truth claims as involving some 'transcendent,' 'regulative,' normative surplus of meaning beyond 'what we happen to agree upon at this particular time and place.' "[42]

IV

Sometimes a coherentist epistemological position is confused with, or is thought to presuppose or entail, an anti-realist position. But epistemological coherentism is inconsistent neither with scientific realism nor—more important, for present purposes—with moral realism. Epistemological coherentism is a position about the nature of rationality (reasoning, justification). Realism, whether scientific or moral, is a position about the world, including ourselves as a part of the world: that it is *real*—that it really exists—and, especially, that its existence is mind-independent, that it "is as it is whatever we think about it".[43] We can be *both* epistemological coherentist *and* scientific and/or moral realists.[44]

But, what is the "cash value" of realism: the real-world, practical value or point of the realist position, either in science or in morals? Does realism have any practical value? After all, whether one is a realist or not, one's practice of reasoning or justification, both particular instances and generally, can be only what the coherentist conception of rationality portrays; it cannot be more than that. Is the realism/anti-realism debate therefore merely a philosophical sideshow with little if any practical import for those of us concerned with the nature of reasoning or justification? Does the ideal of self-critical rationality require the support of the realist position?[45] Can't one embrace self-critical reflective practices without embracing realism?[46] Or does one's embrace of self-critical reflective practices somehow commit one to the realist position?

Rorty has written that "at times like that of Auschwitz, when history is in upheaval and traditional institutions and patterns of behavior are collapsing, we want something which stands beyond history and institutions. . . . I have been urging . . . that we try *not* to want something which stands beyond history and institutions. . . . [A] belief can still regulate action, can still be thought worth dying for, among people who are quite aware that this belief is caused by nothing deeper than contingent historical circumstance."[47] But is Rorty right? Perhaps realism does make a practical difference, and perhaps, contra Rorty, the difference—an existential difference—is this:

> [T]he loss of realism . . . means the loss of any and all realities independent of or transcendent to inquiry. In this respect, God must suffer the same fate as any other transcendent subject or object. Because faith makes sense only when accompanied by the possibility of doubt, Rorty's distancing of scepticism means a concomitant distancing of belief in "things unseen." He, unlike Kant, denies both knowledge and faith; but for what, if anything, is this supposed to make room? Faith may perhaps be given a purely dispositional reading, being seen as a tendency to act in a certain way, but any propositional content will be completely lost. The pull toward religious faith is at best a residue of metaphysical realism and of the craving for metaphysical comfort. The taste for the transcendent usually associated with a religious personality will find little place in a Rortian world. Similarly, hope and love, if thought to have a supernatural object or source, lose their point. The deconstruction of God must leave the pious individual feeling like F. Scott Fitzgerald after his crackup: "a feeling that I was standing at twilight on a deserted range, with an empty rifle in my hand and the targets down." The deconstructed heart is ever restless, yet the theological virtues stand only as perpetual temptations to rest in inauthenticity. We live in a world without inherent *telos*; so there simply is no rest as Christianity has traditionally conceived it.[48]

V

In discussions of the proper relation of religion and morality to politics (as I said at the beginning of this chapter) the issue of rationality often looms large. In this chapter, by way of background to my elaboration and defense, in subsequent chapters, of ecumenical politics, I have sought to explicate and distinguish: the *coherentist* account of rationality (reasoning, justification), the *internalist* account of truth, and the *realist* account of the subject matter of any inquiry, including moral inquiry.[49] It is the first of these positions, the coherentist conception of rationality, that is most relevant to,

because presupposed by, my conception of the proper role of beliefs (including religious beliefs) about human good in political
deliberation and justification. This is not to say that the coherentist
conception entails ecumenical politics. It does not: One can quite
consistently adhere both to the coherentist conception of rationality and to a conception of political deliberation and justification
other than the one I defend in this book. The point is simply that
my argument, in chapter 6, about the possibility of ecumenical
politics in our religiously/morally pluralistic context—in particular,
about the situational/contextual prerequisites to ecumenical political dialogue—presupposes the coherentist understanding of rationality set forth in this chapter. Because that understanding entails a
conception, the coherentist conception, of (rational) discourse, including deliberative discourse and justificatory discourse, my argument presupposes the coherentist conception both of deliberation
and of justification. Catherine Elgin's spare but articulate portrayal
of coherentists justification merits quotation:

> Support for a conclusion comes, not from a single line of argument,
> but from a host of considerations of varying degrees of strength and
> relevance. What justifies the categories we construct is the cognitive
> and practical utility of the truths they enable us to formulate, the
> elegance and informativeness of the accounts they engender, the
> value of the ends they promote. We engage in system-building when
> we find the resources at hand inadequate. We have projects they do
> not serve, questions they do not answer, values they do not realize.
> Something new is required. But the measure of the adequacy of a
> novelty is its fit with what we think we already know. If the finding is
> at all surprising, the background of accepted beliefs is apt to require
> modification to make room for it, and the finding may require revi-
> sion to be fitted into place. A process of delicate adjustments oc-
> curs, its goal being a system in wide reflective equilibrium.[50]

I now want to state a final point about coherentist epistemology.
Just as it is in no way inconsistent with self-critical rationality, the
coherentist conception of rationality is in no way inconsistent with
critical reflection on the beliefs of *other* persons or communities.
Just as our own beliefs can be inadequate to the world, so too can
the beliefs of others be inadequate to the world. Just as "final
truth", as a regulative ideal, supports self-critical reflective practices, so too it supports other-critical reflective practices. In particu-

lar, the coherentist conception of rationality should not be confused with a vulgar cognitive relativism according to which the (coherent) web of beliefs of one person or community is either (a) just as "good" as any other persons's or community's (coherent) web of beliefs or, at least, (b) immune to effective critique from the "outside": from the vantage point of the web of beliefs of another person or community.[51] I develop the point in later chapters, where, in the course of commenting on the implications of coherentism for ecumenical political tolerance, I explain why position (a) is a mistake, a confusion,[52] and, in the course of defending the practice of ecumenical political dialogue, I emphasize something overlooked or minimized by those who advance position (b), namely, that there is often a significant common area among the various webs of belief of different persons and communities.[53]

5

Religion and Morality

My general concern in this book is the proper relation of morality to politics, in particular, the proper role of beliefs about human good in political deliberation and justification. My specific concern, however, is the role of *religious* beliefs: In elaborating and defending the ideal of ecumenical politics, I focus principally on religious beliefs about human good. (As I said in Chapter 3, ecumenical politics institutionalizes a particular conception of "the place of religion in American life" and of "how we should contend with each other's deepest differences in the public sphere.") I do so mainly because in American society the question of the proper relation of religion to politics poses the issues I want to address, about morality and politics, in their most controversial, difficult, and indeed urgent form. But because my focus on religion may be misleading, I want to emphasize here, as I did in the introduction to this book, that much of what I have to say is meant to respond to the general question of morality and politics as well as to the specific question of religion—religious morality—and politics.

Just as it was useful (in my view) to pause to address the issue of rationality, it is useful to pause again, this time to address the question of what makes a morality "religious"—or, put another way, of what it means to say that beliefs about human good are "religious". My elaboration and defense of ecumenical political dialogue, principally in chapter 6, rely on a particular understanding of "religious" morality. In this chapter I clarify that understanding. Such a clarification seems especially important given pervasive misunderstandings, in contemporary intellectual culture, of religion and of allied matters, like theology. "Misunderstanding" is, in some cases, too weak and polite a term. As David Tracy has written, in our society religion is "the single subject about which many intellectuals can feel free to be ignorant. Often abetted by the churches, they need not study religion, for 'everybody' already knows what religion is: It is a private consumer product that some people seem to need. Its former social role was poisonous. Its present privatization is harmless enough to wish it well from a civilized distance. Religion seems to be the sort of thing one likes 'if that's the sort of thing one likes.' "[1] The understanding of "religious" morality and, relatedly, of the enterprise of theology, including moral theology, I present in this chapter is not theologically neutral. There is no such thing as a theologically neutral understanding or account of religion or theology.[2]

I

Charles Taylor has recently argued, in his *Sources of the Self: The Making of the Modern Identity*, that "[t]he problem of the meaning of life is . . . on our agenda, however much we may jibe at the phrase."[3] The problem of the meaning of life does not arise for everyone; it is not on everyone's agenda (even if, as Taylor argues, it is on the agenda of "our" age). But it does arise for many. The problem can even arise *again* for someone, after it had been resolved, or repressed—someone who had been convinced, for whatever reason(s), of the meaningfulness of life, and especially of her own life, but whose conviction has been gradually eroded or perhaps suddenly shattered. As the story of Siddhartha illustrates, a principal occasion of its arising (or arising again)—at least, of its arising in an existential, as distinct from merely intellectual, way— is a searing encounter with such common but elemental events as sickness, old age, and death.[4] Another principal occasion is an encounter, whether personal or vicarious, with evil and the terrible, primal suffering evil causes.[5] Such experiences, and experiences of other kinds, can leave one with a feeling that she is, or might be, a stranger, an alien, an exile, homeless, anxious, vulnerable, threatened, in a world, a universe, that is, finally and radically, unfamiliar, hostile, perhaps even pointless, absurd. Albert Camus wrote: "What, then, is that incalculable feeling that deprives the mind of the sleep necessary to life? A world that can be explained even with bad reasons is a familiar world. But, . . . in a universe suddenly divested of illusions and lights, man feels an alien, a stranger. His exile is without remedy since he is deprived of the memory of a lost home or the hope of a promised land. This divorce between man and his life, the actor and his setting, is properly the feeling of absurdity."[6]

Because of its radically alienating character, any such experience can be an occasion of existential confrontation with the problem of meaning:

> Am I indeed an alien, an exile, homeless, in a world, a universe, that is strange, hostile, pointless, absurd? Or, instead, is the world, finally and radically, familiar, even gracious; does the world have a point, indeed, is it a point, a project; is the world, in that sense, meaningful: meaning-full, full of meaning rather than bereft of it (and therefore meaning-less, absurd)? I am a part of the world. If the world has a point, if it is a project, do I have a part? A part such that the world is hospitable or, instead, inhospitable to me in my deep yearning to be at home, rooted, connected?

For the person deep in the grip of, the person claimed by, the problem of meaning,[7] "[t]he cry for meaning is a cry for ultimate relationship, for ultimate belonging", wrote Abraham Heschel. "It is a cry in which all pretensions are abandoned. Are we alone in the wilderness of time, alone in the dreadfully marvelous universe, of which we are a part and where we feel forever like strangers? Is there a Presence to live by? A Presence worth living for, worth dying for? Is there a way of living in the Presence? Is there a way of living compatible with the Presence?"[8]

One might try to dismiss the problem of meaning by trivializing it.[9] One might contend, for example, that concern with the problem of meaning (and especially a religious response to the problem) is little more than a consequence of a psychological-developmental defect, or a false consciousness, of some sort. But why take seriously such crudely reductionist arguments? As Leszek Kolakowski has observed, "The phenomenon of the world's indifference belongs to fundamental experiences, that is, those it is impossible to intercept as specific cases of another, more primitive need."[10] The drafters of *The Williamsburg Charter* are right in suggesting that "the drive toward meaning and belonging, toward making sense of life and finding community in the world", is not merely "characteristic of humankind" but, indeed, both "natural and inescapable".[11] "Man's concern about a meaning of life is the truest expression of the state of being human."[12]

One polar response to the problem of meaning is to conclude that life is, finally and radically, meaningless, or that, even if meaningful in some ultimate sense, life is not meaningful in a way hospitable to our deepest yearnings for what Heschel called "ultimate relationship, ultimate belonging."[13] Consider, for example, Clarence Darrow's bleak vision (as recounted by Paul Edwards):

> Darrow, one of the most compassionate men who ever lived, . . . concluded that life was an "awful joke." . . . Darrow offered as one of his reasons the apparent aimlessness of all that happens. "This weary old world goes on, begetting, with birth and with living and with death," he remarked in his moving plea for the boy-murderers Loeb and Leopold, "and all of it is blind from the beginning to the end." Elsewhere he wrote: "Life is like a ship on the sea, tossed by every wave and by every wind; a ship headed for no port and no harbor, with no rudder, no compass, no pilot; simply floating for a time, then lost in the waves." In addition to the aimlessness of life and the universe, there is the fact of death. "I love my friends," wrote Darrow, "but they all must come to a tragic end." Death is more terrible the more one is attached to things in the world. Life, he concludes, is "not worthwhile," and he adds . . . that "it is an unpleasant interruption of nothing, and the best thing you can say of it is that it does not last long."[14]

Responses like Darrow's have been more prevalent, increasingly so, since the dawn of modernity, of course: In pre-modern times the demystification/disenchantment and secularization of the world had not yet begun in earnest.

It is an interesting and difficult question, the relation of a life of compassion to a vision as bleak as Darrow's,[15] or, indeed, the relation of any kind of life, of any kind of living, as distinct from dying, from suicide, to such a vision.[16] Is there any difference, in that regard, between Darrow's uncompromisingly honest vision and the (equivocal?) vision of those who say something to the

effect that although life is not ultimately meaningful, it is provisionally meaningful—meaningful in the here and now—and that that's
meaning enough?[17] Is provisional meaningfulness really enough?
Rabbi Heschel wrote that "[a] finite meaning that claims to be an
ultimate answer is specious. The assumption, for example, that the
pursuit of knowledge, the enjoyment of beauty, of sheer being as
an end in itself, is a principle we may utter, not a truth man can live
by. Tell man that he is an end in himself, and his answer will be
despair."[18] That some people feel quite happy even as they believe
that life is ultimately absurd has limited significance. Some people
feel quite miserable even as they believe that life is ultimately
meaningful. Strange things determine or at least affect people's
feelings, after all: drugs, parents, illusions, and so on. And in any
event people's feelings, their affective responses, don't always
make a lot of sense. Or whatever sense they make may require a
lot of psychotherapy to fathom.

II

The other polar response to the problem of meaning is "religious":
the trust that life is ultimately meaningful, meaningful in a way
hospitable to our deepest yearnings. The word "religion" derives
from the Latin verb "religare", which means to bind together again
that which was once bound but has since been torn or broken; to
heal.[19] A "religious" vision, then, etymologically understood, is a
vision of final and radical reconciliation, a set of beliefs about how
one is or can be bound or connected to the world—to the "other"
and to "nature"—and, above all, to Ultimate Reality[20] in a profoundly intimate and ultimately meaningful way. It is a confusion,
on this understanding of religion, to think of an all-encompassing
worldview or ideology (like Marxism?) as "religious", if it is not
grounded in a vision of the ultimately meaningful, the ultimately
reconciled/reconciling, nature of the world.[21]

Throughout human history it has been the so-called religious
mystics who have trusted most deeply and affirmed most passion-
ately the ultimate meaningfulness of life.[22] Although her experience
that life is ultimately meaningful is deeply personal, the religious
mystic denies that the experience is reducible to an idiosyncratic,

perhaps even pathological, psychological state. Notwithstanding its noetic quality, however, and for all its potency, the mystical experience is often, if not invariably, transitory.[23] Moreover, not everyone is graced by such experience (or graced as often, or to the same degree). In the aftermath of mystical experience, therefore, or in its absence, fundamental questions about the meaning of human existence—questions that so thoroughly pervade, and so relentlessly subvert, our lives—remain in need of answers that are intellectually satisfying and emotionally resonant. In Milan Kundera's *The Unbearable Lightness of Being* the narrator, referring to "the questions that had been going through Tereza's head since she was a child", says that "the only truly serious questions are ones that even a child can formulate. Only the most naive of questions are truly serious. They are the questions with no answers. A question with no answer is a barrier than cannot be breached. In other words, *it is questions with no answers that set the limits of human possibilities, describe the boundaries of human existence.*"[24] Communities, especially historically extended communities—"traditions"—are the principal matrices of religious answers to such questions:[25] Who are we? Where did we come from; what is our origin, our beginning? Where are we going; what is our destiny, our end?[26] What is the meaning of suffering? Of evil? Of death? And there is the cardinal question, the question that comprises many of the others: Is life ultimately meaningful or, instead, ultimately bereft of meaning, meaning-less, absurd? If any questions are fundamental, *these* questions—"religious or limit questions"[27]—are fundamental. Such questions—"naive" questions, "questions with no answers", "barriers that cannot be breached"—are "the most serious and difficult . . . that any human being or society must face. . . . To formulate such questions honestly and well, to respond to them with passion and rigor, is the work of all theology. . . . Religions ask and respond to such fundamental questions. . . . Theologians, by definition, risk an intellectual life on the wager that religious traditions can be studied as authentic responses to just such questions."[28]

Theology need not be a practice internal to a community: A theologian can study the religious beliefs of a community of which she is not a member. But understood as an internal practice—a practice embedded in the life of a religious community/tradition—theology represents, in part, the institutionalization of reflection, including self-critical reflection,[29] on the community's religious beliefs (including its religious-moral beliefs), on its answers to the "limit" questions. In its critical aspect, theological reflection is a systematic inquiry into and, if warranted, revision of the beliefs, even the central creedal propositions, that have emerged in the life of an historically extended religious community in the course of its encounter and struggle with fundamental human questions. But the critical aspect of theology is mainly prologue to its constructive aspect: a systematic effort to mediate the faith, the existential trust, that emerges from—or survives, even if transformed—the encounter/struggle of a religious community/tradition with such questions. Theology (understood as an internal practice) is principally aimed at mediating in an ever more adequate way the faith of an historically extended religious community.

Ever more adequate, but never fully adequate. Theological reflection is a recurring moment in an unending dialectic of faith and reflection.[30] The dialectic is unending because, as religious mystics themselves emphatically testify, the Ultimate Reality that is the term (but not the object[31]) of theological reflection—the Uncreated and Indestructible, the Absolutely First and Absolutely Last Reality, which (or whom) Western religions have named "God"—is, finally, beyond all thought and speech. At its best theological reflection is ruthless in its drive to negate, or at least relativize, and transcend every concept of Ultimate Reality. (At its worst, its most primitive, such reflection tends to absolutize one or another such concept.[32]) Indeed, a person of faith need not even be a theist, in the sense of one who finds God-talk meaningful. One of the world's great religions, Buddhism, is predominantly nontheistic. But even a participant in a theistic tradition can be quite wary about God-talk.[33] In any event, God-talk that confuses any particular conceptualization of Ultimate Reality for Ultimate Reality dishonors the Second Commandment: "You shall not make yourself a carved image or any likeness of anything in heaven above or on earth beneath or in the waters under the earth; you shall not bow down to them or serve them. . . ."[34] Rabbi Heschel instructed that "[t]he second commandment implies more than the prohibition of images; it implies rejection of all visible symbols for God."[35] There is a Taoist version of the Second Commandment:

The Tao that can be told
is not the eternal Tao.
The name that can be named
is not the eternal Name.

The unnameable is the beginning
of heaven and earth.
The named is the mother
of ten thousand things.

Free from desire,
you realize the mystery.
Caught in desire,
you see only the manifestations.

Yet mystery and manifestations
arise from the same source.
This source is called darkness.

Darkness within darkness.
The gateway to all understanding.[36]

An important distinction, which has informed my discussion in this chapter, is essential to a proper account of religion and theology: the distinction between religious faith and religious beliefs. Religious faith is best understood as trust in the ultimate meaningfulness of life—that is, the ultimate meaningfulness of the world and of one's own life, one's own being, as part of and related to, as embedded in, the world.[37] Religious beliefs, by contrast, are best understood as religious faith mediated by—understood and expressed in the medium of—words, whether concretely, in stories, or abstractly, in concepts and ideas. "Formulated belief is an attempt to translate into words an unutterable spiritual reality."[38] Thus, religious faith does not necessarily involve assent to creedal propositions, though a person's or community's mediation of her or its faith can eventuate in such propositions. Insisting that "[i]t is . . . necessary to distinguish faith and beliefs", Charles Davis has written:

> Faith is the fundamental religious response. It is an orientation towards the Transcendent, an unrestricted opening of the mind and heart to Reality as Unlimited, or to the Infinite. It can be described as a basic trust in Reality or as a universal love of Reality. It is not

merely relatively transcendent, but absolutely so, inasmuch as it is a thrust beyond every human order of meaning, beyond all the particular forms through which it is mediated in the different religious traditions. As an orientation it has a term, the Transcendent, but no object, because the Transcendent remains unknown. The term of the response of faith is mystery, because we have no proper knowledge of the Transcendent. We cannot grasp the Transcendent as an object; we can merely indicate the Infinite, the Unlimited, through symbols.

The response of religious faith as an awareness of the Transcendent constitutes a fundamental stance on the subject which, like an originating idea, takes possession of the mind and heart and widens the horizon within which the person thinks, judges, decides, and acts. This, in turn, gives rise to a body of religious beliefs. . . . Both kinds of religious beliefs—judgments of value and judgments of fact—are thus the product of interpretive reflection by the human mind within the horizon opened up by faith. . . . Societies begin not with a *tabula rasa,* but with an inherited tradition; religious beliefs are always part of that tradition. Like all human creations, however, religious beliefs are relative, mutable, and limited by culture. . . . Religious beliefs are the changing, limited, culturally particular manifestation of religious faith.[39]

As God-talk (for example) dramatically illustrates, the beliefs a theology comprises, the beliefs it ratifies or systematizes or generates, are, like religious beliefs generally, historically contingent. They are, in that sense, relative and provisional. As a Dutch theologian recently particularized the general point: "[W]e know very well that the message of Christian faith, from the Bible to the present day, can only be expressed in the terms of a particular time, and therefore that it is a prime requirement not to confuse the message and the time."[40] This distinction between faith and beliefs is of course threatening to some religious believers because subversive of some religious beliefs. The distinction opens a space for, even necessitates, a critical stance toward beliefs, including a self-critical stance toward one's own beliefs, which, according to the distinction, are merely contingent and therefore immune neither to change nor reformation. "To suppose otherwise is to fall into idolatry, making the conditional unconditioned and confusing religious beliefs with religious faith."[41] At its best, then, theological discourse, like discourse of any kind (at its best), is self-critical.[42]

John Updike has written that "[t]heology is not a provable accumulation, like science, nor is it a succession of enduring monuments, like art. It must always unravel and be reknit."[43] Because theological articulations are historically contingent and reformable, often the challenge to a theology, especially after a period of unraveling, is to reknit: to speak in a new voice, a voice of the present and accessible to the present, which means in part to mediate—to understand and express—the faith of the community in terms commensurate with what is deeply authoritative for the present, especially the reflective common sense of the present and the widely accepted yield of contemporary intellectual inquiry. This is what the best theology of any period has always done: mine and use the relevant philosophical, scientific, and artistic materials and resources of its present to understand and then speak anew and thereby be heard anew. "Theology's proper task . . . requires the use of philosophical concepts. . . . The historical disciplines are likewise necessary for the theologian's investigations. . . . Finally, a consultation of the 'human sciences' is also necessary. . . . It is the theologian's task to draw from the surrounding culture those elements which will allow him to better illumine one or other aspect of the mysteries of faith. This is certainly an arduous task that has its risks, but it is legitimate in itself and should be encouraged."[44] (One such risk, of course—though it is hardly a risk *just* for theologians—is the risk of trimming self-critical rationality to suit contemporary intellectual fashion.)

III

Now we come to the crux of the matter: religious *morality* (and, inferentially, *moral* theology). Recall one of Rabbi Heschel's questions: "Is there a way of living compatible with the Presence?" For one for whom the problem of meaning has arisen and who trusts that life is ultimately meaningful—in other words, for the "religious" person—to live a "moral" life, a "truly, fully human" life, a life as deeply fulfilling as any of which she is capable, is, above all, whatever else it is, to live a meaningful life: a life oriented by and to the way in which life is trusted and believed to be ultimately meaningful—"a life compatible with the Presence".

Given a choice—a tragically extreme but happily uncommon choice—between, on the one hand, living a life experienced as satisfying ("happy") in all the conventional ways but believed to be unfaithful, meaningless, and, on the other hand, living a life experienced as unsatisfying in all the conventional ways but believed to be faithful, meaningful, the religious person is committed to the latter life. For the person of religious faith, *that* life, not the conventionally "happy" life, is the deeply fulfilling one, as the lives of exemplary religious figures, like Jesus and Buddha, both confirm and illustrate.

As a species of moral beliefs, religious-moral beliefs are about how it is good or fitting for human beings to live their lives.[45] As moral beliefs religious in character, religious-moral beliefs presuppose a vision of the ultimate—the final and radical—meaningfulness of life. They are about how to live in a way that is faithful to that ("religious") vision, faithful to what one believes about the meaningfulness of life. Religious-moral beliefs are about how to live a deeply fulfilling life in the sense of a life that, whether happy or unhappy in some conventional sense, conduces to, even constitutes, a fundamentally rooted, connected, unalienated way of being in the world. Whereas in contemporary political-philosophical parlance a set of beliefs, whether religious or not, about how it is good or fitting for human beings to live is often called a "conception of the good",[46] in the parlance of much religious ethics such a vision is commonly thought of as a conception of the human, of what it means to be "truly" or "authentically" human.[47] For example, the Dutch Catholic theologian Edward Schillebeeckx has written that "[t]he ethical has essentially to do with the question: 'What really is human being?', and because of this, with the question 'How does one want to ultimately live out one's being human?' or 'For which way of being human does one finally decide?' "[48] Consider, too, these comments by James Burtchaell of Notre Dame's Theology Department:

> The Catholic tradition embraces a long effort to uncover the truth about human behavior and experience. Our judgments of good and evil focus on whether a certain course of action will make a human being grow and mature and flourish, or whether it will make a person withered, estranged and indifferent. In making our evaluations, we have little to draw on except our own and our forebears'

experience, and whatever wisdom we can wring from our debate with others. . . .

What we are trying to unpuzzle are things like childbearing and immigration and economic policy and infant mortality and drug use and family fidelity and so much else about which we must frame moral judgments. With our fellow communicants we share commitments and assumptions: that we are happier giving than getting, that there is no greater love than to put down your life for your neighbor, and that your neighbor always turns out to be the most unlikely person.[49]

The preceding passage illustrates a point that bears directly on my argument in this book and that I now want to emphasize: Religions—religious visions—and the theologies, including the moral theologies, that attend them have an essentially political character.[50] As I indicated earlier, a religious vision is a vision of final and radical reconciliation, a set of beliefs about how one is or can be bound or connected to the world—to the "other" and to "nature"—and, above all, to Ultimate Reality in a profoundly intimate and ultimately meaningful way. But every religious vision also comprises beliefs—moral beliefs—about how to live compatibly with the basic religious beliefs: how to live a "moral" life, a "truly human" life, in the sense of a life oriented by and to the way in which life is trusted and believed to be ultimately meaningful, "a life compatible with the Presence" (in Heschel's phrase). "Religions . . . are not only explanations of the meaning of life, but also ways (for example, *Hodos,* Christianity; *Halakah,* Judaism; *Shariah* Islam; *Tao,* Chinese religion) to live according to that explanation. For example, the Buddhist is not only to seek liberation interiorly, but also to practice the virtues of justice, honesty, and compassion."[51] This, then, is the sense in which all religions/theologies—in particular, all religious moralities/moral theologies—are political: They comprise norms governing one's relation to others (as well as to nature and to Ultimate Reality).

However, the political norms embedded in a religious vision, the norms governing one's relation to others, might counsel a politically passivist life rather than a politically activist one. Therefore, although any religion/theology is essentially political, a particular religion/theology might be political only in a weak sense of the term. But some religions/theologies are essentially political in a

strong sense. Certainly the Western religions/theologies with which
we are principally concerned in this book—the "Jerusalem-
based"[52] or semitic spiritualities: Judaism, Christianity, and
Islam—are, in the main, political in a strong sense. They are "prophetic".[53] The religious moralities grounded in Jewish and Christian
religious visions and traditions have at times tended to mandate
efforts to challenge the social-political-economic status quo in the
interests of "the least of our brethren":[54] the poor, the sick, the
abused, and indeed all of society's marginalized persons. (Of
course, religious moralities and moralists have also at times apolo-
gized for the status quo in the interests of the powerful—who sometimes included the moralists themselves and their religious
institutions—or at least to curry favor with the powerful. But there
is another side to the story.) Consider, in that regard, the Prophets
of the Jewish Bible.[55] Consider, too, the prophetic religious leaders
of our own time—like Martin Luther King, Jr., Abraham Joshua
Heschel, and Dorothy Day—and the prophetic religious dimensions of the civil rights movement, the anti-Vietnam War movement, and the anti-nuclear movement. Consider, too, the emergence of liberation theology in Third World countries, especially in
Central and South America.[56]

Schillebeeckx has written (in a statement quoted at the beginning of this book) that "prayer or mysticism without political love
quickly becomes sentimental and irrelevant interiority."[57] Schillebeeckx's statement is firmly rooted in his Christian religious tradition, where the principal commandment given by Jesus (at a Passover seder on the eve of his execution) is to love one another: "I
give you a new commandment: love one another; you must love
one another just as I have loved you."[58] There is no doubt that in
the Gospel vision, this love is to be, in part, what Schillebeeckx
calls "political love". For example, in the Last Judgment scene in
Matthew's Gospel—a passage echoing the Jewish prophets—it is
written:

> He will place the sheep on his right hand and the goats on his left.
> Then the King will say to those on his right hand, "Come, you whom
> my Father had blessed, take as your heritage the kingdom prepared
> for you since the foundation of the world. For I was hungry and you
> gave me food, I was thirsty and you gave me drink, I was a stranger
> and you made me welcome, lacking clothes and you clothed me,

sick and you visited me, in prison and you came to see me." Then
the upright will say to him in reply, "Lord, when did we see you
hungry and feed you, or thirsty and give you drink? When did we
see you a stranger and make you welcome, lacking clothes and
clothe you? When did we find you sick or in prison and go to see
you?" And the King will answer, "In truth I tell you, in so far as you
did this to one of the least of these brothers of mine, you did it to
me." Then he will say to those on his left hand, "Go away from me,
with your curse upon you, to the eternal fire prepared for the devil
and his angels. For I was hungry and you never gave me food, I was
thirsty and you never gave me anything to drink, I was a stranger
and you never made me welcome, lacking clothes and you never
clothed me, sick and in prison and you never visited me." Then it
will be their turn to ask, "Lord, when did we see you hungry or
thirsty, a stranger or lacking clothes, sick or in prison, and did not
come to your help?" Then he will answer, "In truth I tell you, in so
far as you neglected to do this to one of the least of these, you
neglected to do it to me."[59]

According to H. Mark Roelofs, "It takes almost a conscious blind-
ness not to see the social import of [such] lines. And they are not
exceptional. . . . [M]any other passages are just as plain. All are as
clear as anything in the Old Testament that in the biblical perspective to know God and do his will is to heal the sick, tend the poor,
and liberate the oppressed, a message as much distinctively political and social as it is moral."[60]

In the view of Karl Rahner—a view fully consonant with Matthew's Last Judgment scene—there is no tension between the
older commandment to love God and the newer commandment to
love one another. (Jesus the Jew did not mean to, he would not
have presumed to, abrogate the former.) Indeed, in his "Reflections on the Unity of the Love of Neighbor and the Love of God",
Rahner argued for "a radical identity of the two loves."[61] "It is
radically true, i.e. by an ontological and not merely 'moral' or
psychological necessity, that whoever does not love the brother
whom he 'sees', also cannot love God whom he does not see, and
that one can love God whom one does not see only *by* loving one's
visible brother lovingly."[62] (Rahner's reference is to the passage in
John's First Letter in which it is written: "Anyone who says 'I love
God' and hates his brother, is a liar, since whoever does not love
the brother whom he can see cannot love God whom he has not

seen."[63]) Thus, in Rahner's view the two great commandments are really one.[64] (Rahner argued that if and to the extent one loved one's neighbor, one had achieved the ontological/existential state of being/consciousness that constitutes "love of God", even if one did not "believe in God".[65])

The Jewish and Christian religious visions, then, understood as adherents like Heschel, Rahner, and Schillebeeckx understand them, are neither just mystical nor just political but, instead and inseparably, mystical-political.[66] (As Robert McAffee Brown has recently written, even the great German mystic, "Meister Eckhart . . . knew where the saints should be found. Reflecting on the fact that Paul was once lifted to 'the third heaven,' he continued: 'Even if a man were in rapture like St. Paul and knew of a man who was in need of food he would do better by feeding him than by remaining in ecstasy.' "[67]) The mystical aspect of spirituality has often been associated with flight from, or distance from, the world. Johannes Baptist Metz—"the European theologian most sensitive to Third World [religious] views"[68]—has tried to correct such an understanding of mysticism, which, to the extent it purports to be an understanding of Christian mysticism (or, for that matter, of semitic mysticism generally) is a misunderstanding:

> Christian mysticism is neither a kind of pantheistic infinity mysticism, nor an esoteric mysticism of exaltation, tending toward the self-redemption of the individual soul. It is—putting it extremely— a mysticism of human bonding. But it does not proceed from an arbitrary denial of persons and the world, in order to seek to rise toward a direct nearness to God. For the God of Christian faith is found only in the movement of God's love towards persons, "the least," as has been revealed to us in Jesus Christ. Christian mysticism finds, therefore, that direct experience of God which it seeks, precisely in daring to imitate the unconditional involvement of the divine love for persons, in letting itself be drawn into the . . . descent of God's love to the least of God's brothers and sisters. Only in this movement do we find the supreme nearness, the supreme immediacy of God. And that is why mysticism, which seeks this nearness, has its place not outside, beside, or above responsibility for the world of our brothers and sisters, but in the center of it.[69]

Although Metz is a Catholic Christian, his understanding of the mystical as prophetic, or political, is not sectarian. It is an understanding that has characterized, at least since the latter part of the nineteenth century, not just Catholic social teaching but Christian social ethics generally, according to which: "Since the faith of Christians is a faith that does justice, there is no way we can avoid political activity. Whether the political realm is viewed Lutheran-like as a realm of lesser evil or more Calvinistically as the arena of the mediocre good, Christians cannot avoid involvement in the political process."[70] According to Heschel, Rahner, Schillebeeckx, Metz, and many others, a "private"—as distinct from public/political—spirituality is a counterfeit, an inauthentic, spirituality. To try to privatize—private-ize—religious morality, rather than public-ize/politic-ize it, is to misunderstand fundamentally the character of religious moralities of the sort that predominate in the West.[71] And, increasingly, it is to misunderstand as well the character of religious moralities the world over. Partly in consequence of mutually transformative ecumenical encounter and dialogue[72] with one or more of the semitic religions, Indic spiritualities—in particular, Hinduism and Buddhism—are retrieving from their margins their prophetic resources[73] (just as Christianity, for example, is retrieving from *its* margins its *mystical* resources[74]). In that regard, and as I noted in chapter 2, the great religious traditions, Indic as well as semitic, tend to converge with one another in affirming that an essential part of what it means to be fully human, an essential requirement of the meaningful life for everyone, is to accept some responsibility for the basic well-being of the Other (the outsider, the stranger, the alien).

A fundamental problem with conceptions of political justification like those advanced by Bruce Ackerman and Thomas Nagel (and criticized in chapter 1) is that the idealization of, and the related effort to achieve, "neutral" (or "impartial") politics entails repression of the essentially political nature of religion. In their effort to marginalize the role of religious (and other) conceptions of human good in political-justificatory discourse, Ackerman, Nagel, and others presuppose that religious convictions have a personal or private (as distinct from political or public) character; they thereby contribute to the privatization of religious convictions, even prophetic convictions of the sort that have helped inspire some of our most cherished movements for social change. This repression of the essentially political nature of religion is an especially insidious, if unintended, aspect of efforts to imagine a neutral politics. The marginalization/privatization of religious conceptions of human good engenders a counterfeit—inauthentic—spirituality. Moreover, it engenders a politics that, at best, "may often be shrewd but in the end remains no more than a business", as Max Horkheimer and Theodor Adorno said of "politics that does not contain theology within itself, however little considered".[75] Schillebeeckx has warned that at its worst such a politics—"a politics without prayer or mysticism"—can become "grim and barbaric."[76]

This is not to deny what in any event history will not let us deny, and what any serious reflection on religion and politics must acknowledge and accommodate: that both political religion and religious politics have a dark side, that each poses serious problems. But history reveals as well that each also has a liberating side. The matter of religion and politics is complex, not simple,[77] though it may sometimes appear simple to the simple-minded. (Great intelligence is no immunity to simple-mindedness.) Moreover, we should be wary about "project[ing] into the future of the Republic the nightmares, real or fancied, of the past."[78] Neither as individuals nor as communities are we condemned to repeat the mistakes of the past; least of all are we condemned to do so if we take care to remember the mistakes of the past—especially the most tragic mistakes, the darkest and bloodiest mistakes, the "nightmares" most "real" and least "fancied"—and then to guard against them.

The serious question, then, is not *whether* to mix religion and politics. The serious, and difficult, question is *how* to mix them. A principal inquiry pursued in this book is: How, in what way or ways, ought religious (and other) moralities to be politic-ized in a society as religiously and morally pluralistic as American society?[79] I begin addressing that question in the next chapter.

6

Ecumenical Political Dialogue

> "Civilization is formed by persons locked together in argument. From this dialogue the community becomes a political community." This statement . . . exactly expresses the mind of St. Thomas Aquinas, who was himself giving refined expression to the tradition of classic antiquity, which in its prior turn had given first elaboration to the concept of the "civil multitude," the multitude that is not a mass or a herd or a huddle, because it is characterized by civility. . . . Civility dies with the death of dialogue.[1]

The principal constituents of ecumenical politics are two practices: a certain kind of dialogue and a certain kind of tolerance. In chapter 3, in which I introduced the idea of ecumenical politics, I began to elaborate and defend ecumenical political dialogue; I gave several reasons for taking such dialogue seriously. In this chapter I am principally concerned with two types of prerequisites to ecumenical political dialogue: situational or contextual prerequisites and existential prerequisites. Mindful, however, that ecumenical political dialogue is not always productive or even possible, that it does not always or even often lead to agreement—indeed, that it should not always lead to agreement, that agreement is not the true test or measure of the success of such dialogue (a point I develop later in this chapter)—I turn, in chapter 7, to the matter of tolerance (of positions and choices with which one disagrees). I elaborate and defend there the kind of tolerance constitutive of ecumenical politics.

I

The practice of ecumenical political dialogue, like the politics it (along with ecumenical political tolerance) constitutes, is an ideal. To argue that we should take the practice seriously is not to claim that ecumenical political dialogue can actually be achieved in each and every situation or context. To what extent, if any, is the ideal of ecumenical political dialogue achievable in our religiously/morally pluralistic context? What are the situational or contextual prerequisites to such dialogue?

The sort of dialogue at issue here is normative dialogue, which is, whatever else it is, a process for making normative judgments: judgments about what choice to make, what action to take, and so on. Such dialogue can take place between and among persons only if and to the extent they share a common moral "language" or "vocabulary": normative premises—"values"—that can ground and focus their dialogic efforts. "For judgment to be at all possible, there must be standards of judgment. . . ." For dialogic judgment to be at all possible, there must be "a community of judgment. . . . That is, there must be underlying grounds of judgment which [the persons], *qua* members of a judging community, share, and which serve to unite in communication even those who disagree (*and who may disagree radically*). The very act of communication implies some basis of common judgment. . . . The very possibility of communication means that disagreement and conflict are grounded in a deeper unity. This is what may be termed, borrowing Kantian language, a 'transcendental' requirement of discourse."[2] The community of judgment may be a very "thin" community, in the sense that the shared grounds of judgment may be few and quite indeterminate relative to the issues that engage the persons. Or the community may be very "thick": The shared grounds may be many and quite determinate. But whether thin or thick, a community of judgment is a prerequisite to normative dialogue. (To the extent it generates further shared premises, normative dialogue thickens the community between/among the interlocutors. Thus, normative dialogue not only requires community; it can serve as a matrix of, it can engender, community.)

Whereas the fundamental situational/contextual prerequisite to normative dialogue is the existence of community—"a judging community"—the fundamental such prerequisite for political dialogue in particular is the existence of *political* community: There must be underlying grounds of political judgment—grounds concerning how the collective life, the life in common, is to be lived—which citizens, *qua* members of a judging community, share, and which serve to unite them in dialogue, notwithstanding their (sometimes radical) disagreements.

The coherentist conception of discourse set forth in chapter 4 does not entail that there cannot be political dialogue in a religiously/morally pluralistic society like our own. It's easy to see how the members of a single religious community, because of the many basic moral beliefs they share, can engage in productive moral dialogue among themselves. But even the members of a large pluralistic society, which comprises many different religious and other moral communities, might share enough basic moral beliefs that (political-)moral dialogue is often a realistic possibility for them.[3] First, "everything which we can identify as a human being or as a culture will be something which shares an enormous number of beliefs with us. (If it did not, we would simply not be able to recognize that it was speaking a language, and thus that it had any beliefs at all.)"[4] Second, "[a] fully individuable culture [or moral community] is at best a rare thing. Cultures, subcultures, fragments of cultures, constantly meet one another and exchange or modify practices and attitudes."[5] Indeed, moral dialogue among members of different religious/moral communities can be, at its best, as ecumenical religious dialogues have demonstrated,[6] a principal medium through which different communities "meet one another and exchange or modify practices or attitudes". (It is a mistake to conceive of this process as simply or even primarily cognitive. As I suggest later in this chapter, the process is, in important respects, affective as well: a process in which hearts as well as minds are transformed.)

But, to say that ecumenical political dialogue is a possibility in a pluralistic society like ours—to say, that is, that a plurality of religious/moral communities can together constitute a (pluralistic) political community—is not to say that there is in fact such political community in our society or, therefore, that ecumenical political dialogue is a realizable, much less real, practice for us. To what extent, if any, is there such political community in our religiously/ morally pluralistic society? Do we Americans constitute simply a nation of (religious/moral) communities but not a true political community? *E pluribus unum.* We are certainly "plural": We differ from one another in important respects; in particular, we do not all have the same needs and wants; therefore, what is good for some of us may well not be good for all of us, and may even be bad for some (others) of us. We are also—and this is more relevant to the challenge of achieving ecumenical political dialogue in a society like ours—morally and religiously pluralistic: There are among us numerous competing beliefs or convictions about how it is good or fitting for human beings (including, indeed especially, us) to live their (our) lives. In what sense and to what extent, if any, are we also "one"? "The society in which we live (unlike, for instance, Homeric Greece) is just as faction-ridden as it is coherent. We are apt to be misled by the fact that we use a single term, *society,* to designate a complicated system of cultures and subcultures, each with its own values. . . . There are every bit as many contested beliefs as there are shared assumptions in our 'society.' This very fact ought to put us on guard against simply assuming that everyone shares the generalization that they find crystal clear and compellingly reasonable with other members of their society."[7] Some people think this state of affairs makes the United States a City of Babel,[8] that productive political-moral dialogue among all or even most of the various religious/moral communities is impossible to achieve because the basic moral beliefs of so many communities are fundamentally different from those of so many others.

The position that a dialogic politics is beyond the capacity of us Americans is especially troubling when we remember that although the moral culture of the United States is pluralistic, it is certainly no more pluralistic, almost certainly less so, than the moral culture of the human species. Human society comprises a multitude of different religious/moral communities. If we members of American society cannot engage even one another in productive moral dialogue, how can we hope to engage members of other societies very different from our own in such dialogue (about, for example, human rights)? In thinking about the possibility (as well as the desirability) of ecumenical politics in a particular pluralistic country like the United States, perhaps we can achieve insights that will help us meet the challenge of achieving such a politics not merely in our own country but in our pluralistic world as well.

Notwithstanding its substantial religious/moral pluralism, American society *is* a genuine political community. There *are* underlying grounds of political judgment—grounds concerning how the life in common is to be lived—which we Americans, *qua* members of a judging community, share, and which can and do serve to unite us in dialogue, notwithstanding our (sometimes radical) disagreements. The most apparent such shared standards of political judgment derive from our constitutional tradition, especially from that part of the tradition concerned with the rights of citizens and others against the state—standards concerning, for example, religious liberty; political freedom, including the freedoms of speech and of the press; racial and other sorts of discrimination; "due process" and other procedural rights (most prominently, perhaps, rights pertaining to the criminal justice system); and so on. Such constitutional standards are, for most of us Americans, fundamental standards of political morality. Most of us who think about political morality at all embrace these standards. This is not to suggest that these are the only standards of political morality any of us embraces. Nor is it to suggest that we all interpret these standards the same way in particular situations of conflict. Of course we don't. Members of religious communities don't all interpret their standards the same way in particular situations of conflict. (The generality or indeterminacy of normative standards invites competing interpretations. I address the problem, and the promise, of such indeterminacy later in this chapter.) Nor, finally, is it to suggest that we don't ever question the standards. Of course we do. Members of religious communities sometimes question their standards. If not even one's most fundamental religious convictions should be immune to such questioning,[9] why should our most fundamental political standards be immune? That some among us do not embrace the constitutional standards does not change the fact that these standards are, for most of us, *qua* Americans, authoritative standards of political morality. Of course, these standards are also authoritative standards of legality. But it would be a mistake to conclude that constitutional norms are morally authoritative for us because they are legally authoritative for us. Rather, they are legally authoritative for us—we have established them and we maintain them as our "fundamental" law—because they are morally authoritative for us. Their moral authority, not their legal authority, is paramount—a moral authority that, at the end of the twentieth century, seems to be claiming more and more people around the world. Consider, for example, the internationalization of the movement for human rights in the period since the end of World War II.[10]

The underlying grounds of political judgment with which I am principally concerned, however, are not constitutional standards.[11] The fundamental standards of American political morality with which I am principally concerned in this book, standards that have been formative for and that continue to inform American political institutions and practices, derive from the religious traditions of American society, in particular the biblical heritage.[12] (A recent joint statement, "Moral Education in the Public Schools", issued by the Committee for Ecumenical and Interreligious Affairs of the National Conference of Catholic Bishops and the Interreligious Affairs Committee of the Synagogue Council of America emphasized that "values like honesty, compassion, integrity, tolerance, loyalty, and belief in human worth and dignity are embedded in our respective religious traditions. . . ."[13]) In that regard, I want to discuss John A. Coleman's argument for "a larger role for biblical religion in our public ethics".[14] Coleman's argument, which I largely endorse, needs to be broadened to support a larger role for more than just biblical religion. More about that later.

Coleman, an American Jesuit theologian and sociologist, writes that "the tradition of biblical religion is arguably the most powerful and pervasive symbolic resource" for a public ethics in the United States today. "[O]ur tradition of religious ethics seems . . . to enjoy a more obvious public vigor and availability as a resource for renewal in American culture than either the tradition of classic republican theory or the American tradition of public philosophy."[15] Coleman observes that "the strongest American voices for a compassionate just community always appealed in public to religious imagery and sentiments, from Winthrop and Sam Adams, Melville and the Lincoln of the second inaugural address, to Walter Rauschenbusch and Reinhold Niebuhr and Frederick Douglass and Martin Luther King." In Coleman's view, "The American religious ethic and rhetoric contain rich, polyvalent symbolic power to command sentiments of emotional depth, when compared to 'secular' language, . . . [which] remains exceedingly 'thin' as a symbol system."[16]

Coleman is not unmindful of the problematic potential of using religious language and symbols in public discourse: "[T]he 'thicker,' more powerfully evocative language of the Bible can become exclusive, divisive in public discourse and overly particularistic. It can rally hearts which share its history and nuances without providing an opening to those who stand as linguistic outsiders to its forms of discourse." However, Coleman does "not find the mere 'particularism' of the biblical heritage an overwhelming drawback." He explains: "[P]retensions to a universal language and traditions are delusions. Every language is particular. Every language stands within a very particular tradition of interpretation. Every language is caught in the conflict of interpretations. To prefer a speciously 'neutral' language of secular humanism to the biblical language seems to me either to be naive about the pretended neutrality and universality of the secular language or to give up on the claims of the Judaeo-Christian heritage to be illuminative of the human situation."[17] (It seems to me that Coleman's point would not be changed, nor would it lose whatever force it has, if instead of relying on the problematic notion of "the Judaeo-Christian heritage" he were to talk about "the claims of *the Jewish and Christian traditions* to be illuminative of the human situation.")

Nonetheless, the problematic potential of using religious language and symbols in public discourse persists. The challenge, therefore, is to explain "how religion can essay a public theology without being sectarian"—how "a religiously based public ethics" can avoid being sectarian.[18] I address that challenge in section III of this chapter; here I want to note two ways in which Coleman responds. First, Coleman emphasizes that "when used as a public discourse, the language of biblical religion is beyond the control of any particular, denominational theology. It represents a common American cultural patrimony. . . . American public theology or religious ethics . . . cannot be purely sectarian. The biblical language belongs to no one church, denomination, or sect." In Coleman's estimate,

The genius of public American theology . . . is that it has transcended denominations, been espoused by people as diverse as

Abraham Lincoln and Robert Bellah who neither were professional theologians nor belonged to any specific church and, even in the work of specifically trained professional theolgians, such as Reinhold Niebuhr, has appealed less to revelational warrant for its authority within public policy discussions than to the ability of biblical insights and symbols to convey a deeper human wisdom. . . . Biblical imagery . . . lies at the heart of the American self-understanding. It is neither parochial nor extrinsic.[19]

Second, Coleman is careful to delimit the proper place or role of religious language, stories, and symbols in public discourse, thus minimizing the potential for sectarian exclusiveness and divisiveness. Coleman's position is not "that specifically formulated, theological *arguments* [should] enter societal debates about public policy." He is concerned, rather, "that these debates be informed by a religious vision and orienting value preference. . . . [T]he most important place for theological symbols in public debate is more as an ethical horizon and set of value preferences than in specific and concrete policy discussion."[20]

Coleman's argument in support of "a larger role for biblical religion in our public ethics" is richly suggestive of the possibility, in our pluralistic context, of ecumenical political dialogue. The argument can be modified, however—and, given the increasing religious pluralism of American society, *should* be modified—to support a larger role in our public ethics not just for biblical religion or religions but for other religious traditions as well, for example, the Islamic, Hindu, Buddhist, and Native American traditions.[21] There is little reason to fear that such a public discourse would resemble Babel, or at least would resemble Babel any more than it already does: As I noted in chapters 2 and 5, the great religious traditions, Indic as well as semitic, tend to converge with one another in affirming that an essential part of what it means to be (truly, fully) human, an essential requirement of the meaningful life for everyone, is to accept (some) responsibility for the basic well-being of the Other (the outsider, the stranger, the alien).[22] My arguments in this chapter and in this book generally, I want to emphasize, do not presuppose that the Jewish and Christian traditions are normative insofar as religious participation in American public discourse is concerned.

I began this section of the chapter by asking about the situational/ contextual prerequisites of ecumenical political dialogue. The principal such prerequisite, I have explained, is the existence of community—political community. But that is not the only such prerequisite. The extent of a person's participation in ecumenical political dialogue—indeed, whether he participates at all—surely depends on the extent to which he enjoys such things as material well-being, personal security, educational attainment, and political freedom, including freedom of speech and freedom of religion. A context in which the material well-being of the people, or their personal security, or their educational attainment, or their political or religious freedom, is minimal or imperiled is not a context in which we should expect much genuine dialogue, ecumenical or otherwise, much less realization of the ideal of ecumenical political dialogue. A commitment to ecumenical political dialogue, and to the sort of political community it helps cultivate, requires a commitment to the various conditions in which such dialogue may realistically be expected to flourish—and, so, a commitment to attack those conditions that militate against, that are subversive of, such dialogue and community.

A commitment to ecumenical political dialogue also requires a commitment to the establishment and maintenance of social, economic, and political institutions and practices that encourage and facilitate, even nurture, such dialogue, as opposed to institutions and practices that discourage, impede, and otherwise frustrate it. The flourishing of ecumenical political dialogue requires a congenial institutional/practical environment. Such an environment, conducive to dialogue, is yet another situational/contextual prerequisite. An important issue that belongs on the intellectual agenda of theorists of dialogic politics is the question of what institutions and practices are likely to maximize rather than minimize authentic dialogue.[23]

II

Ronald Beiner has written that "inquiry into the intersubjective basis of moral and political rationality may contribute to a fuller understanding of what [Hannah] Arendt and [Jürgen] Habermas call a public realm or public space, what Charles Taylor has called a deliberative culture, and what in the traditional vocabulary goes by the name of a republic."[24] I have been addressing, in this chapter, the question of the intersubjective basis of political-moral rationality for us Americans as we engage one another dialogically in our public life. Normative premises derived from our constitutional tradition constitute one major dimension of our intersubjective basis. Normative premises derived from our religious traditions constitute a second major dimension—the dimension with which I am principally concerned in this book. *E plurius unum.* Earlier I said that we are both "plural" (in our needs and wants) and pluralistic (in our moral and religious beliefs about human good) and asked in what sense, if any, we are also "one". We are a political *community,* as distinct from a mere nation of communities, in the sense that, notwithstanding our plurality (the fact that we are many and various) and, more relevantly, our religious/moral pluralism (the fact that among us there are many competing views about human good), there are constitutional and religious premises about the human that constitute the intersubjective basis of our political-moral rationality. In particular, there are constitutional premises about the proper relation between human beings and their government and religious premises about our responsibility for one another's basic well-being.

Moreover, the two sorts of premises are not unrelated: Some religious premises, interpreted in certain ways, offer strong support, arguably even essential support,[25] for some constitutional premises, especially premises about basic human rights.[26] (I discussed human rights, and their religious ground, in chapter 2.) Anyone tempted to think that religious premises inevitably have a conservative character should reflect on the fact that some biblical premises, interpreted in certain ways—in particular, premises concerning our responsibility for one another's well-being, a responsibility emphasized by the commandment to "love one another"— are at the root of liberation theology,[27] and at the root, too, of Marxist moral imperatives. Marxism, after all, in its normative (as distinct from its putative social-scientific) aspect, is a kind of secularized biblical prophecy. Some religious premises are as radical as political-moral premises get.[28]

Of course, the standards of political judgment authoritative for us as Americans do not exhaust the standards authoritative for us as members of the various other communities to which we belong. For example, and in particular, they do not exhaust the standards authoritative for us as members of particular religious communities— or, at least, as persons claimed by, persons in the grip of, particular religious or other moral convictions. Because each of us participates in more than one community, a problem arises: When someone engages in moral dialogue, "which community is appealed to for the intersubjective criteria or grounds of judgment, since the latter will vary as one varies the community appealed to. . . . [W]here allegiances conflict, it is not decided in advance which community will supply the basis of judgment. Does my commitment to a particular people outweigh, or is it outweighed by, my commitment to" some other group? "[I]t [is not] immediately apparent to whom the judgment is addressed: a community of the past or one projected into the future; a particular national community or a community of nations; a tiny circle of associates or universal mankind. . . . Thus, the claim—judgment implies judging community—gives rise to the question: which community?"[29] With respect to political-moral dialogue in American public life—as distinct from such dialogue in, for example, the Catholic Church—with respect, that is, to ecumenical political dialogue, whether justificatory or deliberative or both, the right answer to "which community?" seems clear. The community appealed to for the fundamental "intersubjective criteria or grounds of judgment" is the American *political* community.[30]

The grounds or standards of judgment that constitute our "intersubjective basis of moral and political rationality" are certainly not determinate with respect to all the controversial political issues that engage and divide us—as the issue of abortion, for example, engages and deeply divides us. The standards or premises relevant to such conflicts are often quite indeterminate—or, more precisely, "underdeterminate".[31] They often underdetermine resolution of such conflicts. (Recall, in that regard, Coleman's point that "the most important place for theological symbols in public debate is more as an ethical horizon and set of value preferences than in specific and concrete policy discussion."[32]) If the moral premises were not indeterminate, they would not be so widely shared: "[O]ur actual shared moral principles . . . have been rendered indeterminate in order to be adequately shared, adequately shared for the purposes of practical life, that is, with persons of quite different and incompatible standpoints."[33]

To say that the shared premises are (often) indeterminate is not to say that they, or the sharing of them, is inconsequential. The shared premises are what makes political judgment possible. They are, for us in the United States, the "underlying grounds of judgment which" we, "*qua* members of a judging community, share, and which serve to unite in communication even those who disagree (*and who may disagree radically*)." Indeed, without such shared (albeit indeterminate) standards of judgment, articulate disagreement would not even be possible. "Even divergent judgments of the most deep-seated and fundamental kind are rooted in some relation of community, otherwise one would lack the concepts with which to disagree."[34] But how, precisely, do shared premises make political judgment possible, if they are indeterminate?

Imagine a disagreement between two persons about how to resolve a problem implicating, for example, the ideal of freedom of religion. A dialogic effort to resolve the disagreement isn't likely to get very far, or even begin, if only one of the parties is committed to the ideal. A dialogic effort stands a better chance of making progress, even if not eventuating in complete agreement, if both parties accept the ideal. But, since it *is* indeterminate, what work can the ideal really be expected to do in diminishing, if not resolving, the disagreement? To accept the ideal of freedom of religion, or any other general political-moral principle, is almost certainly to accept that a particular governmental policy (or policies) would be illegitimate, for example, a policy requiring persons to pledge allegiance to religious doctrines they do not in fact embrace and may even reject. Like other general principles (premises, standards, values), the ideal of freedom of religion is, in part, a memorandum of particulars,[35] and in the political community that embraces the ideal, there will be, at any given time, some particulars (at least one)—such as the belief that government may not legitimately compel allegiance to religious doctrines—as to which there is a virtual consensus and which therefore constitute the uncontested core of the principle.[36] So, parties who accept a general political-moral principle but disagree as to whether a particular policy violates it can engage in dialogue with one another about the respects in which the policy is relevantly like, or relevantly unlike, another policy (or policies) that would consensually violate the principle. They can also engage in dialogue about the respects in which the policy is relevantly like or unlike another policy that was earlier and authoritatively concluded by the people, their representatives, or their courts to violate the principle (assuming that the earlier conclusion is not then in question). In this way, then, the sharing of values, even relatively indeterminate ones, serves to ground and focus dialogic efforts that would otherwise stand little chance even of getting started.

In thus grounding and focusing dialogic efforts aimed at diminishing conflict, the indeterminacy of shared moral premises serves an essential social function: It is an occasion of *the mediation of dissensus*. In particular, the indeterminacy of moral premises authoritative for the American political community is a principal occasion of the mediation of the dissensus of the community. (While there is consensus as to the premises themselves, there is often dissensus as to particular interpretations of the premises: Particular interpretations are often not shared/authoritative. As I noted earlier, even in religious communities there is often dissensus as to how shared convictions should be interpreted in particular situations. It is difficult to imagine a community of any size, religious or political, of which that is not true. Dissensus, as well as consensus, is a typical feature of communities.[37]) David Levine has written that "the inherently ambiguous character of legal rules permits . . . parties who submit contending interpretations . . . to participate, through the open forum of the court, in the continuous reestablishment of a rule of law that stands as their common property and their warrant of real community."[38] The point can be generalized beyond legal rules to political-moral norms generally, as Levine himself seems to suggest when he explains that "ambiguous talk makes modern politics possible . . . by tempering the assertion of particular interests and parochial understandings with symbols whose common use, in the face of diverse interpretations, provides a mooring for social solidarity and a continuing invitation to engage in communal discourse. And that continuing invitation, finally, engages us as well in quests for meanings that transcend whatever univocal determinations we have achieved at any given moment."[39]

We may say of indeterminate moral norms, then, including moral premises authoritative for the American political community—"the intersubjective criteria or grounds of judgment" of the community—that their indeterminate character permits persons who submit contending interpretations to participate, through the open forum of the public square, in the continuous reestablishment of the values that stand as their common property and their warrant of real (political) community. It permits us Americans to participate in the continuous reestablishment of the values that constitute our *political* conception of human good: our conception of how it is good or fitting for us to live our collective life, our life in common. In so participating, we redeem "the distinctive promise of political freedom", which is, writes Hannah Pitkin, "the possibility of genuine collective action, an entire community consciously and jointly shaping its policy, its way of life. . . . A family or other private association can inculcate principles of justice shared in a community, but only in public citizenship can we jointly take charge of and responsibility for those principles."[40]

As I said, while there is, in American society, consensus as to general moral premises, there is often dissensus as to particular interpretations of such premises. Given that dissensus, a shared-premises requirement of the sort explicitly endorsed by Bruce Ackerman[41] is impossibly restrictive: Because general moral premises as to which there is a consensus are often indeterminate, resort must often be had to particular interpretations. But a particular interpretation or specification of a general moral premise is itself a (further) premise: a more specific, less indeterminate, perhaps even (relative to the controversy at issue) determinate premise. Because particular interpretations are often the object of dissensus, however, particular interpretations would often fail Ackerman's and any similar shared-premises constraint on political justification. A major difference between Ackerman's approach and mine, then, is that whereas we both want to ground political justification (and, in my case, political deliberation, too) in shared premises, Ackerman seems to insist on grounding political justification *only* in shared premises. His approach tolerates only shared premises. It does not tolerate particular interpretations (which are themselves premises, albeit more specific than the general premises they interpret) when they are not shared. Such an approach is impossibly restrictive: Shared moral premises are often indeterminate; further premises, *determinate* premises, are therefore required, but often are not available, under Ackerman's approach, because they often are not shared. (I have just explained how the indeterminacy of shared norms serves an important social function.[42] But such indeterminacy is obviously a severe problem for an approach like Ackerman's.) Ecumenical political dialogue, by contrast, tolerates particular interpretations even when, as is often true, they are not shared. It tolerates particular, disputed interpretations of authoritative moral premises because, realistically, it must: The alternative is, to say it a final time, impossibly restrictive. An ideal of politics according to which justification of controversial political choices may proceed *only* on the basis of premises that are shared, premises as to which there is a consensus, is, in a word, quixotic.

As we have now seen, ecumenical political dialogue requires a context, namely, a political "community of judgment". But the ecumenical political dialogue our authoritative moral premises permit to get started, in part in virtue of their very indeterminacy ("ambiguity"), can itself be, and at its best is, a matrix of political community: Such dialogue can strengthen existing bonds of political community, by generating shared interpretations of authoritative premises; it can even forge new bonds, by generating new authoritative premises. In that sense, ecumenical political dialogue can be an occasion of what Hans-Georg Gadamer has called "a fusion of horizons". (Recall Bernard Williams' point that "[a] fully individuable culture [or moral community] is at best a rare thing. Cultures, subcultures, fragments of cultures, constantly meet one another and exchange or modify practices and attitudes."[43]) That we are a *pluralistic* political community, comprising many different and sometimes competing religious/moral communities, ought not to obscure the "integrating" potential of ecumenical political dialogue:

> [Gadamer's model] suggests that understanding is possible between forms of life, and looks upon differences between their presuppositions as opportunities for fuller understanding (self-understanding as well as understanding of the other) rather than as impediments to it. . . . Gadamer describes this process as a "fusion of horizons". Although he discusses this in relation to historical understanding,

we can easily reformulate his point in relation to forms of life. . . . This is not to deny that to some extent forms of life differ from one another, presuppose somewhat different standards of meaning and value, and are constituted in part by rules which vary from one form of life to another. It is to suggest, however, that understanding is a task which involves the creation as well as the discovery of shared structures of meaning and value. Perhaps the most disturbing aspect of the contemporary belief in the absence of any such shared standard between different forms of life is that it invites resignation and passivity rather than dialogue, disagreement, and the eventual creation of mutual understanding.[44]

As I noted earlier in this chapter, such a process of fusion is not only, or even always primarily, cognitive: a process in which ideas or thoughts are exchanged and minds are sometimes changed. It is, as well, an affective process, in which feelings and sensibilities are sometimes transformed, and sometimes mutually transformed, through human contact and noncognitive modes of human communication. To conceive of the process of dialogue, including ecumenical political dialogue, as always primarily cognitive is to overlook what personal experience teaches: that dialogue can be a process through which hearts as well as minds are changed. This might happen less because of anything in particular that is said than because of the way or ways in which one comes to know the person of the other (one's interlocutor) in dialogue. (In ecumenical dialogue one's interlocutors are strangers, outsiders, to one's primary religious or moral community.) Political theorists, like other intellectuals, are often obsessively cognitive and therefore prone to overlook the important affective dimension of dialogue. "[I]f we think of understanding as something that happens in our heads and something that is confined to our heads, then understanding is not adequate to express the goal of dialogue. The word 'integration' is intended to point to the fact that genuine understanding has implications for our life and practice. Integration is something that happens 'in our guts.' In dialogue, more than just our theory is transformed."[45] To discount the affective dimension of dialogue is to miss much of the transformative potential of dialogue—a potential crucially relevant to the challenge of strengthening and extending the bonds of human community.[46]

III

Thus far in this chapter I have been discussing issues related to the contextual/situational prerequisites of ecumenical political dialogue. In this section I address a different but related matter: "existential" prerequisites. A certain constellation of attitudes and virtues or habits of character[47] is prerequisite to fruitful participation in the practice of ecumenical political dialogue. Whether one can participate in such dialogue and, especially, the quality of one's participation depend on the extent to which one embodies the requisite attitudes and virtues.

a

Let's begin with a basic example: cognitive competency. One who would engage in ecumenical political dialogue should of course always take care to be accurately and fully informed, or to get accurately and fully informed in the course of the dialogue, as to such matters as (1) the various moral arguments relevant to the issue or issues) addressed in the dialogue, especially, of course, the arguments of one's interlocutors, and (2) whatever "empirical" or "technical" data may be relevant to the issue.[48]

Other basic virtues are respect for one's interlocutors—for example, "a willingness to probe [their] arguments . . . rather than question their motives"[49]—and, even better, empathy with one's interlocutors, so that one can better understand the affective as well as cognitive dimensions of their position. Moral positions, after all, are a matter of feeling as well as thinking;[50] indeed, they are more fundamentally a matter of feeling, or sensibility, than of thinking: "[M]oral reality . . . [is] about an interaction between persons and the world which can only be known from the reports of those who experience that interaction."[51] Habits of respect and of empathy help us guard against practicing the kind of self-serving, manipulative talk, the kind of feigned dialogue, too often characteristic of political discourse.[52]

David Tracy suggests other basic dialogic virtues—including honesty and sincerity[53]—when he writes that "[c]onversation is a game with some hard rules: say only what you mean; say it as accurately as you can; listen to and respect what the other says, however different or other; be willing to correct or defend your opinions if challenged by the conversation partner; be willing to argue if necessary, to confront if demanded, to endure necessary conflict, to change your mind if the evidence suggests it. These are merely some generic rules for questioning. As good rules, they are worth keeping in mind in case the questioning does begin to break down." Tracy adds: "In a sense [these rules] are merely variations of the transcendental imperatives elegantly articulated by Bernard Lonergan: 'Be attentive, be intelligent, be responsible, be loving, and, if necessary, change.' "[54]

b

Two attitudes essential to the practice of ecumenical political dialogue are fallibilism and pluralism.[55] To be a fallibilist is essentially to embrace the ideal of self-critical rationality.[56] To be a pluralist, in the sense relevant here, is to understand that a morally pluralistic context, with its attendant variety of ways of life, can often be a more fertile source of deepening moral insight—in particular, a more fertile soil for dialogue leading to deepening moral insight—than can a monistic context.[57] Ways of life different from our own can test our beliefs about what ways of life are good for human beings and, moreover, fuel our efforts to imagine better ways of life. "Certainly . . . 'self-knowledge' . . .—knowledge of one's wants, needs, motives, of what kind of life one would find acceptable and satisfying—is something agents are very unlikely to attain in a society without extensive room for free discussion and the unrestrained play of the imagination with alternative ways of living. . . . [Self-knowledge requires] knowledge of . . . [one's] own human possibilities and . . . [the ability to] see . . . [one's] form of life against a background of envisaged alternatives."[58] (Many of the attitudes and virtues I'm discussing here are allied; for example, just as cognitive competency is enhanced by empathy, pluralism is supported by fallibilism.)

The notion that a *religious* person or community can be fallibilist probably seems strange to some. But it is not at all strange. (This is not to deny that the virtue of fallibilism has not loomed large among many—most?—religious persons and communities.) Recall the crucial distinction, elaborated in chapter 5, between religious faith and religious beliefs. The existential or affective condition called "faith", not the cognitive condition of subscribing to particular religious beliefs, is "the fundamental religious response".[59] At its most authentic, religious faith supports ongoing political critique:

> Religious faith may be seen as following a narrow ridge between the two abysses of nihilism and idolatry. Nihilism denies the validity of all truths and values and reduces human life and human society to a context of unrestrained selfishness and exploitation. Idolatry, in contrast, makes one set of truths and values absolute and seeks to freeze human life and society into conformity with those beliefs. Both nihilism and idolatry refuse the authority of rational political argument. . . . Religious faith is best viewed not as a set of beliefs, but as an unrestricted openness to Reality. As such, it is a critical foundation for the permanent argument that constitutes political society. . . .
> . . . Religious faith, by pushing us towards the Transcendent, relativizes every existing order. In so far as any existing social order absolutizes itself, religious faith becomes subversive and revolutionary in the usual political sense. . . . Since every social order tends to make itself absolute, it is the constant function of religious faith to remind human beings that even basic principles are subject to revision as human understanding grows. Religious faith protects human creativity from social inertia.[60]

For the same reason it supports ongoing political critique, religious faith also supports self-critical reflective practices. A religious community no less than a political one—especially, a religious bureaucracy no less than a political one—can tend to absolutize itself and, so, can need reminding "that even basic principles are subject to revision as human understanding grows". Authentic religious faith and the virtue of fallibilism are intimately connected.[61]

This is an appropriate point (in connection with the discussion of fallibilism) at which to comment on J. Bryan Hehir's expression of skepticism about Coleman's argument that (in Hehir's words) "a more explicitly theological style of assertion, using religious symbols to interpret and adjudicate justice claims, is more appropriate to the questions faced by the [Catholic] Church in the United States today."[62] Hehir distinguished "the need for shaping 'the mind of the Church' (as a community and an institution) regarding social questions from the task of *projecting the perspective of the Church into the societal debate about normative questions of public policy.*" Whereas the language and symbols of scripture, and other religious language and symbols, are essential, in Hehir's view, "in efforts [inside the Church] both to identify the social issues facing the Christian conscience and to mobilize the Church in a coherent approach to specific issues", such language and symbols are peripheral to the "significant task of *sharing the [Church's] vision with the wider society.* . . . [I] hesitate about the usefulness of public theology in policy discussions [involving the wider society]." The pluralistic character of American society, and even more so of international politics, "points toward the need for systemic solutions which are persuasive for a multiplicity of actors with widely varying 'faith visions.' "[63] Hehir's position has an apparent affinity with the Catholic Church's traditional predilection for a putatively nonsectarian, "natural law" style of moral discourse—a style that aspires to be more "universalistic" than "particularistic".[64]

There are two basic problems with the position Hehir seems to offer as an alternative to Coleman's. Hehir seems to presuppose that when the Church enters the public square—when it joins "the societal debate about normative questions of public policy"—it does so only for the strategic purpose of persuasion ("projecting the perspective of the Church into the societal debate", "sharing the Church's vision with the wider society") or perhaps justification (or perhaps both): to persuade others ("the wider society") to support a particular political choice, probably for the same reasons the Church supports it but conceivably for different reasons, or perhaps to justify a particular political choice, in the sense of arguing that the choice is permitted, or supported, or even required, by the relevant, nonsectarian justificatory criteria (for example, constitutional criteria). Arguments contained in legal briefs submitted on behalf of the U.S. Catholic bishops in constitutional cases involving, for example, public aid to religious schools, or abortion, are justificatory in that sense.

Such a presupposition is problematic. Why shouldn't the Church—that is, members of the Church—and, more generally, members of other religious communities, and religious persons even if they identify with no religious community, enter the public square, join the societal debate, for purposes of deliberation as well: to deliberate about what political choice the Church, and others, *should* support. Why assume that "the mind of the Church" or other community is to be shaped only by internal dialogue: deliberation *within* the religious community, among its members? Why shouldn't the mind of the Church or other community be shaped by external dialogue as well: deliberation between those who are members of the religious community and those who are not?

Hehir would likely agree that the ideal of self-critical rationality, which I discussed in chapter 4, is an ideal for religious communities no less than for other sorts of human communities (moral, political, intellectual), and for theology no less than for other sorts of inquiry. Religious communities, too, consist of broken, fallible human beings and broken, fallible institutions. History discloses that "the mind of the Church", like the minds of countless other religious and moral communities, is from time to time shaped in distorted, even perverse ways. A robust internal deliberation is certainly an essential part of the process of self-critical rationality for a religious community. But a robust external deliberation is no less important a part of the process.[65] Religious persons sometimes say something to the effect that "the world needs the church". For example, in a statement issued late in 1987, in connection with the beginning of the 1988 season of presidential primaries, the Catholic bishops said: "Precisely because the moral content of public choice is so central today, the religious communities are inevitably drawn more deeply into the public life of the nation. *These communities possess long and systematically developed moral traditions which can serve as a crucial resource in shaping the moral vision needed for the future.*"[66] What is *not* often said by religious persons, however—and what is implicitly overlooked in Hehir's assumption that the Church enters the public square only for purposes of persuasion and/or justification—is that "the church needs the world". Religious communities need a robust external deliberation to protect them from themselves. "There is, of course, much to gain by sharpening our understanding in dialogue with those who share a common heritage and common experience with us. . . . Critical understanding of the [religious] tradition and a critical awareness of our own relationship to it, however, is sharp-ened by contact with those who differ from us. Indeed, for these purposes, the less they are like us, the better."[67]

I suspect Hehir would agree that there must be external deliberation as well as internal.[68] (In any event, the point is not controversial—at least, not among those likely to be reading this book.) Hehir would likely insist, however, that his point about the limited value, if not disvalue, in the public square ("the wider society"), of religious language and symbols nonetheless obtains. But, clearly, external deliberation cannot serve as a significant part of a religious community's self-critical reflective practices unless the community communicates to others, outsiders to the community, its understanding (mediation) of its faith—in particular, its interpretation of its tradition, especially the moral aspects of its tradition—and, moreover, unless it communicates such information in language and symbols that clarify rather than obscure the scriptural and other religious/theological warrants for its understanding/interpretation: Only in that way can the community render its understanding, its interpretation, and its scriptural/religious warrants vulnerable to the possibility of critique by those outside the community. If there is to be external deliberation, a religious community cannot closet its religious language and symbols and thereby, in effect, immunize from the possibility of external challenge its scriptural/religious warrants.

The distinction between religious faith and religious beliefs is once again relevant. "Religious beliefs are the changing, limited, culturally particular manifestations of religious faith. Therefore, in political argument, religious people must be prepared to see their religious beliefs challenged."[69] Religious people must be more than prepared to see their religious beliefs challenged in the course of political argument. If I am right in what I have said, to this point, about Hehir's position, religious people must actively submit their relevant beliefs, especially religious-moral beliefs, to challenge. Relgous beliefs are best submitted to challenge in political argument by being advanced in political argument. That religious beliefs be advanced is therefore important. (But, as I amplify below, *how* they are advanced is important too: "The religious, and religious institutions, can only help to complete the project of modernity (that is, releasing the social enterprise from all false necessity) if they advance their beliefs as something other than unchanging and unquestionable. Those beliefs can then enter fruitfully into the political argument."[70])

There is another reason that it is important that relevant religious beliefs—and the attendant religious language and symbols—be advanced in political argument: The Church's (or other religious community's or person's) contribution to political argument, the position it means to advance in political argument, is finally and radically incomplete without such beliefs. As David Hollenbach has contended, striking a rather different note from Hehir's, "[I]f the church is intent on making a contribution to debates about social, political, and economic life, it must state forthrightly and publicly its own most basic convictions about the nature and destiny of human beings. . . . [The church] must respond to the most basic questions about the meaning of human life in its social teachings as well as in doctrinal theology. . . . [Such questions] are religious questions, demanding religious and theological answers." Hollenbach reports that "[t]he [Second Vatican C]ouncil highlighted a few of these questions: 'What is the human person? What is this sense of sorrow, of evil, of death, which continues to exist despite so much progress? What is the purpose of these victories, purchased at so high a cost? What can human beings offer to society? What can they expect from it? What follows this earthly life? . . . What recommendations seem needful for the upbuilding of contemporary society? What is the ultimate significance of human activity throughout the world?' "[71]

We have now arrived at the second problem with Hehir's position: the assumption that for the Church (and, inferentially, for any religious community or person) to advance, "in the societal debate about normative questions of public policy" (Hehir), "its own most basic convictions about the nature and destiny of human beings" (Hollenbach)—and, therefore, for it to rely, in the debate, on religious language, stories, or symbols—is for the Church to act in a sectarian way (and, therefore, given our religious/moral pluralism, in a divisive way as well). That assumption is mistaken, as I am about to explain.

c

Now we come to two truly cardinal dialogic virtues: public intelligibility and public accessibility. The virtue of public intelligibility is the easier one to specify: It is the habit of trying to elaborate one's position in a manner intelligible or comprehensible to those who speak a different religious or moral language—to the point of translating one's position, to the extent possible, into a shared ("mediating") language.[72] That public intelligibility is a dialogic virtue is clear. As John Courtney Murray emphasized, "Argument ceases to be civil . . . when its vocabulary becomes solipsist, premised on the theory that my insight is mine alone and cannot be shared; when dialogue gives way to a series of monologues. . . . When things like this happen, men cannot be locked together in argument. Conversation becomes merely quarrelsome or querulous. Civility dies with the death of dialogue."[73] (Murray's point, it will soon be clear, applies as well to the allied virtue of public accessibility.)

What we may call, for want of a better term, the virtue of public accessibility is the habit of trying to defend one's position in a manner neither sectarian nor authoritarian. A defense of a disputed position is sectarian if (and to the extent) it relies on experiences or premises that have little if any authority beyond the confines of one's own moral or religious community. A defense is authoritarian if it relies on persons or institutions that have little if any authority beyond the confines of one's own community. Of course, to defend one's position in a nonsectarian and nonauthoritarian way is not necessarily to render one's position accessible, much less persuasive, to each and every member of the public. But, with that caveat, I shall continue to speak, I hope not too misleadingly, of "public accessibility".

The standard or criterion of public accessibility is not uncontroversial, of course. (The virtue of public accessibility is the habit of trying to satisfy that standard.) But it *is* difficult to understand how *religious* convictions can play a deliberative or, much less, a justificatory role in American politics that is not only not divisive but constructive, unless some such standard[74] is honored. The point is not that failure to honor such a standard is, as some argue, invariably politically destabilizing.[75] Sectarian (or authoritarian) argument in the public square, including sectarian religious argument, is not, in my view, invariably politically destabilizing. Without denying that some imaginable instances of sectarian religious argument in the public square could, with other factors, precipitate political instability, I am nonetheless inclined to agree that as a general matter "the risk of major instability generated by religious conflict is minimal. Conditions in modern democracies may be so far from the conditions that gave rise to the religious wars of the sixteenth century that we no longer need worry about religious divisiveness as a source of substantial social conflict."[76]

Nor is the point that failure to honor such a standard somehow denies fellow citizens the respect due them as "free and equal persons".[77] Sectarian religious argument in the public square is no more problematic in that regard than sectarian nonreligious argument, and sectarian argument of neither kind can fairly be understood *necessarily* to deny either the moral or political freedom or the moral or political equality of persons.[78] (This is not to deny that particular sectarian arguments, whether religious or not, can deny the moral or political freedom or the moral or political equality of persons: most obviously, arguments *that* certain persons are not morally or politically free or that they are moral or political inferiors.)

The point, rather, is simply that failure to honor a standard like that of public accessibility dooms argument in the public square, including religious argument, to play a role that is anything but constructive; it dooms such argument to play at best a marginal and ineffective, and sometimes even divisive, role. "Even when their fundamental inspiration comes from a religious belief in God," writes Edward Schillebeeckx, "ethical norms . . . must be rationally grounded. None of the participants in [religious-moral discourse] can hide behind an 'I can see what you don't see' and then require [the] others to accept this norm straight out."[79] Even if we assume *arguendo* that Schillebeeckx's principle should not govern religious-moral discourse in *all* contexts—for example, in the context of a small, monistic, charismatic religious community—the principle should certainly govern religious-moral discourse, and moral discourse generally, in *some* contexts, especially the context of a large, pluralistic, liberal political community like the United States. In words of J. Bryan Hehir (who, as the principal drafter of the U.S. Catholic bishops' 1983 letter on nuclear deterrence,[80] has some experience in the matter):

> [R]eligiously based insights, values and arguments at some point must be rendered persuasive to the wider civil public. There is

legitimacy to proposing a sectarian argument within the confines of
a religious community, but it does violence to the fabric of pluralism
to expect acceptance of such an argument in the wider public arena.
When a religious moral claim will affect the wider public, it should
be proposed in a fashion which that public can evaluate, accept or
reject on its own terms. The [point] . . . is not to banish religious
insight and argument from public life[, but only to] establish a test
for the religious communities to meet: to probe our commitments
deeply and broadly enough that we can translate their best insights
to others.[81]

Although the allied virtues of public intelligibility and public
accessibility do not guarantee eventual agreement,[82] they do inhibit sectarian imperialism, which is the very antithesis of ecumenical dialogue.[83] Defending the moderate style of his participation in
public discourse about abortion and other issues implicating what
he has famously called "the consistent ethic of life", Cardinal Joseph Bernardin, archbishop of Chicago, has said: "The substance
of the consistent ethic yields a style of teaching it and witnessing to
it. The style should . . . not [be] sectarian. . . . [W]e should resist
the sectarian tendency to retreat into a closed circle, convinced of
our truth and the impossibility of sharing it with others. . . . The
style should be persuasive, not preachy. . . . We should be convinced we have much to learn from the world and much to teach it.
A confident church will speak its mind, seek as a community to live
its convictions, but leave space for others to speak to us, help us
grow from their perspective. . . ."[84] (It bears mention, even emphasis, in this time of renascent, fundamentalist religious fanati-
cism, domestic as well as foreign, that not all sectarian imperialism
is religious in character—a point to which the twentieth century
bears painful witness.[85])

The virtue of public accessibility is not an insurmountable obstacle for religious persons who would bring their deepest convictions
about the human to bear in political dialogue. As John Coleman
correctly observes (in a passage that bears traces of "natural law"
thinking), "[M]any elements and aspects of a religious ethic . . .
can be presented in public discussion in ways that do not presume
assent to them on the specific premises of a faith grounded in
revelation. Without being believing Hindus, many Westerners, after all, find in Gandhi's social thought a superior vision of the

human than that of ordinary liberal premises."[86] Indeed, to embrace a religious premise, including a biblical premise, about what it means to be human, about how it is good or fitting for human beings to live their lives, and then to rely on the premise in public discourse is not necessarily to count oneself a participant in the tradition that has yielded the premise (or the particular interpretation of it); indeed, it is not even necessarily to count oneself as a religious person—not, at least, in any conventional sense. Billboards in New York City used to proclaim that you didn't have to be Jewish to love Levy's rye bread. You certainly don't have to be Jewish to recognize that the prophetic vision of the Jewish Bible is profound and compelling, any more than you have to be Catholic or Presbyterian or Methodist or even Christian to recognize that the Gospel vision of what it means to be human is profound and compelling. Gandhi wasn't a Christian, but he recognized the Gospel vision as profound and compelling.[87] Moreover, we should be wary of assuming that traditions other than our own, including religious traditions, cannot become our own. They can, to some extent, through acts of appropriation. Robert Cover, who took his Jewish tradition very seriously, once commented: "It is strange to me that Jews claim Moses or Abraham or Maimonides as ancestors. What does it mean to claim them as ancestors. . . . [I]t seems that if we can claim those people, whom we do not know anything about, even whether they ever existed, claim them as our fathers or mothers, then we can claim Martin Luther King, too. The claiming of ancestry is an act of appropriation. It is not an act of descent. It is something that you do actively, that you grab and work for and with. . . ."[88]

Consider, in connection with the virtue of public accessibility, the practice of religious narrative or storytelling as an element in moral, including political-moral, discourse. It is one thing to tell a religious story—for example, about the Good Samaritan—for the purpose of indicating what a sacred text obligates the listener to do. Even if storytelling for that purpose is sometimes appropriate in a religious community for which the text itself, or a particular interpretation of it, is authoritative, such a practice is sectarian and would certainly be divisive in a religiously/morally pluralistic context.[89] It is another thing altogether to tell a religious story for the purpose of providing some (human) insight into the question of what it means, in some context or other, to be human—truly, fully human. Such a narrative practice, which may even draw on a religious tradition or traditions not one's own, is not sectarian nor any more divisive, in our pluralistic context, than "secular" narrative about how it is good or fitting for human beings to live their lives. Indeed, the person telling the religious story or interpreting the religious symbol may identify with no religious community. As David Tracy has emphasized: "Some interpret the religious classics not as testimonies to a revelation from Ultimate Reality, . . . but as testimonies to possibility itself. As Ernst Bloch's interpretations of all those daydreams and Utopian and eschatological visions that Westerners have ever dared to dream argue, the religious classics can also become for nonbelieving interpreters testimonies to resistance and hope. As Mircea Eliade's interpretations of the power of the archaic religions show, the historian of religions can help create a new humanism which retrieves forgotten classic religious symbols, rituals, and myths."[90] Tracy continues: "If the work of Bloch and [Walter] Benjamin on the classic texts and symbols of the eschatological religions and the work of Eliade and others on the primal religions were allowed to enter into the contemporary conversation, then the range of possibilities we ordinarily afford ourselves would be exponentially expanded beyond reigning Epicurean, Stoic, and nihilistic visions."[91]

But if the work of Bloch and Benjamin and Eliade and other "nonbelievers" should be allowed to enter (directly or indirectly) the public *political* conversation—indeed, should be invited and welcomed—then why not, as well, the work of Tracy and other "believers", so long as religious stories and symbols are interpreted not in a sectarian or authoritarian way "but as [human] testimonies to [human] possibility itself"? First: As statements above by Murray, Schillebeeckx, and Coleman suggest, reliance on biblical premises about the human—or, more broadly, on premises about the human from whatever religious tradition—need be neither sectarian nor authoritarian. Recall Coleman's point that in the American tradition such reliance has "appealed less to revelational warrant for its authority within public policy discussions than to the ability of biblical insights and symbols to convey a deeper human wisdom."[92] Second, and relatedly: Consider the approach to, and understanding of, religious morality sketched by James Burtchaell of Notre Dame's Theology Department: "Our judgments of good and evil focus on whether a certain course of action will make a human being grow and mature and flourish, or whether it will make a person withered, estranged and indifferent. In making our evaluations, we have little to draw on except our own and our forebears' experience, and whatever wisdom we can wring from our debate with others."[93] In the context of such an approach to, and understanding of, religious morality, it is difficult to know how to administer the putative distinction between "secular" premises about the human, which are certainly allowed to enter political dialogue, and "religious" premises about the human, which according to some should not be allowed to enter—or, at least, should not be allowed to have the same status or play the same (dispositive) role as secular premises.[94]

Indeed, the appeal of the virtue of public accessibility (if it is appealing) helps us see the two basic problems with a strategy—endorsed by Kent Greenawalt, among others—I criticized in chapter 1:[95] the strategy of distinguishing between controversial moral premises (premises not "widely shared") that are nonreligious in character and controversial premises that are religious and then disfavoring the latter relative to the former, even excluding the latter, insofar as political-justificatory practices are concerned. First: The strategy I have defended in this chapter, unlike Greenawalt's strategy, largely avoids the difficulty of administering any sharp or strong distinction between "religious" and "nonreligious" moral premises. Second: The strategy I have defended seems fairer than Greenawalt's strategy: (1) Religious argument that survives the standard of public accessibility (or some such standard) should be admitted to the public square no less than nonreligious, or "secular", argument that survives the standard, and (2) nonreligious/secular argument that fails the standard of public accessibility should be excluded no less than religious argument that fails the standard.[96]

The extent to which the foregoing existential prerequisites to ecumenical political dialogue are satisfied within the American polity is uncertain. Because such dialogue, like the (ecumenical) politics it constitutes, is an ideal—a practice to be encouraged and cultivated—the various attitudes and virtues sketched here should

be understood as ideals, too, grounded partly in the ideal of ecumenical political dialogue. They are attitudes and virtues to be
encouraged and cultivated whether or not they are now widely and
deeply embodied by the polity.

IV

If a conception of politics is to be taken seriously as an ideal for
American society, the conception should comport with the relevant
basic features of the American constitutional tradition. A conception of politics that is in tension with, much less violates, those
traditions is not an attractive ideal for American society. Ecumenical politics is, in part, a *religious* politics, in this sense: a politics in
which persons with religious convictions about the good or fitting
way for human beings to live their lives rely on those convictions,
not only in making political choices but in publicly deliberating
about and in publicly justifying such choices. Is such a politics
consistent with the provision of the United States Constitution that
forbids government—both the federal government and the governments of the fifty states—to make any "law respecting an establishment of religion"? Is ecumenical politics in tension with "the establishment clause"?[97]

The establishment clause is understood (by its principal and
authoritative interpreter, the United States Supreme Court) to forbid government to establish a religion—in the way, for example,
the Church of England is established in England—or otherwise to
act for the purpose of endorsing the institutions, theologies, or
practices of one or more religions (churches, sects, denominations,
communities of faith) as against the institutions, theologies, or
practices of one or more other religions.[98] More controversially,
the clause is understood to forbid government to act for the purpose of endorsing religion generally—religious institutions, systems of belief, or practices—as against irreligious or nonreligious
institutions, systems of belief, or practices.[99]

Not surprisingly, the establishment clause is not understood to
proscribe, as a basis for political deliberation, justification, or
choice, moral beliefs: beliefs about the good or fitting way for
human beings to live their lives. (This is not to say that each and

every political choice based on such beliefs—in effect, each and every political choice—is constitutional. A political choice consistent with the establishment clause may not be consistent with a different constitutional provision.) Such an understanding would be patently ridiculous: On what basis, then, *could* political deliberation, justification, and choice proceed? Moreover, the establishment clause is not understood to proscribe moral beliefs (as a basis for political deliberation and so on) just because they are "religious" in character: beliefs about the "truly, fully" human way to live, the way to live that is compatible with the ultimate meaningfulness of life, with what Rabbi Heschel called the "Presence".[100] (This is not to deny that the clause proscribes some moral beliefs religious in character; the point is that the clause does not proscribe religious-moral beliefs just because they are religious. More about that momentarily.) Such an understanding would be utterly implausible: Do we really want to insist that Martin Luther King, Jr., sinned against the establishment clause when he based his call for civil rights legislation on a biblical vision of the "truly, fully human"? Or, more generally, that religious persons sin against the clause when they base their cry for economic justice, for human rights, on that, or on a similarly religious, vision?[101] There is no accepted interpretation of the establishment clause, nor, more important, is there any plausible interpretation of the clause (whether accepted or not), according to which citizens or their political representatives act in a constitutionally problematic way if they make political choices partly or even wholly on the basis of religious convictions about the good or fitting way for human beings to live their lives, or, much less, if they publicly deliberate about or publicly justify political choices on that basis.

The present issue, however, is more specific. The particular sort of politics—a partly religious politics—whose consistency with the establishment clause is in question is ecumenical politics. With respect to *that* issue—in particular, with respect to the question of the consistency of ecumenical political dialogue with the establishment clause—what I have already said, in the preceding section of this chapter, about public accessibility as a constitutive virtue of ecumenical political dialogue is directly relevant here: The sort of reliance on religious premises about the human that is a feature of ecumenical politics is *not* sectarian or authoritarian. To adapt a (related) point I made in the preceding section: It is difficult, in the context of a nonsectarian and nonauthoritarian approach to, and understanding of, religious morality (like that sketched by Notre Dame's James Burtchaell[102]) to know how to administer the putative distinction between "secular" premises about the human, the dialogic role of which in politics the establishment clause certainly tolerates, and "religious" premises about the human, the dialogic role of which the clause, on some imaginable if farfetched interpretation, would proscribe.

Although the establishment clause is not understood to proscribe moral beliefs (as a basis for political deliberation, justification, or choice) if and just because they are religious in character— that is, although the clause is not understood to proscribe *all* religious-moral beliefs—the Supreme Court has interpreted the clause to require, *inter alia*, that laws "have a secular legislative purpose".[103] In that sense, as Kent Greenawalt's elaboration and defense of the requirement in effect suggest, the establishment clause *is* understood to proscribe (as a basis for political deliberation and so on) *some* religious-moral beliefs. (According to Greenawalt, the "secular purpose" requirement is at least as much a matter of sound liberal political theory as it is of sound establishment clause doctrine.) "[W]e can identify one kind of religious reason that should not count for good liberal citizens in a liberal democracy. . . . [A] certain kind of religious reason . . . is not consonant with liberal democracy."[104] The kind of religious reason that, according to Greenawalt, is an inappropriate basis for legislation, especially coercive legislation, is a belief that some way of acting or living is morally wrong (because God says so?) *even if the way of acting or living involves no physical or psychological harm either to persons who act or live that way or to any other person or entity.*[105] (Mere "offense" in knowing that someone is acting or living a particular way presumably does not, and in any event should not, count as an instance of the requisite "psychological harm", since if that is the only harm, the harm or offense is apparently parasitic on a belief that the way of acting or living is morally wrong even though it involves no harm to persons who act or live that way and no harm, other than the offense itself, to any other person or entity.) As Greenawalt himself emphasizes, "Conceptually, the claimed bar on this sort of reason is not one that relates peculiarly to religious reasons. The analysis can be generalized to conclude that a simple belief that acts are morally wrong, whether religiously based or not, is never an appropriate ground of prohibition. To support prohibition in a liberal society, one must be able to point to some genuine damage to individuals or society (or other entities). So understood, the bar on this basis for legislation extends to some possible nonreligious as well as religious views of wrong." He adds: "However, because a nonreligious moral view is much less likely than a religious one to have notions of wrong that can be detached from notions of ordinary harm, the bar I have discussed does mainly concern religious reasons for prohibition. Further, given the special concern over imposition of religious positions, historically grounded and reflected in the religion clauses of the constitution, the bar is of particular practical importance as it applies to religious notions of wrong."[106]

Assuming *arguendo* that the kind of reason Greenawalt specifies is an inappropriate basis for legislation, the bar on such reasons—whether understood as an element of establishment clause doctrine or simply as a feature of liberal political theory—is largely inconsequential. It is virtually *never* the case that coercive legislation is grounded, or need be grounded, on (or solely on) such a reason. Coercive legislation is virtually *always* based (in part, at least) on a belief that the prohibited way of acting or living involves either physical or psychological harm (or both), whether to persons who live or act the prohibited way, to other persons or entities, or to both. That is, coercive legislation, like legislation generally, virtually always has an "earthly" or "worldly" or, to use the Supreme Court's word, "secular" purpose: a purpose (goal, objective) intelligible or comprehensible in earthly terms as distinct from solely "heavenly" or "otherworldly" or "spiritual" terms.[107] Basil Mitchell's observation is relevant here: "Christians [for example] would presumably want to argue . . . that the Christian revelation does not require us to interpret the nature of man in ways for which there is otherwise no warrant but rather affords us a deeper understanding of man as he essentially is."[108]

In any event, ecumenical politics—which, after all, is the issue here—does not come close to offending the bar Greenawalt defends or the Supreme Court's equivalent requirement, inferred from the establishment clause, that laws have a "secular" purpose.

Indeed, the standard of public accessibility—satisfaction of which is, as I said, a constitutive virtue of ecumenical political dialogue— seems to subsume Greenawalt's bar. It is difficult to imagine reasons that would fail Greenawalt's bar but not fail the accessibility standard: Claims to the effect that some way of acting or living is morally wrong independent of any physical and/or psychological harm to self and/or other persons or entities seem to require supporting arguments of a kind that are not publicly intelligible/ accessible. It is not difficult, however, to imagine reasons that would survive Greenawalt's bar but not survive the accessibility standard: A claim that some way of acting or living is morally wrong because (or partly because) of physical and/or psychological harm to self and/or other persons or entities might be supported by an argument that is not publicly intelligible/accessible.

I want to use the cacophonous and deeply divisive political debate about abortion to illustrate a point and also to make a point. The point I want to illustrate is the point I just made: that coercive legislation is virtually never grounded, or virtually never need be grounded, on the kind of reasons subject to Greenawalt's bar, which are the kind of reasons that would make it difficult to conclude that a law has a "secular" purpose. The (new) point I want to make is that religious argument in support of coercive legislation often can and does satisfy the public accessibility standard. The latter point bears emphasis because of a tendency to overestimate the extent to which political argument religious in character, even if not violative of Greenawalt's bar—and, therefore, not violative of the (equivalent) secular-purpose requirement—is nonetheless (and, relative to nonreligious political argument, especially) sectarian or authoritarian.

It is sometimes suggested, in the course of political argument about abortion, that legislation outlawing abortion violates the establishment clause. While such legislation has been held (by a majority of the Supreme Court) to violate the due process clause of the Fourteenth Amendment[109]—and while government's refusal to permit a woman to have an abortion at least in certain situations (for example, when her pregnancy is the result of rape), arguably violates the equal protection clause of the Fourteenth Amendment[110]—the warrant for concluding that legislation outlawing abortion violates the establishment clause is quite opaque.

(And, indeed, the Supreme Court has never been tempted to so hold.[111]) Such legislation certainly has a purpose no less "secular" than, for example, the purpose of legislation outlawing the slaughter of Alaskan wolves: the protection of fetal life. Relatedly, the most prominent religious argument advanced in the United States today in support of such legislation—the argument advanced most prominently, perhaps, by the American Catholic bishops—easily passes Greenawalt's bar: Abortion involves physical harm to the fetus. The bishops' abortion argument also easily satisfies the standard of public accessibility, as the following excerpts from various statements of the argument illustrate. A premise of the bishops' argument is that a fetus of the sort in question is a human life, in the sense that a fetus has life and is human. The premise is not problematic: Unless a fetus is dead, it is alive and "has life" in that quite ordinary sense; and a fetus (of the sort in question) is a member of the human species and "is human" in that equally ordinary sense.[112] Those are biological facts, not interpretations of scripture or deliverances of religious revelation or of other epistemically privileged insight.

> [A]bortion . . . negates two of our most fundamental moral imperatives: respect for innocent life and preferential concern for the weak and defenseless. . . . Because victims of abortion are the most vulnerable and defenseless members of the human family, it is imperative that we [who are] called to serve the least among us give urgent attention and priority to this issue.[113]

> We would do well to pay special heed to the implications of the great commandment [to love our neighbor as ourselves, which requires] that we value the lives and needs of others no less than our own. The right to life of the unborn baby, of the ill and infirm grandparent, of the despicable criminal, of the AIDS patient, is to be affirmed and protected as though it belonged to us. In addition, the refugee from Indochina, the lives of the welfare recipient from Illinois and the homeless in our own community each possess a dignity that matches our own. When we respond to that need, we acknowledge not only their dignity but ours as well.[114]

> When people say abortion is a matter of choice, they're forgetting someone. "Pro-choice" is a phrase that is incomplete; it lacks an object. One must ask the natural follow-up: the choice to do what? If it were the choice to poison an elderly person, or to smuggle

drugs, or to embezzle from a bank, no one would defend that choice. In this case, its the choice to take [an unborn] child's life. Who defends . . . the child's inalienable right to life?[115]

Catholic teaching sees in abortion a double failure: A human life is taken, and a society allows or supports the killing. Both concerns, protecting life and protecting the society from the consequences of destroying lives, require attention. Both fall within the scope of civil law. Civil law, of course, is not coextensive with the moral law, which is broader in its scope and concerns. But the two should not be separated; the civil law should be rooted in the moral law even if it should not try to translate all moral prohibitions and prescriptions into civil statutes.

When should the civil law incorporate key moral concerns? When the issue at stake poses a threat to the public order of society. But at the very heart of public order is the protection of human life and basic human rights. A society which fails in either or both of these functions is rightfully judged morally defective.

Neither the right to life nor other human rights can be protected in society without the civil law. . . . [O]ur objective, that the civil law recognize a basic obligation to protect human life, especially the lives of those [like unborn children] vulnerable to attack or mistreatment, is not new in our society. The credibility of civil law has always been tested by the range of rights it defends and the scope of the community it protects. To return to the analogy of civil rights: The struggle of the 1960s was precisely about extending the protection of the law to those unjustly deprived of protection.[116]

Of course, and as I emphasized in the preceding section of this chapter, to say that an argument satisfies the accessibility standard is not to suggest that everyone who hears the argument will embrace it. Often opposed arguments each satisfy the standard. For example, one could quite intelligibly/accessibly contend, against the call by the bishops and others for legislation outlawing all abortions (except those necessary to save the life of the mother), that a fetus, although a human life, has not attained—at least not in the early stages of a pregnancy—the moral status (worth, value) of a more fully developed human life,[117] that a woman may *sometimes* have a compelling reason, all things considered, to choose abortion, and that, in any event, there are good, even compelling, reasons not to deal with the problem of abortion by means of criminal legislation. (I mean merely to suggest the contours of an argument, which would have to be filled in.) Again, not every intelligible/accessible argument is persuasive to, much less conclusive for, everyone. The important and illustrative point, for present purposes, is that not even the argument against abortion advanced by the bishops and others—which is one of the most prominent religious arguments in American public life today—violates the establishment clause, Greenawalt's bar, or the standard of public accessibility.

I can anticipate a question to which that last observation will give rise: *In what sense is the bishops' argument in support of legislation outlawing abortion really a "religious" argument at all? More generally, is any political argument "religious" in character if it satisfies the accessibility standard?* In response to this inquiry (and to another inquiry I anticipate in the next paragraph) I need to rehearse some points I developed in previous chapters. What makes the bishops' argument in support of restrictive abortion legislation a "religious" argument is that at its very foundation is a set of related religious convictions: the conviction *that* life is ultimately meaningful, a conviction about *how* it is meaningful, and, in particular, a conviction about the ultimately meaningful way for human beings to live their lives, about the "truly, fully human" way to live, the "way of living [that is] compatible with the Presence".[118] In the bishops' view, the truly/fully human way of life involves both protection and nurture of the life and well-being even—indeed, especially—of society's most helpless, defenseless members.

Let me anticipate another question: *Given what makes the bishops' argument religious in character—given, that is, the foundational, religious convictions about the ultimate meaningfulness of life—in what sense can the argument be said to satisfy the accessibility standard? After all, not everyone agrees (or could be persuaded to agree) with the bishops (and others) about how life is meaningful or about the meaningful way for human beings to live their lives; indeed, not everyone agrees that life is meaningful (ultimately or otherwise).* Many convictions, including (especially?) fundamental convictions about human existence—for example, the conviction that life is ultimately meaningless—are not shared. That a conviction is not shared does not mean that reliance on it in political argument is necessarily inconsistent with the accessibility standard. It's difficult to imagine how political argument of any kind, even political argument steadfastly "secular" in character, could satisfy a standard *that* strict.[119]

What makes the bishops' religious argument consistent with the accessibility standard is that the foundational convictions are not defended in political argument on sectarian or authoritarian grounds. They are not defended, for example, as the yield of some epistemically privileged insight: religious revelation to, or infallible communication with the will of God on the part of, a particular religious community or its leaders. In American society the foundational convictions are not usually in question—not, at least, in political argument. Certainly the central such conviction—that a life animated by love for others is more truly, fully human than any other kind of life, especially a life bereft of such love—is not usually in question, even implicitly, in American political argument. But were that conviction in question, it could, should, and—certainly by the Catholic bishops and the moral theologians who advise them—would be defended, in American political argument, *as the yield of the lived experience of many historically extended communities struggling to discern what it means to be human.* "Nothing is specifically Christian about this method of making judgments about human experience. That is why it is strange to call any of our moral convictions . . . sectarian, since they arise from a dialogue that ranges through so many communities and draws from so many sources."[120]

Many secular moralities, no less than religious, presuppose some view as to the meaningfulness or meaninglessness, ultimate or otherwise, of human existence—a view that is neither rational nor irrational but, finally, nonrational.[121] (Not every secular morality is agnostic with respect to that deep question.[122]) Greenawalt seems less than fully sensitive to the point: "This complicated reliance on personal experience, and tradition, that I have described is largely what I mean to capsulize by saying that *religious* beliefs are largely 'nonrational'. . . ."[123] But some *nonreligious* ("secular") moral beliefs, too—specifically and especially beliefs about matters as fundamental as the meaningfulness *vel non* of human life—are no less "nonrational". A standard that would rule out moral premises grounded on what is, at the end of the day, a nonrational apprehension of the meaningfulness or meaninglessness of life is impossibly restrictive (and thus reminiscent of the standard, criticized in chapter 1, that would tolerate justificatory reliance only on moral premises shared among all the interlocutors[124]).

What often underlies the two inquiries I've just anticipated is a particular understanding of religion—in particular, of religious morality—according to which religious fundamentalism is paradigmatic of religion/religious morality. Religious fundamentalists themselves encourage that (mis)understanding, which some others, nonreligious or irreligious, uncritically embrace (in part, perhaps, because the [mis]understanding confirms them in their dismissive stereotypes of religion).[125] So, it is difficult for some people to understand either how an argument that is thoroughly nonfundamentalist is really a religious argument at all, or how an argument that is religious, and is therefore (according to the misunderstanding) thoroughly or at least partly fundamentalist, can possibly satisfy a standard of public accessibility. We "moderns" (or "postmoderns") would never embrace an outdated, superseded conception of "science" (of scientific inquiry, of the methodology of science, and so on), but we often embrace an outdated and outlandish conception of "religion" (and of "theology"). Chapter 5 was addressed partly, if implicitly, to such misconceptions, which, in some circles, are regrettably quite widespread. What the British philosopher Stephen Clark said in a review of a book by the evolutionary biologist Richard Dawkins is relevant here:

> [In commenting critically on religious arguments about creation,] Dawkins cannot simply ignore theological and philosophical discussion of what it would mean to speak of God's design, or God's existence, and what forms of 'the' argument from design are currently at issue. It really will not do to take Bishop Montefiore's book, *The Probability of Theism,* as a representative text, any more than the Bishop should have relied on Arthur Koestler, Fred Hoyle or Gordon Rattray Taylor for his up-to-the-minute biological information. Dawkins readily admits that he is no physicist or chemist, and feels no shame at consulting specialists in those disciplines; it does not occur to him that history, theology, and philosophy are also disciplines as scholarly and truth-oriented as his own, and that he is, just possibly, not entirely expert in them all.[126]

Clark's point can be adapted: In commenting critically on the proper role of religious arguments in politics, one cannot simply ignore the impressive range of such arguments (some of which, of course, are anything but impressive). It really won't do to take fundamentalist religious arguments (for instance, "homosexuality is a sin because the Bible says so") as representative.[127] (It won't do, either, to dismiss such arguments as altogether marginal. That's where the existential prerequisites to ecumenical political dialogue come in, especially the virtue of public accessibility.)

V

What are the prospects for achieving ecumenical political dialogue in the context of contemporary, pluralistic American society (and in any similar context), and for achieving the kind of politics that ecumenical political dialogue (in conjunction with ecumenical political tolerance) constitutes? And what, for us, is the promise of such dialogue/politics?

There are significant examples of ecumenical political dialogue in American society even now; and, indeed, there always have been such examples, as John Coleman has reminded us.[128] For significant contemporary examples, consider the dialogues that led to—and, in turn, the dialogues that were precipitated by—the two letters issued by the National Conference of Catholic Bishops on, respectively, nuclear deterrence (1983) and the U.S. economy (1986).[129] Consider, too, the contributions by various religious organizations, in the form of "friend of the court" briefs, to discussion of the "right to die" in the recent constitutional case of *Nancy Beth Cruzan v. Director, Missouri Department of Health* (1990).[130] Older examples concern such fundamental national questions as slavery, war, and civil rights. My argument in this book has been that such dialogue should be a central, not peripheral, feature of American politics—a constitutive, definitive feature. Echoing John Courtney Murray, who spoke of "the growing edge of tradition", Cardinal Joseph Bernardin, archbishop of Chicago, has said that "[t]he significance of Vatican II is not that it said brand new things, but that it took . . . ideas from the edge of the [Catholic] church's life and located them at the center."[131] At its most vital, a tradition is always growing at the edge and participants in the tradition are often taking ideas and practices from the edge to the center. In those terms, my argument has been that we should take ecumenical politi-

cal dialogue from the edge of the American political tradition—
when it is on the edge, when it has been marginalized—and (re)lo-
cate it at the center.

There are many who are understandably skeptical that a practice
like ecumenical political dialogue can be achieved to any significant extent in a society as religiously and morally pluralistic as
ours—and many others who, though they acknowledge that such
dialogue can sometimes (in some contexts, around some issues) be
achieved to some extent, are nonetheless skeptical that it can go
very far toward resolving disagreement and achieving consensus.
Given the dispiriting alternatives to dialogue, there is surely little
to be gained by discounting the possibility of productive political-
moral discourse. In any event, the best rejoinder to the skeptic is
Philippa Foot's: We don't know how far dialogue can go in resolving *particular* disagreements between *particular* individuals or
groups until it is tried. "One wonders . . . why people who say this
kind of thing [that dialogue can't be productive] are so sure that
they know where discussions will lead and therefore where they
will end. It is, I think, a fault on the part of relativists, and subjectivists generally, that they are ready to make pronouncements
about the later part of moral arguments . . . without being able to
trace the intermediate steps."[132] What Beiner has said of argument
we may say of dialogue:

> The question here is not whether there is some ascertainable moral-
> political framework that will guarantee a resolution in all cases; but
> rather, whether there is, in principle, any limit to the possibility of
> overcoming incommensurability. . . . [T]here is no such limit: at no
> point are we justified in terminating an unresolved argument, for it
> always remains open to us to persevere with it still further. The next
> stage of argument may yet bring an enlargement of moral vision to
> one of the contending parties, allowing this contender to integrate
> the perspective of the other into his own in a relation of part to
> whole. . . . Therefore at any point there remains the possibility,
> though not the guarantee, of resolving deep conflict. . . . Con-
> fronted with apparent stalemate, there is no need to give in to moral
> or intellectual "pluralism", for it always remains open to us to say
> "Press on with the argument".[133]

Moreover, it is a basic mistake—a basic misunderstanding—to
think that the point of ecumenical political dialogue is invariably

agreement. Such dialogue is not, cannot be, an unfailing solvent of political-moral conflict. Plurality and pluralism, after all, are ineliminable features of our social situation. As Arendt insisted: "Men, not Man, live on earth and inhabit the world."[134] Perhaps the idealized (and stylized) dialogues of philosophers are unfailing solvents of political-moral conflict, but not the actual dialogues and conversations of real-world, flesh-and-blood human beings.[135] We cannot realistically hope always to achieve agreement in the midst of our plurality and, especially, our pluralism. Nor, if we are pluralists—persons who understand that a religiously/morally pluralistic context can be a particularly fertile source of deepening insight—will we want always everyone to agree.[136]

Community, not agreement, is the fundamental test or measure of the success of ecumenical political dialogue. The invariable point—the hoped-for yield—of ecumenical political dialogue is *political* community of a certain sort: constituted by the sharing and the cultivation, in dialogue, of certain basic, albeit indeterminate, political-moral norms, and embodied, at its best, in a polity that is committed to certain dialogic virtues and aspires to mediate its conflicts, as much as possible, discursively rather than manipulatively, coercively, violently. (Thus, as I remarked earlier, ecumenical political dialogue not only requires a context of community—a political "community of judgment"—it also holds out the promise of, it makes possible the flourishing of, such community.) "Perhaps the time has come when we should endeavor to dissolve the structure of war that underlies our pluralistic society, and erect the more civilized structure of the dialogue. It would be no less sharply pluralistic, but rather more so, since the real pluralisms would be clarified out of their present confusion. And amid the pluralism a unity would be discernible—the unity of an orderly conversation. The pattern would not be that of ignorant armies clashing by night but of informed persons locked together in argument in the full light of a new dialectical day. Thus we might present to [the world] the spectacle of a civil society."[137]

To ideal-ize ecumenical political dialogue, then, is not to imagine that if we could only talk long enough with one another, and under some "ideal" conditions, we would all finally, at the end of the day, agree. There is, after all, our plurality and our pluralism: We are not all the same person, with the same affective makeup and the same traces on our being of the same religious or other moral tradition. To affirm the ideal of such dialogue is to avoid other extremes as well: in particular, the skeptical position "that there is no point in going on discussing [the] issues [that divide us]" and the "realist" position that such issues "are always resolved by power struggles between factions."[138] To affirm the ideal, and to cultivate the practice, of ecumenical political dialogue is to pursue a middle way: "to recognise that political dialogue is *neither* futile *nor* conclusive: that it issues in political decisions which are ad hoc, contingent, and always liable to be challenged: but nevertheless that the process of public dialogue is something variable in itself."[139]

Ecumenical political dialogue is valuable in itself because it is a principal constituent of a politics neither neutral/impartial nor sectarian/authoritarian but ecumenical: a politics in which citizens meet one another in the public square, sometimes to reach consensus, more often to diminish dissensus, and most often, perhaps, simply to clarify, to better understand, the nature of their disagreement, but always to cultivate the bonds of (political) community, by reaffirming their ties to one another, in particular their shared commitment to certain authoritative political-moral premises. They may, if only occasionally, succeed in strengthening existing bonds (by generating shared interpretations of existing authoritative premises). They may even, in exceptional, critical moments, forge new bonds (by generating new authoritative premises). But even when they do not succeed in strengthening the bonds of political community, much less in forging new bonds, they can, in ecumenical political dialogue, reaffirm the bonds they currently enjoy.

David Lochhead has written that "[a] truly dialogical relationship has no other purpose than itself. Dialogue is the end of dialogue."[140] I disagree. Ecumenical political dialogue does have purposes other than itself. (I mentioned several in chapter 3;[141] for example, such dialogue is a principal way for us to achieve knowledge of ourselves that is both truer and fuller than that which otherwise we could achieve.) The central purpose of the ecumenical dialogue, however, is itself, in this sense: Its central purpose is the political community of which it is a principal constituent. "In more biblical terms, the choice between monologue and dialogue is the choice between death and life. If to be human is to live in community with fellow human beings, then to alienate ourselves from community, in monologue, is to cut ourselves off from our own humanity. To choose monologue is to choose death. Dialogue is its own justification."[142]

If ecumenical political dialogue promises us, even as it presupposes, political community—a political "community of judgment"—is the community it promises an unself-critical one, unable to challenge, and unable to take seriously any challenge to, its fundamental, authoritative "standards of judgment"? There is no reason to assume that a political community nourished in part by ecumenical political dialogue would be unself-critical, especially since (as I explained earlier in this chapter) self-critical rationality is a regulative ideal for such dialogue.[143] Certainly such a community is not *necessarily* unself-critical. Not only would (or do) conflicting interpretations of authoritative political-moral premises compete with one another in the public square. Given the regulative ideal of self-critical rationality, any of the authoritative premises of the political community—any of its basic standards of political judgment—can itself be put in question, it is itself vulnerable to challenge, albeit on the basis of what Michael Walzer has termed "internal critique": criticism rooted in and inspired by other premises/standards of the community not then in question.[144] Ecumenical political dialogue, in both its justificatory and deliberative aspects, can be a matrix of such critique. (Of course, to say that an authoritative premise of a community has genuinely been put in question in the community is to say that the authority of the premise has been, to that extent, suspended, perhaps later to be reaffirmed, but not necessarily.)

It is a feature of many historically extended communities ("traditions") that they acknowledge, implicitly if not explicitly, the provisional and therefore revisable character of their beliefs and thus allow for, even encourage, the exercise of self-critical rationality. Traditions vary, of course, in the extent to which they allow for or encourage—in the extent to which they institutionalize—self-critical reflective practices. Ecumenical political dialogue and the kind of politics and political community it makes possible ideal-ize self-critical rationality, as I have emphasized throughout this book. And in any event, self-critical reflective practices—bolstered in part by authoritative constitutional premises regarding political freedom—are hardly a peripheral feature of the American political tradition. Walzer writes that "[p]erhaps there are some societies so closed in upon themselves, so rigidly confined even in their ideological justifications, that they require asocial criticism; no other kind is possible. Perhaps—but it is my own belief that such societies are more likely to be found in social science fiction than in the real world."[145] Whether or not such societies are more fictive than real, our society is not and has not been such a society, in part, no doubt, because of its congenital pluralism. (We are more pluralistic now than we once were, but even in the beginning we were pluralistic.[146])

Moreover, the authoritative premises or standards of judgment of the American political community/tradition are not themselves invariably unself-critical. Indeed, as I noted earlier, some of the standards—for example, biblically rooted premises concerning our responsibility for one another's well-being—are prophetic and, in that sense, support radical critique of existing practices and institutions. Conservative interpretations of the standards—interpretations congenial to maintenance of the status quo—may come to prevail at any given time, in which case the accompanying politics may be conservative. But the politics that prevails at any given time may be anything but conservative, depending on which interpretations of the standards come to prevail. As the emergence of liberation theology powerfully and dramatically confirms, radical interpretations of prophetic standards do not a conservative politics make.

As I said at the beginning of this chapter, the principal constituents of ecumenical politics are two practices: a certain kind of dialogue and a certain kind of tolerance. I have discussed ecumenical political dialogue at some length in this chapter. I turn now to ecumenical political tolerance.

7

Ecumenical Political Tolerance

Ecumenical political dialogue is not possible with everyone, of course; or, if possible in some weak or trivial sense, it cannot be productive with everyone. Although we should be wary of *a priori* generalizations about the categories of persons with whom dialogue is not possible (or cannot be productive)—why not in concrete situations give dialogue a chance?—it seems fair to say that dialogue is difficult with those who reject the relevant authoritative norms and impossible with those who utterly lack the virtues or habits of character and mind prerequisite to such dialogue. With particular reference to Nazis (or neo-Nazis) and members of the Klu Klux Klan, David Lochhead has written that "there are some individuals and groups who are not capable of dialogue. . . . [C]ertain groups and individuals behave in a way that continually subverts the dialogical process. The problem is not that we could have dialogue with these groups but choose not to. The problem is that dialogue itself is not possible."[1] Moreover, even with those with whom dialogue is possible and can be productive, dialogue does not always or even often eventuate in agreement. (Indeed, as I argued in chapter 6, ecumenical political dialogue should not always end in agreement; agreement is not the true test or measure of the success of such dialogue.) Often dialogue runs out before agreement is reached. Or even if it has not run out, dialogue often fails to achieve agreement before a political choice has to be made—before, for example, a vote has to be case for or against a proposed policy choice.

That dialogue is not always possible, or, even when possible, does not always, or even often, eventuate in agreement, brings us to the issue of tolerance. It would be a mistake to say that tolerance begins when dialogue ends (inconclusively). Tolerance is surely an important element of the social soil in which dialogue must grow, if it is to grow at all. Tolerance is an important precondition of dialogue. There is no, or little, authentic dialogue among, or with, the intolerant. But the inconclusive ending of dialogue is a principal occasion of tolerance. The kind of tolerance with which I am centrally concerned here, the kind that (in conjunction with ecumenical political dialogue) constitutes ecumenical politics, is (a) political tolerance, tolerance on the part of us and our representatives acting politically, *qua* state, and (b) of beliefs judged false and of behavior judged immoral. To practice such tolerance, therefore, is not to refuse to judge true from false, right from wrong, good from bad (or evil), moral from immoral. ("Properly speaking, one can 'tolerate' only beliefs or practices of which one disapproves."[2]) To practice ecumenical political tolerance is, rather, to make such judgments, and sometimes to make them publicly, perhaps in the course of or as a conclusion to ecumenical political dialogue, but to refrain from coercing others on the basis of the judgments, especially to refrain from using the apparatus of the state to coerce others.

I

Why should we refrain from coercing others to revise beliefs we judge to be false? Why, at least, should we refrain from coercing others to modify behavior we judge to be immoral?[3] Of course, radical tolerance—"we should never coerce"—is no more plausible a position than radical intolerance—"we should always coerce." Given that sometimes we should coerce and sometimes we should not, the serious question is whether a particular instance of political coercion is defensible or not. More generally, the question is what considerations (principles, criteria) should inform or guide our judgment whether to tolerate (what we believe to be) a person's immoral behavior or, instead, to coerce her to modify her behavior, to do something she does not want to do or to refrain from doing something she wants to do?[4]

Two misconceptions need dispelling. The first concerns the relation among moral cognitivism, moral skepticism, and tolerance. The morally cognitivist position, in contrast to the morally skeptical one, holds that moral beliefs can have truth value, that they can bear the predicate true/false or some equivalent predicate, such as rationally acceptable/unacceptable, and that therefore they can be objects of knowledge. Religious moralities are, of course, morally cognitivist. (They are hardly unique in that regard: *Any* morality that affirms that moral beliefs can bear the predicate true/false is morally cognitivist.) The first misconception is that moral cognitivism entails, or at least is conducive to, intolerance both of moral beliefs judged false and of the behavior such beliefs animate—and that moral skepticism entails, or at least is conducive to, tolerance of moral behavior different from one's own. This position about moral cognitivism, moral skepticism, and intolerance and tolerance is both incorrect and misguided, as Hilary Putnam has explained:

> [C]ommitment to ethical objectivity [should not] be confused with what is a very different matter, commitment to ethical or moral authoritarianism. . . . [D]iehard opposition to all forms of political and moral authoritarianism should not commit one to . . . moral scepticism. The reason that it is wrong for the government to dictate a morality to the individual citizen is not that there is no fact of the matter about what forms of life are fulfilling and what forms of life are not fulfilling, or morally wrong in some other way. (If there were no such thing as moral *wrong,* then it would not be wrong for the government to impose moral choices.) The fact that many people fear that if they concede any sort of moral objectivity out loud then they will find some government shoving *its* notion of objectivity down their throats is without question one of the reasons why so many people subscribe to a moral subjectivism to which they give no real assent.[5]

The second misconception concerns the relation between epistemological coherentism—the position I elaborated in chapter 4—and tolerance. According to this misconception, an epistemological coherentist cannot consistently hold that any moral belief comfortably nested in a coherent moral system, in a coherent set of moral beliefs, is false or, therefore, that any choice made in accordance with such a belief is immoral. This position is confused. Epistemological coherentism does not entail that any belief comfortably nested in a coherent system of beliefs is true. Rather, it holds merely that any belief about the truth/falsity of another belief— including another person's belief, however comfortably nested in a coherent system of beliefs—is itself true (or false), in the sense of rationally acceptable (or unacceptable), only "relative to" a particular web of beliefs. There is no inconsistency in adhering to epistemological coherentism and, at the same time, insisting that a particualr moral belief of another person, even if comfortably nested in a coherent moral system, is false, just as there is no inconsistency in adhering to epistemological coherentism and insisting that the position of the members of the Flat Earth Society is false.[6] As I said at the end of chapter 4: Just as it is in no way inconsistent with self-critical rationality, the coherentist conception of rationality is in no way inconsisent with critical reflection on the beliefs of *other* persons or communities; just as our own beliefs can be inadequate to the world, so too can the beliefs of others be inadequate to the world; just as "final truth", as a regulative ideal, supports self-critical reflective practices, so too it supports other-critical reflective practices.[7] In particular, the coherentist conception of rationality should not be confused with a vulgar cognitive relativism according to which the (coherent) web of beliefs of one person or community is just as good as any other person's or community's (coherent) web of beliefs. Richard Rorty is right: "[T]here is a difference between saying that every community is as good as every other and saying that we have to work out from the networks we are, from the communities with which we presently identify. . . . The view that every tradition is as rational or as moral as every other could be held only be a god, someone who had no need to use (but only to mention) the terms 'rational' or 'moral,' because she had no need to inquire or deliberate. Such a being would have escaped from history and conversation into contemplation and metanarrative."[8]

So, moral cognitivism does not entail intolerance and coercion. Nor does epistemological coherentism entail tolerance and noncoercion. Let's return, then, to this question: What considerations should inform our judgment whether to tolerate a person's immoral behavior or, instead, to coerce her to modify her behavior?[9]

II

Whether to pursue a coercive political strategy is a (political-) moral question, of course, and any list of criteria for answering that question is rooted in a set of moral beliefs. The considerations I am about to sketch presuppose—indeed, express—a set of normative commitments. But the commitments are fairly standard ones: beliefs/commitments common to many religious communities in American society as well as to many persons who identify with no religious community. The considerations are, in that sense, an appropriate and even authoritative ground for ecumenical political deliberation about tolerance.

Several basic considerations counsel against pursuit of coercive political strategies. A principal such consideration is the fact that human judgment is fallible. There is always the possibility that the moral judgment in the service of which a coercive strategy has been proposed is mistaken.[10] That possibility is especially likely with respect to paternalistic coercion. John Stuart Mill's point seems right as a *general* matter (there are always counterexamples): "[W]ith respect to his own feelings and circumstances the most ordinary man or woman has means of knowledge immeasurably surpassing those that can be possessed by anyone else. The interference of society to overrule his judgement and purposes in what only regards himself must be grounded on general presumptions which may be altogether wrong and, even if right, are as likely as not to be misapplied to individual cases, by persons no better acquainted with the circumstances of such cases than those are who look at them merely from without."[11] The consideration of human fallibility should not be discounted. History is littered with examples of mistaken judgments that a choice or behavior different from the evaluator's own in some or many respects was not merely different but immoral. Thus, one of the most important existential prerequisites to ecumenical political dialogue—fallibilism—is also conducive to tolerance. (I explained in the preceding chapter why the existential condition called religious faith supports a fallibilist attitude—why, that is, it supports taking very seriously the ideal of self-critical rationality.)

Another important prerequisite to ecumenical political dialogue is conducive to tolerance: pluralism. To be a pluralist, in the relevant sense, is (as I explained in chapter 6) to understand that a morally pluralistic context, with its attendant variety of ways of life, can often be a more fertile source of deepening moral insight than can a monistic context.[12] Thus, a pluralist sensibility serves as a brake on the regrettable tendency to condemn and outlaw choices, behavior, and ways of life different from one's own. Fallibilism, then, in conjunction with pluralism, should make us wary about interfering, through coercion, with behavior and ways of life different from our own.[13] Fallibilism and pluralism are conducive to tolerance. (And tolerance, like fallibilism and pluralism, is conducive to dialogue. Again, there is no or little dialogue among or with the intolerant.)

Another consideration counseling against pursuit of coercive political strategies is simple self-interest. A strong tradition or spirit of tolerance—that is, a strong wariness about political coercion—can help protect us in the event the winds change. We may be members of the politically dominant coalition today, but there is no guarantee we will be tomorrow. Governor Mario Cuomo made the point in addressing a group of fellow Catholics at Notre Dame:

> [Catholic public officials don't always] love what others do with their freedom, but . . . they realize that in guaranteeing freedom for all, they guarantee our right to be Catholics. . . .
>
> The Catholic public official lives the political truth which most Catholics through most of American history have accepted and insisted on: the truth that to assure our freedom we must allow others the same freedom, even if it occasionally produces conduct by them which we would hold to be sinful.
>
> I protect my right to be a Catholic by preserving your right to believe as Jew, a Protestant or non-believer, or as anything else you choose. We know that the price of seeking to enforce our beliefs on others is that they might some day force theirs on us. This freedom is the fundamental strength of our unique experiment in government. In the complex interplay of forces and considerations that go into the making of our laws and policies, its preservation must be a pervasive and dominant concern.[14]

Another consideration is compassion. To coerce someone to make a choice she does not want to make is to cause her to suffer.[15] If we are empathetic, we will be sensitive to such suffering. If we are compassionate, we will be wary about imposing that suffering on another. A related consideration is the friendship or fellowship that nourishes community. For the politically dominant coalition to coerce a member of the political community to make a choice she does not want to make is to provoke resentment in her. If we respect the other with whom we disagree, and especially if we value friendship/fellowship and the sort of community it makes possible, we will be wary about provoking such resentment, which is corrosive of community. Consider what we might call extreme coercion: coercing someone to refrain from doing something she not merely wants to do but believes essential to her well-being, even obligatory, that she do; or coercing someone to do something she not merely does not want to do, but believes destructive of her well-being to do, even forbidden for her to do. Extreme coercion causes extreme suffering. And extreme resentment. It can tear the fabric of public civility essential to civil politics,[16] even engender alienation from community, lack of respect for "authority" and the law, political instability, and the reactive repression that often attends political instability. (It is difficult to imagine dialogue flourishing in such a context.) Commenting on Aquinas' view of the relationship between religion and law, Mulford Sibley writes: "Human beings vary widely in their social and moral development. To make impossible demands on many of them might provoke rebellion and civil war—consummations far worse in their consequences for humanity, perhaps, than those which result from not embodying every moral offense in human law. St. Thomas is constantly emphasizing contingencies in human life, and awareness of them tends to modify what might otherwise be inflexible and absolutist principles."[17] John Noonan has said that "[t]he central problem . . . of the legal enterprise is the relation of love to power."[18] If we are compassionate, and if we value community, we will be especially wary about relying on extreme coercion: The costs—extreme suffering and extreme resentment—are great and sometimes terrible.

Extreme coercion entails another cost as well, and another consideration, counseling against reliance on extreme coercion, concerns this cost. To coerce someone to refrain from doing something she believes herself obligated to do, or to do something she believes herself forbidden to do, is to ask her to act contrary to her conscience. A moral community that values individual conscientiousness or personal integrity—that believes that ultimately, after careful, informed deliberation, a person should choose on the basis of conscience—will be wary, therefore, about pursuing a political strategy of extreme coercion. In an essay elaborating "A Catholic Perspective on Morality and the Law", Joseph Boyle writes that the Catholic

> conception of morality . . . is based on the assumption that human beings have choices to make, and that it is by making the choices which they believe to be the correct ones that they become good persons. Moral norms in this conception of morality are acknowledged guidelines for choices. These norms are known within the human conscience, and human dignity lies in choosing to act in accord with these norms. [In a footnote at this point, Boyle writes: "This formulation is based on Vatican Council II, *Pastoral Constitution on The Church in the Modern World (Gaudium et Spes)*, paragraph 16."] Thus, what is morally central is making the correct choices in the light of personally acknowledged moral standards . . . [The] legal imposition of moral prohibitions can have effects contrary to the moral goal of making choices that conform to one's conscience. For, it might be the case that what one person or group regards as morally prohibited is regarded by others as morally required. The legal enforcement of the moral views of some thus becomes a significant temptation for others not to act in accord with their consciences. Those who regard morality as choosing to conform to conscience can hardly regard this to be acceptable.[19]

This concern that coercive legislation not subvert individual conscientiousness partly undelies the statement of John Courtney Murray that "the moral aspirations of the law are minimal. Law seeks to establish and maintain only that minimum of actualized morality that is necessary for the healthy functioning of the social order. It does not look to what is morally desirable, or attempt to remove every moral taint from the atmosphere of society. It enforces only what is minimally acceptable, and in this sense socially necessary."[20]

That various considerations counsel against pursuit of coercive political strategies, and that we should therefore be wary, as a general matter, about pursuing such strategies, is not to say that no such strategy should ever be pursued. That position—radical tolerance—would be extreme and extremely silly.[21] The principal consideration supporting, even necessitating, a coercive political strategy is the fact, if it is a fact, that the strategy is an essential means of protecting a fundamental interest or interests: interests the satisfaction of which significantly enhances one's level of well-being and the frustration of which significantly diminishes it. This consideration has special force if the coercive strategy is an essential means of protecting one or more of the fundamental interests of human beings themselves relatively incapable of protecting those interests, and if those considering the strategy are committed to protecting the weak among them ("the least of my brethren"[22]). The protection of fundamental interests is, after all, a principal aspect of the very *raison d'etre* of government. "Thomas Aquinas, a natural lawyer if ever these was one, . . . argues that the law should not seek to prohibit all vices, but only the more serious ones, and 'especially those which involve harm to others, without whose prohibition human society could not be preserved. . . . ' "[23] ("In the heat of the civil rights debate, Martin Luther King Jr. was accused of wanting to legislate morality. He replied that the law could not make people love their neighbors, but it could stop their lynching them."[24]) Relatedly, a coercive strategy is supported by the fact that it is an important means of safeguarding basic social institutions— the courts, for example—institutions whose effective functioning is itself crucial to the protection of fundamental interests.[25]

Inevitably there are disagreements as to which interests are fundamental. And there are disagreements, too, as to when an entity (a slave, for example, or an unborn child) is a member, or to what extent a member, of the human community.[26] (An instance of this disagreement looms very large in the abortion controversy.) In a religiously/morally pluralistic society like our own, however—a relatively democratic society—the views of no single religious or other moral community can be determinative, and the chance that truly idiosyncratic views might prevail is thereby diminished.[27]

II

The kind of politics I am defending in this book—ecumenical politics—is, in part, a *religious* politics, in this sense: a politics in which persons with religious convictions about the good or fitting way for human beings to live their lives, about the "truly, fully human" way to live, rely on those convictions, not only in making political choices, but in publicly deliberating about and in publicly justifying such choices. Many people are frightened by the prospect of a religious politics. They think that any such politics must be, or almost certainly is, sectarian and authoritarian. (I argued to the contrary in the preceding chapter.) But above all they think that a religious politics must be intolerant, even fanatical. At points in this book I argue, in effect, that a religious politics need not be intolerant any more than it need be authoritarian or dogmatic: In chapter 2, I discussed the religious ground of human rights,[28] and in chapter 6, I suggested that some religous premises, interpreted in certain ways, offer strong support, arguably even essential support, for some constitutional premises, especially premises about basic human rights.[29]

In this chapter I have continued the argument by specifying several considerations that militate against pursuit of coercive political strategies: fallibilism (in conjunction with pluralism), self-interest, compassion, community, and conscientiousness. Those considerations are not exhaustive, but they are, I think, the principal ones.[30] (Others that have been mentioned include not enacting "laws which are difficult to enforce and whose enforcement tends, therefore, to be patchy and inequitable", "laws which are likely to . . . produce . . . evils such as blackmail", or laws "punishing people for what they very largely cannot help."[31]) Both individually and, especially, cumulatively, the considerations set forth here—considerations that are, as I said earlier, an authoritative ground for ecumenical political deliberation about tolerance—call for a strong reluctance to rely on coercive political strategies and, so, for a tolerant political agenda. They inform a sensible, discriminating wariness about the use of coercive state power.

With respect to ideals of politics, the opposition between a politics that is "liberal" and one, like ecumenical politics, that is (partly) religious is quite false. Ecumenical politics *is* a liberal ideal. Granted, the liberal character of the ideal does not inhere in some putatively "neutral" or "impartial" practice of political justification. It inheres, rather, in certain of the values that animate ecumenical politics, in certain of the existential prerequisites to ecumenical politics I detailed in the preceding chapter: fallibilism, pluralism, public intelligibility, and public accessibility.[32] Above all the liberal character of ecumenical politics inheres in the fact that, for the various reasons I have specified in this chapter—including, perhaps most prominently, the importance of conscientiousness, a contemporary name for which seems to be "autonomy"[33]—tolerance is a principal constituent of ecumenical politics. Although liberalism-as-neutrality is a dead end (as I explained in chapters 1 and 2), liberalism-as-tolerance is not. "[O]nce the ideal of liberal neutrality is recognized as empty, the remaining choice is between tolerance and intolerance. . . . [T]olerance is the only viable way of preserving the liberal commitment to individual freedom in a genuine political community."[34]

At one time the subtitle to this book was "A Postliberal Reflection on Religion and Politics"; chapter 1 was titled "The Liberal Project: Neutral Politics", and chapter 3, "The Postliberal Project: Ecumenical Politics". I concluded, however, that it was seriously misleading to cast the alternatives in terms of "liberal" and "postliberal". The alternative are better understood as representing (among other things) two kind of liberalism. One kind can be understood, and often is, as "neo-Kantian", because it aspires to a neutral politics: a politics in which different and competing conceptions of human good are to play no or little role in political justification. Such a politics is sometimes called a "deontological", or Right-prior-to-Good, politics.[35] Chapters 1 and 2 of this book are, in effect, a critique of that kind of liberalism. The other kind of liberalism is "neo-Aristotelian": It aspires to a politics that, while "teleological" or "Good-prior-to-Right" in character[36]—that is, a politics in which convictions about human good or well-being play a fundamental justificatory (and, in the case of ecumenical politics, deliberative) role—is at the same time tolerant: a politics in which convictions about human good justify, even mandate, great toleration for beliefs judged false and behavior judged immoral (and mandate, more generally, great respect for human rights).[37] The liberalism of ecumenical politics is a neo-Aristotelian liberalism.[38]

Conclusion

I

I started writing this book in the spring of 1989; I largely finished writing it—except for this conclusion—in the summer of 1990. As I write this conclusion it is November 1990. During the last few months I have received thoughtful comments from several persons kind enough to read the book and share their critical reactions with me. I want to report and respond to one such reaction.

In a letter I received this fall, David M. Smolin, a law professor[1] who identifies himself as an evangelical Christian, claimed that two of the existential prerequisites to participation in ecumenical political dialogue I set forth and defend in chapter 6—namely, fallibilism and pluralism—have the effect of "excluding from dialogue a number of culturally significant religious communities in America, including various Christian groups (evangelicals, fundamentalists, pentecostals, traditionalist Roman Catholics) and theologically conservative representatives of other monotheist[ic] religions (Orthodox Jews, and certain Muslims)." He continued: "None of these groups accepts fallibilism [or pluralism] in the sense you describe [them]; none of them accepts the dichotomy and definitions of religious faith and religious belief that you describe [in chapters 5 and 6]." My position with respect to fallibilism, pluralism, and the faith/beliefs distinction, Profesor Smolim observed, "favor[s] cer-

tain religious groups: in particular modernist or theologically liberal forms of Catholicism and Protestantism, Reform (and perhaps
Conservative) Judaism, and also probably religions (such as Hinduism and Buddhism) that may suggest a 'pluralistic' view of truth."[2]
He concluded: "The gist of your book seems to be that members of
these favored religious groups, along with those of a more 'secular'
mindset, are allowed to enter into public dialogue; less 'enlightened' religious groups are presumed unworthy."

My argument in chapter 6, including my discussion of the existential prerequisites to participation in ecumenical political dialogue,
proceeds against the background of a particular understanding of
"religion"—in particular, of "religious" morality—and of the enterprise of theology, including moral theology. I elaborate that understanding in chapter 5, where I emphasize that there is no such thing
as a theologically neutral understanding or account of religion or
theology.[3] Deep theological differences between Professor Smolin
and me account, at least in part, for our different evaluations of
fallibilism and pluralism and our different understandings of "faith"
and "belief". But perhaps meaningful participation in ecumenical
political dialogue *is* possible even for those who are not fallibilists or
pluralists. Perhaps fallibilism and pluralism are better understood,
not as prerequisites *to* ecumenical political dialogue, but as attitudes
or positions for which it is sometimes fitting to contend, depending
on the particular question at issue, *in* ecumenical political dialogue.[4]
(It does seem to me, however, that the kind, or quality, or participation in ecumenical political dialogue available to one who is neither
fallibilist nor pluralist is inferior to that available to one who is both
fallibilist and pluralist.[5])

In any event, the essential criterion is less fallibilism or pluralism
than public accessibility. I explain, in chapter 6, why "[t]he virtue
of public accessibility is not an insurmountable obstacle for religious persons who would bring their deepest convictions about the
human to bear in political dialogue."[6] If I am wrong about that, I
am eager to hear why. Moreover, if someone thinks, contrary to
my argument in chapter 6, that meaningful religious (or nonreligious) participation in political dialogue is possible in a religiously and morally pluralistic society like the United States even if
the criterion of public accessibility (or some such criterion) is not

honored, I am eager to hear the argument. It seems to me that the realistic choice is between, on the one hand, a criterion like that of public accessibility and, on the other, giving up on the possibility of ecumenical political dialogue or anything like it.

Let me emphasize (as Professor Smolin thought I should) that the various prerequisites to participation in ecumenical political dialogue for which I contend in chapter 6, including public accessiblity, are not intended as *legal* prerequisites. I do not think that, for the most part, participation in political dialogue—whether the participation be religious or not—is, or should be, subject to legal regulation. Such regulation would be deeply problematic under the First Amendment's protection of freedom of speech. I am merely proposing an ideal of religious (and nonreligious) participation in political dialogue—specifically, in the political dialogue of a religiously and morally pluralistic society. What ideal of religious participation in political dialogue would Professor Smolin, or anyone with a similar theological orientation, propose as an alternative to the ideal I elaborate and defend in this book? Religious argument that is either sectarian or authoritarian, or both,[7] and thus fails the criterion of public accessiblity seems, at best, singularly unhelpful to the project of political dialogue in a religiously and morally pluralistic political community like the United States.

I should recur here to something I have sought to emphasize throughout the book: My effort has been to propose an *ideal* of politics (in particular, of political deliberation and justification). The ideal of neutral politics I criticize in chapters 1 and 2 does not—cannot—work as an ideal. The fact that the ideal of ecumenical politics for which I contend in this book, or some part of it, may be, at the level of theory, problematic—or the fact that the ideal may be, at the level of practice, difficult to achieve in the real world of American politics—cannot count as a reason to adhere to the failed ideal of neutral politics. The challenge to those who criticize the ideal of ecumenical politics is to propose their own ideal of (nonneutral) politics—or perhaps to modify the ideal of ecumenical politics. (Of course, no one will be interested in proposing a dialogic ideal of politics who is deeply skeptical that the project of political dialogue can succeed in a society as religiously and morally various as our own.)

II

If aspects of my argument prove troubling for fundamentalist Christians, Orthodox Jews, and some other religious persons, different aspects will surely prove no less troubling for those who, at the other end of the spectrum, prefer to keep a safe distance from any and all religion—and who prefer, too, that religion keep a safe distance from them. In particular: The argument I develop in *Love and Power,* for an ideal of political deliberation and justification that does not exclude religiously based argument—indeed, that welcomes such argument—will undoubtedly provoke those who, for various reasons, are prejudiced against religion and want to marginalize (repress?) it as much as possible.[8] (Included in that group, of course, are many intellectuals—alas, too many—who are religiously illiterate.) However, religion is a quintessentially human expression and endeavor—at least as much as so as, say, art or science. Religion should no more be marginalized, in politics or elsewhere, than should art or science. Of course, there has been and continues to be bad, or inhumane, religion (religious institutions, practices)—far too much of it—as well as good religion. But there has been and continues to be bad science (silly science, brutalizing science) as well as good science. There has been and continues to be bad art (degrading art, misogynist art) as well as good art. It makes as much sense—which is to say, *no* sense at all—to think that the persistence of bad science is a reason to marginalize science generally, or to think that the persistence of bad art is a reason to marginalize art generally, as it does to think that the persistence of bad religion is a reason to marginalize religion generally. Religion no less than art and science struggles with fundamental, ineliminable human questions. (As I explain in chapter 5, religion arguably struggles with the deepest human questions, "limit" questions.) Religion, no less than science and art, is a fundamental, ineliminable human endeavor. May I suggest that any reader who doubts that fact—or, especially, any reader who *laments* that fact—take time to read Robert Coles's recent wonderful book, *The Spiritual Life of Children.*[9] None of this is to say that religious endeavor is central to everyone's life. Far from it. Artistic endeavor is not central to everyone's life either. Nor is scientific endeavor. It is not even to say that everyone is religiously literate. Not everyone is artistically or scientifically literate.

After commenting critically on the prejudice against religion one often encounters in the intellectual environment of elite law schools, Mary Ann Glendon (of the Harvard Law School) wrote recently that "[t]he most commonly *stated* reasons for drawing a *cordon sanitaire* around legal political discourse, however, are not that moral and religious beliefs are essentially arbitrary or foolish, or that ordinary men and women are unfit to rule. They are, rather, that religion has often been a source of civil strife, and that particularistic groups are often intolerant and 'illiberal.' All too frequently, what is implied is that religion and particular communities are *presumptively* intolerant and socially divisive."[10] Professor Glendon's measured response bears repeating here:

> Academics and others who express dismay at the prospect of a greater role for religious voices in political life seem to believe that because some religious adherents have committed atrocities in the name of their beliefs, there must be something wrong with religion itself. The dismal record reflects, however (to paraphrase Chesterton), not that religion has been tried and found wanting, but that it has been tried and found hard. If the fears of proponents of [a "neutral" politics] are terror, intolerance, and oppression, the historical evidence reveals that the excesses of the Crusades, the Inquisition, or the Iranian revolution pale before those of the thoroughly secular regimes of Hitler, Stalin, and Pol Pot. On the whole, the world's religions and their followers (however fallen, misguided, or inept) have probably done more to moderate the worst human impulses than to call them forth.[11]

I do not mean to minimize the serious problems some kinds of religion or religiosity, and some styles of religious participation in politics, pose for American public life.[12] But it is precisely to address those problems (among others) that I essayed: in chapter 6, the existential prerequisites to constructive religious participation in political deliberation and justification, and, in chapter 7, the considerations, including *religious* considerations, that support a tolerant rather than a coercive politics.

III

I just acknowledged that some kinds of religion and some styles of religious participation in politics pose serious problems. At its best, as I argue in chapter 5, religion is liberating. At its worst, however, religion is oppressive. Any argument in support of a significant role for religious convictions about the human in political deliberation and justification will understandably give pause to those, such as feminists, who correctly discern the extent to which much religion—the Bible, for example—is not only used as an instrument of oppression but is itself, in some of its (central, not peripheral) parts, oppressive.[13] But of course much secular thought is oppressive too—as feminists understand at least as well as anyone else. One of the most appropriate responses to oppressive ideologies, whether religious or secular, is surely to take them on, to contend against them—and, where fitting, to do so in the context and course of political dialogue.

IV

Any politics comprises more—*much* more—than dialogue and tolerance, of course. Ecumenical politics is no exception. Any politics, realistically conceived, including a relatively nonviolent politics, comprises such sometimes unruly practices as campaigning, advertising, lobbying, bartering, strikes, even civil disobedience, and so on. (Not all these practices always compete with dialogue. Sometimes a practice can complement dialogue: For example, civil disobedience can enable a stalled dialogue to begin again, with new vigor and promise.[14] I think here of the movements led by Gandhi in India and by Martin Luther King in the United States.) So, any complete conception of politics must make room for a host of (sometimes competitive, sometimes complementary) practices, not all of them polite.

But dialogue and tolerance of the sorts I have sought to portray in this book certainly constitute a politics quite unlike any politics in which such dialogue and tolerance are, for the most part, devalued and marginalized. They nourish, even as they presuppose, a form of political community quite unlike any political association in which the practices of ecumenical political dialogue and ecumenical political tolerance are largely unknown—a form of political community in which, notwithstanding our sometimes radical disagreements with one another, we always strive to understand one another, to know one another, to serve one another, better than we now do. It is a form of political community that takes very seriously an image—a moral image that is also a political image that is, finally, a religious image—central to "[t]he Jerusalem-based religions": an image that "[stresses] equality and also fraternity, as in the metaphor of the whole human race as One Family, of all women and men as sisters and brothers."[15] As that image suggests, it is a form of political community, an *ideal* of political community, in which love (*agape*) and power—*political* love[16] and *political* power—are intimately connected: an ideal of political community in which love both inspires and inhibits the exercise of political power (including power exercised *against* the state, as in civil disobedience,[17] as well as power exercised *by* the state), in which the exercise of political power, and the decision not to exercise it, are, at their best, acts of love.[18]

The central problem of politics for some of us, given our deepest convictions—*religious* convictions—about the truly, fully human way to live, is the relation of love to power.

Notes

Introduction

1. On the meaning of "morality", see chapter 5, notes 45 and 49.
2. See K. Wald, Religion and Politics in the United States (1987). See also G. Wills, Under God: Religion and American Politics (1990). For a collection of historical essays on religion and politics in the United States, see M. Noll, ed., Religion and American Politics: From the Colonial Period to the 1980s (1990).
3. The Williamsburg Charter: A National Celebration and Reaffirmation of the First Amendment Religious Liberty Clauses 13 (1988).
4. M. Perry, Morality, Politics, and Law 181–82, 183 (1988).
5. J. Murray, We Hold These Truths x (1960).
6. *Love and Power* is also, in part, a response to Richard John Neuhaus's invitation "to make the argument for the connections between bibilical faith and democratic governance. . . . In the past that argument was made in part by thinkers such as Reinhold Niebuhr, John Courtney Murray, Jacques Maritain, and A. D. Lindsay. The argument has been sorely neglected in our recent history." R. Neuhaus, The Naked Public Square: Religion and Democracy in America xi (2d ed. 1986). As I later emphasize, however, I am concerned not only with "biblical" faith but with religious faith generally.
7. Woodward, "Noonan's Life in the Law," Newsweek, Apr. 1, 1987, at 82. Noonan made the statement in the foreword to his *Persons and Masks of the Law* (1976) (at p. xii).

Chapter 1

1. J. Murray, We Hold These Truths 27 (1960). Murray added: "This fact created the possibility of a new solution; indeed, it created a demand for a new solution. The possibility was exploited and the demand was met by the American Constitution." Id. For a discussion of the constitutional provision most relevant to

the subject matter of this book, the establishment clause of the First Amendment, see pp. 112–17.

2. I use "citizen" here and throughout the book in a nontechnical sense. A person may reside in the United States, may intend to do so for the rest of her life, and may habitually and even prominently participate in arguments about issues that engage American politics, without being an American citizen, even without intending to become one, in the technical, legal sense.

3. For a complementary discussion, see M. Perry, Morality, Politics, and Law, chs. 3 & 4 (1988).

4. Ackerman uses the term "neutral". See B. Ackerman, Social Justice in the Liberal State (1980); Ackerman, "What Is Neutral about Neutrality?," Ethics, Jan. 1983, at 372. (So do kindred political theorists like Ronald Dworkin and Charles Larmore. See Dworkin, "Liberalism," in S. Hampshire, ed., Public and Private Morality 113 [1978]; Dworkin, "What Liberalism Isn't," New York Rev., Jan. 20, 1983, at 47; Larmore, Patterns of Moral Complexity [1987]; Larmore, "Political Liberalism," Political Theory [forthcoming 1990].) I have commented elsewhere on Ackerman's basic position in *Social Justice in the Liberal State*: M. Perry, note 3, at 63–66; Perry, "Neutral Politics?," 51 Rev. Politics 479, 480–81 (1989). I comment here on a recent essay by Ackerman. See note 5.

5. Ackerman, "Why Dialogue?," 86 J. Philosophy 5, 17–18 (1989).

6. Ackerman, note 5, at 22. See note 16 (quoting Thomas Nagel: requirement that "the premises be *actually* accepted" is an "impossibly restrictive condition on [the exercise of] political power"). When is a normative premise "shared"? What counts as evidence that a premise is shared? Reading Ackerman's *Social Justice in the Liberal State* (note 4) retrospectively through the lens of his later essay "Why Dialogue?" (note 5), we may fairly interpret Ackerman to be suggesting that a distribution-of-scarce-resources-according-to-worth principle (see M. Perry, note 3, at 65) is shared across American society. But is it? People mean such different things by "worth": worth-in-God's-eyes, worth-according-to-the-laws-of-nature, and so on. Superficial sharing may conceal deep disagreement. See id. at 155–56.

7. See note 29.

8. See W. Quine & J. Ulian, The Web of Belief (2d ed. 1978).

9. See Smith, "Separation and the 'Secular': Reconstructing the Disestablishment Decision," 67 Texas L. Rev. 955, 1010 (1989): "[T]he common denominator argument [is] fraudulent. Suppose Dad and Daughter are discussing what to have for dinner. Daughter proposes: 'Let's just have dessert.' Dad suggests that it would be better to have a full meal, with salad, meat, fruit, cooked vegetables, and *then* dessert. Daughter responds: 'Obviously, Dad, we disagree about a lot of things. But there is one thing we agree on; we both want dessert. Clearly the fair and democratic solution is to accept what we agree on. So let's just have dessert.' Although he might admire Daughter's cleverness, Dad is not likely to be taken in by this common denominator ploy. The argument that secular public discourse provides a common denominator that all citizens share is comparably clever—and equally unpersuasive."

10. Nagel, "Moral Conflict and Political Legitimacy," 16 Philosophy & Public Affairs 215, 218 (1987). Nagel emphasizes that by "justification" he does not mean

"persuasion": " 'Justification' . . . is a normative concept: arguments that justify may fail to persuade, if addressed to an unreasonable audience; and arguments that persuade may fail to justify. Nevertheless, justification hopes to persuade the reasonable. . . . " Id.

11. Id. at 223. Nagel explains: "This would be implied, on one reading, by the second formulation of Kant's categorical imperative—that one should treat humanity never merely as a means, but always also as an end. If you force someone to serve an end that he cannot share, you are treating him as a mere means—even if the end is his own good, as you see it. . . . " Id. at 223 n. 8.

12. Cf. id. at 223: "If liberalism is to be defined as a higher-order theory rather than just another sectarian doctrine, it must be shown to result from an interpretation of impartiality itself, rather than from a particular conception of the good that is to be made impartially available. Of course any interpretation of impartiality will be morally controversial—it is not a question of rising to a vantage point above all moral disputes—but the controversy will be at a different level."

13. Id. at 229.

14. Id. at 230.

15. See id. at 230 (emphasis added & deleted):

> The idea is that when we look at certain of our convictions from outside, however justified they may be from within, the appeal to their truth must be seen merely as an appeal to our beliefs, and should be treated as such unless those beliefs can be shown to be justifiable *from a more impersonal standpoint*. If not, they have to remain, for the purposes of a certain kind of moral argument, features of a personal perspective—to be respected as such but no more than that.
>
> This does not mean that we have to stop believing them—that is, believing them to be true. Considered as individual beliefs they may be adequately grounded, or at least not unreasonable: the standards of individual rationality are different from the standards of epistemological ethics. It means only that from the perspective of political argument we may have to regard certain of our beliefs, whether moral or religious or even historical or scientific, simply as someone's beliefs, rather than as truths—unless they can be given the kind of impersonal justification appropriate to [the perspective of political argument], in which case they may be appealed to as truths without qualification.

16. Id. at 231, 232. Nagel goes on to emphasize that "[b]y a common ground I do not mean submerged agreement on a set of premises by which the claim could in principle be settled in a way that all parties would recognize as correct." Id. See id. at 231–32:

> [Impartial justification involves] neither an appeal to my own beliefs nor an appeal to beliefs that we all share. It cannot be the latter because it is intended precisely to justify the forcible imposition in some cases of measures that are not universally accepted. We need a distinction between two kinds of disagreement—one whose grounds make it [all right] for the major-

ity to use political power in the service of their opinion, and another whose grounds are such that it would be wrong for the majority to do so.

For this purpose we cannot appeal directly to the distinction between reasonable and unreasonable beliefs. It would be an impossibly restrictive condition on political power to say that its exercise may be justified only by appeal to premises that others could not reasonably reject (though less restrictive than the condition that the premises be *actually* accepted by all). . . .

Reasonable persons can disagree not only over religious doctrines and ultimate conceptions of the good life, but over levels of public provision of education and health care, social security, defense policy, environmental preservation, and a host of other things that liberal societies determine by legislative action. What distinguishes those disagreements from the ones where liberalism rejects majority rule?

17. See id. at 232:

Public justification in a context of actual disagreement requires, first, preparedness to submit one's reasons to the criticism of others, and to find that the exercise of a common critical rationality and consideration of evidence that can be shared will reveal that one is mistaken. This means that it must be possible to present to others the basis of your beliefs, so that once you have done so, *they have what you have,* and can arrive at a judgment on the basis. . . .

Public justification requires, second, an expectation that if others who do not share your belief are wrong, there is probably an explanation of their error which is not circular. That is, the explanation should not come down to the mere assertion that they do not believe the truth (what you believe), but should explain their false belief in terms of errors in their evidence, or identifiable errors in drawing conclusions from it, or in argument, judgment, and so forth. One may not always have the information necessary to give such an account, but one must believe there is one, and that the justifiability of one's own belief would survive a full examination of the reasons behind theirs. These two points may be combined in the idea that a disagreement which falls on objective common ground must be open-ended in the possibility of its investigation and pursuit, and not come down finally to a bare confrontation between incompatible personal points of view.

18. Cf. Lovin, "Empiricism and Christian Social Thought," Annual of Society of Christian Ethics 25, 41 (1982): "[M]oral reality . . . [is] about an interaction between persons and the world which can only be known from the reports of those who experience that interaction."

19. See Burtchaell, "The Sources of Conscience," 13 Notre Dame Mag. 20, 20 (Winter 1984–85). See also Ladd, "Politics and Religion in America: The Enigma of Pluralism," in J. Pennock & J. Chapman, eds., Religion, Morality, and the Law 263, 279 (1988) (commenting on and recommending "the pragmatic attitude that . . . most people in America take towards particular religions [and particular religious doctrines]," in which they are understood not as absolutist, dogmatic,

authoritarian systems but simply as "experiments in living with other people in a shared world of suffering and hope"). Cf. Battaglia, " 'Sect' or 'Denomination'?: The Place of Religious Ethics in a Post-Churchly Culture," 16 J. Religious Ethics 128, 137 (1988): "[David] Tracy's aim is to reintroduce into public life a reasonable discussion of the possibilities of human life. His great accomplishment is to make comprehensible to both believers and outsiders his willingness to let the public explanation of Christianity stand on that basis—as profound and challenging disclosure of what it means to be human."

20. Raz, "Facing Diversity: The Case of Epistemic Abstinence," 19 Philosophy & Public Affairs 3, 40 (1990). See id. at 43:

> We are left in a frustrating position. We know that the test of "sharing all the evidence" must be relaxed. But nothing in the rest of Nagel's discussion suggests how to relax it. I suspect that the principle of impartiality, when relaxed to admit all acceptable reasons, fails in the task that Nagel assigns it. . . . It can rule out only blatantly irrational beliefs. It does not rule out as grounds for coercive political action any beliefs that individuals are justified in holding to be true. No one is justified in holding beliefs that are not based on acceptable reasons. But the heart and soul of Nagel's argument is for epistemic restraint in appealing to truth, for the contention [is] that some truths which individuals are justified in believing, they are not justified in relying on politically. This seems an impossible task, given that to be personally justified in believing a proposition one must accept that one's belief is in principle subject to impersonal, impartial standards of correctness. Those who comply with this condition do subject their beliefs to valid impersonal tests. It may be that others do not see it that way, and deny the validity of those tests. But given that the tests are both valid and publicly, objectively, and impartially available, it seems impossible that others can *reasonably* deny the validity of those tests, unless they lack information. And that lack can be remedied, and so cannot serve as the basis for Nagel's theory. Ultimately Nagel's principle is bound to fail because it depends on driving a wedge between appeal to truth and acceptance of objective standards of justification; and that wedge comes unstuck.

21. Surely he means much more than the exercise of common logic. That would be a trivially weak requirement. Cf. A. MacIntyre, Whose Justice? Which Rationality? 351 (1988): "It is not then that competing traditions do not share some standards. All the traditions with which we have been concerned agree in according a certain authority to logic both in their theory and in their practice. Were is not so, their adherents would be unable to disagree in the way in which they do. But that upon which they agree is insufficient to resolve the disagreements." Does "the exercise of a common critical rationality" partly involve, in Nagel's view, "consideration [only] of evidence that can be shared", so that the evidence-that-can-be-shared requirement is simply an aspect of the common-critical-rationality requirement?

22. Not that Nagel has done so wittingly. Cf. note 16 (quoting Nagel: requirement that "the premises be *actually* accepted" is an "impossibly restrictive condition on [the exercise of] political power").

23. See Ackerman, note 5.

24. See Nagel, note 10, at 231–34.

25. For a critical comment on such question-begging moves in political theory, see Ackerman, note 5.

26. See note 29.

27. See Nagel, note 10, at 232–33.

Nagel struggles but, in my view, ultimately fails to specify, much less administer, a distinction, which he acknowledges to be "vague" and problematic, between (1) moral disagreements, including religious-moral disagreements, that "come down finally to a pure confrontation between personal [religious or] moral convictions", and (2) a "perceptibly different" kind of disagreement: "disagreement[s] in judgment over the preponderant weight of reasons bearing on an issue" (id. at 233). See id. at 233 et seq. "Perceptibly different" to whom? To Nagel? Certainly not to me. But then perhaps my perceptual apparatus isn't up to snuff. In any event, by the second kind of disagreement Nagel cannot mean either disagreements merely about the facts or even disagreements in reasoning from shared premises. Nagel specifically disclaims to be addressing political conflicts in which there is "submerged agreement on a set of premises by which the claim could in principle be settled in a way that all parties would recognize as correct." Id. at 232. See note 16.

28. See note 9. Cf. The Williamsburg Charter: A National Celebration and Reaffirmation of the First Amendment Religious Liberty Clauses 221 (1988) ("The Framer's intention is indisputably ignored when public policy debates can appeal to the theses of Adam Smith and Karl Marx, or Charles Darwin and Sigmund Freud but not to the Western religious tradition in general and the Hebrew and Christian scriptures in particular.").

In a letter to me, dated March 20, 1990, Thomas Nagel wrote that "I don't know whether it will please or disappoint you to learn that I have decided, since publishing the essay you criticize, that the attempt fails." (This is not to say that Nagel agrees that the goal of impartial political justification is impossible. In his letter Nagel expresses the hope that he can reinterpret and vindicate the notion of such justification.) I critize Nagel's important essay not to beat a dead horse but because I think Nagel's failure is instructive.

29. See T. Nagel, What Does I All Mean? ch. 10 (1987) ("The Meaning of Life"). Cf. Nagel, "Agreeing in Principle," Times Literary Supp., July 8–14, 1988, at 747 (reviewing A. MacIntyre, Whose Justice? Which Rationality? [1988]). See also B. Ackerman, note 4, at 368: "There is no meaning in the bowels of the universe." Cf. R. Neuhaus, The Naked Public Square: Religion and Democracy in America 86 (1984): "In minds of some secularists the naked pubic square [i.e., neutral/impartial political discourse] is a desirable goal. They subscribe to the dogma of the secular Enlightenment that, as people become more enlightened (educated), religion will wither away; or, if it does not wither away, it can be safely sealed off from public consideration, reduced to a private eccentricity." For examples of a rather different attitude in contemporary Anglo-American philosophy, see D. Braine, The Reality of Time and the Existence of God (1988); S. Clark, From Athens to Jerusalem: The Love of Wisdom and the Love of God (1984). See also L. Kolakowski, Metaphysical Horror (1988).

30. K. Greenawalt, Religious Convictions and Political Choice 7 (1988).
31. Id. at 26. See also id. at 20–21. The requirement that laws have a secular purpose seems to mean, for Greenawalt, that a belief that an act is wrong without regard to any physical or psychological harm it might do, directly or indirectly, to the actor or to others, indeed, even if it does no such harm, is not a good reason for restricting someone's liberty. See id. at 87–95.
32. Greenawalt summarizes his basic (twofold) argument at several points. See, e.g., id. at 12, 49, 87, 144–45. Cf. id. at 37: "For our purpose, a person is relying on religious convictions if their abandonment would force him seriously to reconsider a position he takes." For critical comments on Greenawalt's basic argument, see Audi, "Religion and the Ethics of Political Participation," 100 Ethics 386 (1990); Richards, Book Review, 23 Georgia L. Rev. 1189 (1989). For Greenawalt's tentative, inconclusive comments on whether reliance on religious convictions is appropriate if shared premises or reasoning from shared premises *is* determinate, see K. Greenawalt, note 30, at 203–11. To claim that such reliance is inappropriate because shared premises and reasoning from shared premises, if determinate, are dispositive is in effect to privilege a particular set of beliefs about human good: beliefs common to the various conceptions of human good prevalent in the society. Of course, there is nothing "liberal", in the sense of neutral/impartial, about such privileging. See pp. 14–16.
33. For example, see id. at 17: "To say that a liberal government rests on secular justification is not necessarily to deny that government generally, or liberal government in particular, may also be ordained by God. Supplemental justifications accepted by religious believers need not be at odds with unifying justifications that can be accepted by citizens regardless of their religious beliefs."
34. Id. at 155–56. See also id. at 215: "[S]ome people believe that the premises of liberal democracy, properly understood, either do not reach at all to the actual decisions of individual citizens or set very few restraints on them; it is on this view when citizens enter the political process more actively by engaging in public justifications of their positions or by becoming officials that constraints derived from liberal democratic premises really matter."
35. See id. at 156: "This substantive position turns out to be the one I largely endorse, as Chapter 12 in particular reflects."
36. For example, see id. at 12.
37. Not that Greenawalt is alone in disfavoring religious convictions. For a recent example of a liberal theorist who contends against reliance on religious convictions in the making (as well as the justifying) of political choices, see Audi, note 32; Audi, "The Separation of Church and State and the Obligations of Citizenship," 18 Philosophy & Public Affairs 259 (1989).
38. K. Greenawalt, note 30, at 215.
39. Id. at 216.
40. Id. at 218.
41. Id. at 220.
42. Id. at 216–17.
43. Id. at 228.
44. Greenawalt believes that the "ground rules" derive from the fact, as

Greenawalt sees it, "that now in the United States there is (1) a substantial consensus on the organizing political principles for society; (2) a shared sense that major political discussions will be carried on primarily in secular terms; (3) a respect for religious belief and activity and a hesitancy to attack religious practices as nonsensical; and (4) an assumption that one can be a seriously religious person *and* a liberal participant in a liberal society." Id. 216.

45. Id. at 219.

46. Id.

47. See pp. 75–77.

48. See pp. 72–73.

49. Greenawalt, "Religious Convictions and Political Choice: Some Further Thoughts," 39 DePaul L. Rev. 1019, 1022 (1990).

50. Id. In Greenawalt's view, "[c]ivility and respect for minorities counsel that public advocacy be [so] conducted". Id.

51. See K. Greenawalt, note 30, at 157–62.

52. Id. at 157, 159.

53. For an argument that reliance on religious convictions in political argument is not more problematic than reliance on nonreligious convictions, see Carter, "The Religiously Devout Judge," 64 Notre Dame L. Rev. 932, 940–42 (1989).

54. See K. Greenawalt, note 30, at 217.

55. See id. Greenawalt offers strategic advice in setting forth many of his exceptions. With respect to this second exception, for example, he counsels: "The Catholic bishops' statement [on the use of nuclear arms] should make some effort to root the positions it takes in Catholic understanding about war and military weapons, but if the statement is designed to have general influence, it should also contain language and ideas that have a broader appeal. In part, the effort should be to cast ideas that conform to Catholic understandings in as generalized a form as is possible." Id.

56. Id. at 218.

57. See id. at 217–18.

58. See id. at 218.

59. See id. at 218–19.

60. See id. at 219–20. I discuss John Coleman's position at length in chapter 6.

61. Rawls has argued that the following interpretation of his early effort is mistaken. See Rawls, "Justice as Fairness: Political, Not Metaphysical," 14 Philosophy & Public Affairs 223 (1985). But see Ackerman, note 5, at 15 n. 7: "Despire Rawls's subsequent disavowal of this interpretation, . . . I do not believe critics were simply engaged in tea-leaf reading in finding this theme (uneasily co-existing with many others) in Rawls's major works."

62. See M. Perry, note 3, at 60–62.

63. See id. at 59–63. See also Ackerman, note 5, at 15–16.

64. On the distinction between GpR theories and RpG theories, see Taylor, "Hegel's Ambiguous Legacy for Modern Liberalism," 10 Cardozo L. Rev. 857, 857–58 (1989).

65. Raz, "Liberalism, Autonomy, and the Politics of Neutral Concern," 7 Midwest Studies in Philosophy 89, 105 (1982). See id.: "[T]he common feature of most

routes will be the reliance on a rational reconstruction of a process of bargaining by which the common overriding goal to reach an agreement leads the parties to compromise by accepting a less than perfect doctrine as the optimally realizable second best."

66. See J. Rawls, A Theory of Justice (1971).

67. Rawls, note 61, at 225–26.

68. Although Rawls sometimes distinguishes loosely between "comprehensive doctrines" and "conceptions of the good", the distinction is unimportant for present purposes. See Rawls, "The Idea of an Overlapping Consensus," 7 Oxford J. Legal Studies 1, 4 (1987): "[A workable conception of justice] must allow for a diversity of general and comprehensive doctrines, and for the plurality of conflicting, and indeed incommensurable, conceptions of the meaning, value and purpose of human life (or what I shall call for short 'conceptions of the good') affirmed by the citizens of democratic societies." See also Rawls, "The Priority of Right and Ideas of the Good," 17 Philosophy & Public Affairs 251, 252–53 (1988): "[A moral conception (as distinct from a political conception of justice)] is said to be general when it applies to a wide range of subjects (in the limit to all subjects); it is comprehensive when it includes conceptions of what is of value in human life, ideals of personal virtue and character, and the like. . . . There is a tendency for religious and philosophical conceptions to be general and fully comprehensive. . . ."

69. Rawls, note 61, at 247.

70. Rawls, "The Idea of an Overlapping Consensus," 7 Oxford J. Legal Studies 1, 19 (1987).

71. Rawls, "The Priority of Right and Ideas of the Good," 17 Philosophy & Public Affairs 251, 251 (1988).

72. Id. at 252, 253. "A doctrine is fully comprehensive when it covers all recognized values and virtues within one rather precisely articulated scheme of thought, whereas a doctrine is only partially comprehensive when it comprises certain (but not all) nonpolitical values and virtues and is rather loosely articulated." Id. at 253.

73. I have addressed only the first sense, a weak sense, in which the priority of right is a feature of Rawls' political liberalism: The justification at which Rawls aims does not privilege any particular conception of the good (though it does privilege a particular range of such conceptions). The priority of right is a feature of Rawls' political liberalism in a second sense as well. But the second sense is even weaker than the first. Rawls writes that in his theory of justice "the priority of right implies that the principles of (political) justice set limits to permissible ways of life; hence the claims citizens make to pursue ends that transgress those limits have no weight (as judged by that political conception)." Id. at 251. See also id. at 252, 253. However, this is just to make the tautologous point that principles of political justice trump other moral principles if political justice is the aim. Charles Taylor has recently discussed "three separate theses which are advanced at different times under the slogan of the priority of the right over the good." See C. Taylor, Sources of the Self: The Making of the Modern Identity 532–33 (1989).

Given the turn in Rawls' thinking, as marked in particular by his 1985 essay (note 61), it is not surprising that Richard Rorty has revised his earlier characterization of Rawls as a Kantian and now sees him as more Deweyan than Kantian. See Rorty,

"The Prioity of Democracy to Philosophy," in M. Peterson & R. Vaughan, eds., The Virginia Statute of Religious Freedom 257, 264–65 (1987). However, the fact that Rawl's theory is fundamentally of the Good-prior-to-Right sort has implications that Rorty, in his recent discussion of Rawls, seems not to understand. Such a theory implicitly claims that, contrary to what Rorty maintains, there *is* a need, sometimes, for "a religious or a philosophical preface to politics" (id. at 264), especially in circumstances like our own, in which there is no political conception of justice supported by an overlapping consensus and there are only few determinate shared political-moral premises. Rawls seems to understand this—e.g., see Rawls, note 70, at 14 ("in affirming a political conception of justice we may eventually have to assert at least certain aspects of our own comprehensive . . . religious or philosophical doctrine")—even if Rorty does not. For an excellent critical commentary on Rawls' recent writings and, in particular, an argument that political philosophy must be "metaphysical", see Hampton, "Should Political Philosophy Be Done without Metaphysics?," 99 Ethics 791 (1989). See also K. Greenawalt, note 30; M. Perry, note 3, at 87 & 102–4. Cf. J. Murray, note 1, at ix–x: "[For a Catholic] the principles of Catholic faith and morality stand superior to, and in control of, the whole order of civil life. The question is sometimes raised, whether Catholicism is compatible with American democracy. The question is invalid as well as impertinent; for the manner of its position inverts the order of values. It must, of course, be turned round to read, whether American democracy is compatible with Catholicism." (Murray went on to say that "[a]n affirmative answer to [the question] . . . is one of the truths I hold." Id.)

74. Rawls, note 70, at 5.

75. Id. at 7.

76. Raz, note 20, at 45. For an interesting argument that "a Christian affirmation of [Rawls' political conception of justice] is impossible," see Jackson, "To Bedlam and Part Way Back: John Rawls and Christian Justice" (forthcoming). Compare Beckley, "A Christian Affirmation of Rawls's Idea of Justice as Fairness: Part I," 13 J. Religious Ethics 212 (1985); Beckley, "A Christian Affirmation of Rawls's Idea of Justice as Fairness: Part II," 14 J. Religious Ethics 229 (1986).

77. Raz, note 20, at 45.

78. In his 1988 essay on "the priority of right" Rawls distinguishes among (1) "procedural neutrality", (2) three kinds of "neutrality of aim," and (3) "neutrality of effect or influence". See Rawls, note 71, at 260–64. He acknowledges that his political conception of justice is neither procedurally neutral nor neutral in effect or influence. He acknowledges, too, that his conception is neutral in aim only in the weak sense that "the state is to secure equal opportunity to advance any permissible conception [of good, i.e., any conception not ruled out by the political conception; and the social, political, and economic] . . . institutions are not intended to favor any [one of the permissible conceptions of the good]." Id. at 262. This is a weak sense of neutrality because the political conception of justice tolerates only some, not all, conceptions of the good; not every conception of the good is "permissible". See Macedo, "The Politics of Justification," 18 Political Theory 280, 289 (1990): "What does a liberal say about a range of religious beliefs that include ecumenical Catholicism, fundamentalist Protestantism, and sects that require holy war against

nonbelievers? There are, says Rawls, 'no sources within the political view to judge those conflicting conceptions. They are equally permissible provided they respect the limits imposed by the principles of political justice.' Underline 'provided': All religions compatible with liberalism will be respected; those not compatible will be opposed. The liberal *must* in this way imply that religious convictions incompatible with liberalism are unsupportable." (The statement of Rawls quoted by Macedo is from Rawls, note 70, at 9.)

79. Ackerman, note 5, at 12–13.

Chapter 2

1. It's not that Ackerman doesn't advance positions on issues of human rights. See B. Ackerman, Social Justice in the Liberal State (1980). It's just that his doing so is inconsistent with his ideal of neutral political justification. See, in addition to chapter 1 of this book, M. Perry, Morality, Politics, and Law 63–66 (1988).

In the period since the end of World War II discourse about human rights has been rich and important. See R. Drinan, Cry of the Oppressed: The History and Hope of the Human Rights Revolution (1987); J. Nickel, Making Sense of Human Rights: Philosophical Reflections on the Universal Declaration of Human Rights (1987); J. Donnelly, Universal Human Rights in Theory and Practice (1989).

Like feminist critical-theorist Nancy Fraser, and "unlike some communitarian, socialist, and feminist critics, I do not believe that rights talk is inherently individualistic, bourgeois-liberal, and androcentric—rights talk takes on those properties only when societies establish the *wrong* rights, for example, when the (putative) right to private property is permitted to trump other, social rights." N. Fraser, Unruly Practices: Power, Discourse, and Gender in Contemporary Social Theory 183 (1989).

2. To claim that a right ought to be conferred by some specified entity is not necessarily to claim that the entity (or anyone else) ought always to respect the right, that is, ought never to violate the right. Not all rights that ought to be conferred are "absolute" rights.

3. A prescriptive legal-rights-claim, too, may concern a human right: The claim may be that such-and-such a (legal) right ought to be conferred on (virtually) all human beings. Even a descriptive rights-claim may concern a human right: For example, the United States confers some human rights by means of the U.S. Constitution. But I'm here interested in human-rights-claims as a species of prescriptive moral-rights-claims. For useful analyses of "rights", see L. Sumner, The Moral Foundation of Rights, ch. 2 (1987); J. Nickel, note 1, ch. 2.

4. Some rights theorists argue that the basic point of conferring rights on human beings (and of respecting rights that have been conferred; cf. note 2) is to protect the well-being of the human beings on whom the rights are or should be conferred. Other rights theorists contend that the basic point is to protect not well-being but autonomy. Yet others argue—sensibly, in my view—that the basic point of conferring rights on human beings, whether some human beings or all human beings, is sometimes to protect well-being and sometimes to protect autonomy and some-

times to do both. See J. Nickel, note 1, at 23–24. Compare L. Sumner, note 3, at 203–5. Indeed, if autonomy is a particular, and particularly important, constituent of human well-being (on the relation of well-being and autonomy, see Raz, "Liberalism, Skepticism, and Democracy," 74 Iowa L. Rev. 761 [1989]), then protecting autonomy is protecting (an important constituent of) of human well-being and protecting human well-being in its entirety requires protecting autonomy. Let's assume that the basic point of conferring rights on (some or all) human beings is to protect human well-being, including autonomy.

5. It bears emphasis that to accept the universalist presupposition of common human needs is to deny neither (1) that it might be possible to satisfy such a need in various ways (see note 8) nor (2) that particular beliefs about human needs are, in Nancy Fraser's words, "culturally constructed and discursively interpreted". N. Fraser, note 1, at 181. Cf. note 15 and accompanying text. At the same time, however, to accept that particular beliefs about human needs, including beliefs about what needs human beings have in common, are socially constructed "is not to say that any need interpretation is as good as any other." N. Fraser, note 1, at 181. See id. at 181–82. For a brief, commonsensical discussion of "social constructionism", "essentialism", etc., see Boswell, "Gay History," Atlantic, Feb. 1989, at 74 (review of D. Greenberg, The Construction of Homosexuality [1988]).

6. Cf. H. Putnam, Reason, Truth and History 148 (1981):

> If today we differ with Aristotle it is in being much more pluralistic than Aristotle was. Aristotle recognized that different ideas of Eudaemonia, different conceptions of human flourishing, might be appropriate for different individuals on account of the difference in their constitution. But he seemed to think that ideally there was some sort of constitution that every one ought to have; that in an ideal world (overlooking the mundane question of who would grow the crops and who would bake the bread) everyone would be a philosopher. We agree with Aristotle that different ideas of human flourishing are appropriate for individuals with different constitutions, but we go further and believe that even in the ideal world there would be different constitutions, that diversity is part of the ideal. And we see some degree of tragic tension between ideals, that the fulfillment of some ideals always excludes the fulfillment of some others.

(As Putnam goes on to emphasize, however: "[B]elief in a pluralistic ideal is not the same thing as belief that every ideal of human flourishing is as good as every other. We reject ideals of human flourishing as wrong, as infantile, as sick, as one-sided." Id. See id. at 140 [referring to "sick standards of rationality" and "sick conception(s) of human flourishing"] and 147: "We have just as much right to regard some 'evaluational' casts of mind as sick (and we all do) as we do to regard some 'cognitional' casts of mind as sick.") See also B. Williams, note 25, at 153:

> [T]here are many and various forms of human excellence which will not all fit together into a one harmonious whole, so any determinate ethical outlook is going to represent some kind of specialization of human possibilities. That idea is deeply entrenched in any naturalistic or . . . historical conception of human nature—that is, in any adequate conception of it—and I find it hard

to believe that it will overcome by an objective inquiry, or that human beings could turn out to have a much more determinate nature than is suggested by what we already know, one that timelessly demanded a life of a particular kind.

7. Cf. R. Rorty, "Solidarity or Objectivity?," in J. Rajchman & C. West, eds., *Post-Analytic Philosophy* 3, 9 (1985) ("[T]he distinction between different cultures does not differ in kind from the distinction between theories held by members of a single culture. The Tasmanian aborigines and the British colonists had trouble communicating, but this trouble was different only in extent from the difficulties in communication experienced by Gladstone and Disraeli."); A. Rorty, "Relativism, Persons, and Practices," in M. Krausz, ed., *Relativism: Interpretation and Confrontation* 418, 418 (1989): "Sometimes there is unexpectedly subtle and refined communication across radically different cultures; sometimes there is insurmountable bafflement and systemic misunderstanding between relatively close cultures. For the most part, however, we live in the interesting intermediate grey area of partial success and partial failure of interpretation and communication. The grey area is to be found at home among neighbors as well as abroad among strangers. . . . "

8. As I said in the introduction to this book, different ways of life can be good, or bad, for different persons, and different ways of life can be good for the same person. Cf. S. Hampshire, *Two Theories of Morality* 48–49 (1977):

> The correct answer to the old question—"why should it be assumed, or argued, that there is just one good for man, just one way of life that is best?"—is . . . an indirect one and it is not simple. One can coherently list all the ideally attainable human virtues and achievements, and all the desirable features of a perfect human existence; and one might count this as prescribing the good for man, the perfect realization of all that is desirable. But the best selection from this whole that could with luck be achieved in a particular person will be the supreme end for him, the ideal at which he should aim. It is obvious that supreme ends of this kind are immensely various and always will be various. There can be no single supreme end in this particularized sense, as both social orders and human capabilities change. . . .
>
> That there should be an abstract ethical ideal, the good for men in general, is not inconsistent with there being great diversity in preferred ways of life, even among men living at the same place at the same time. The good for man, as the common starting-point, marks an area within which arguments leading to divergent conclusions about moral priorities can be conducted. The conclusions are widely divergent, because they are determined by different subsidiary premises. Practical and theoretical reason, cleverness, intelligence and wisdom, justice, friendship, temperence in relation to passions, courage, a repugnance in the face of squalid or mean sentiments and actions; these are Aristotle's general and abstract terms, which do not by themselves distinguish a particular way of life, realizable in a particular historical situation. The forms that intelligence and friendship and love between persons,

and that nobility of sentiment and motive, can take are at least as various as human cultures; and they are more various still, because within any one culture there will be varieties of individual temperament, providing distinct motives and priorities of interest, and also varieties of social groupings, restricting the choice of ways of life open to individuals.

9. Inevitably, too, there are differences as to which universalist position is most credible. Such differences have figured prominently in international political debates about human rights, for example, between proponents of liberal-democratic human rights of the sort advanced in the First World and proponents of social human rights of the sort advanced in the Second World. See D. Hollenbach, Claims in Conflict: Retrieving and Renewing the Catholic Human Rights Tradition, esp. ch.1 (1979); M. Stackhouse, Creeds, Society, and Human Rights: A Study in Three Cultures (1984). Moreover, some Third World participants in debates about human rights argue that First World universalist rhetoric is sometimes just another strategy for imposing Western values on non-Western cultures. See J. Nickel, note 1, at 65–68. For a recent discussion of the problem in the context of traditional African cultures, see Nhlapo, note 37.

10. See, e.g., R. Rorty, Contingency, Irony, and Solidarity, esp. introduction & ch. 9 (1989). See also Williams, "Auto-da-Fé," New York Rev., Apr. 28, 1983, at 33: "Rorty is so insistent that we cannot, in philosophy, simply be talking about human beings, as opposed to human beings at a given time. . . . Rorty . . . contrasts the approach of taking some philosophical problem and asking . . . 'What does it show us about *being human*?' and asking, on the other hand, 'What does the persistence of such problems show us about *being twentieth-century Europeans*?' " (Emphasis in original.) Rorty's position is reminiscent of Joseph de Maistre's statement two centuries ago, commenting on then-recent developments in revolutionary France: "I have seen in my time Frenchmen, Italians, Russians. I even know, thanks to Montesquieu, that one may be a Persian, but as for Man, I declare that I have never met him in my life; if he exists it is without my knowledge." Quoted in E. Leach, Social Anthropology 56 (1982). For a critical discussion of Rorty's position, see M. Perry, note 1, at 44–48.

11. Foot, "Moral Relativism," in J. Meiland & M. Krausz, eds., Relativism: Cognitive and Moral 152, 164 (1982). For an excellent defense of a non-relativist position on human good, see Nussbaum, "Non-Relative Virtues: An Aristotelian Approach," 13 Midwest Studies in Philosophy 32 (1988). See also Jacobs, "Practical Wisdom, Objectivity, and Relativism," 26 American Philosophical Q. 199 (1989); Kekes, "Human Nature and Moral Theories," 28 Inquiry 231 (1985); Matilal, "Ethical Relativism and Confrontation of Cultures," in M. Krausz, ed., Relativism: Interpretation and Confrontation 339, 357 (1989) ("The common dispositions, constitutive of the concept of 'the naked man,' may be recognized as numerous simple facts about needs, wants, and desires, for example, removal of suffering, love of justice, courage in the face of injustice, pride, shame, love of children, delight, laughter, happiness."); A. Rorty, note 7 (a relevant passage of this essay is quoted in note 15).

12. R. Rorty, note 10, at xiii. Rorty writes approvingly of "this historicist turn," which, he says, "has helped free us, gradually but steadily, from theology and

metaphysics—from the temptation to look for an escape from time and chance. It has helped us substitute Freedom for Truth as the goal of thinking and of social progress." Id. For an excellent critique of this and related aspects of Rorty's views, see Jackson, "The Theory and Practice of Discomfort: Richard Rorty and Pragmatism," 51 Thomist 270 (1987). See also McShea, "Making Truth," London Rev. Books, Dec. 4, 1986.

    13. For a discussion of one group of such thinkers, see West, "Feminism, Critical Social Theory, and the Law," U. Chicago Legal Forum 59 (1989).

    14. N. Chomsky, For Reasons of State 404 (1973). See also McShea, note 12.

    15. See A. Rorty, note 7, at 418–19 (emphasis added):

> [R]elativists are quite right to insist that even such dramatically basic activities as birth, copulation, and death, such basic processes as eating and sleeping, physical growth and physical decay, are intentionally described in ways that affect phenomenological experience. Events and processes are encompassed and bounded, articulated and differentiated, within the web of a culture's conceptual and linguistic categories; their meaning is formed by its primary practices and sacred books, songs and rituals. Even the conceptions of social practices and meaning are sufficiently culturally specific so that it is tendentious to refer to conceptions *of* culture practices [*sic*], as if *culture* or *practice* were Platonic forms, waiting to be conceptualized this way or that. Indeed the very practices of interpretation and evaluation are themselves culturally variable.
>
> But nothing follows from this about the impossibility of crosscultural interpretation, communication, or evaluation, particularly among cultures engaged in practical interactions with one another. The core truth of relativism—the intentionality of practice and experience—does not entail that successful communication and justified evaluation require strict identity of meaning. *There are, furthermore, basic culturally invariant psychophysical and biosocial salience markers that set the boundaries of attention, however variously these foci may be identified, interpreted, or evaluated.*

See also Nussbaum, note 11, at 33: "[Aristotle's] account [of the human good, or human flourishing,] is supposed to be objective in the sense that it is justifiable with reference to reasons that do not derive merely from local traditions and practices, but rather from features of humanness that lie beneath all local traditions and are there to be seen whether or not they are in fact recognized in local traditions." Cf. Lovin, "Perry, Naturalism, and Religion in Public," 63 Tulane L. Rev. 1517, 1532–33 (1989):

> . . . Perry speaks of "human good" in nonrelativist terms, not because he thinks that there is universal agreement about what is good for persons, nor even because he believes that there is some single ideal of human flourishing that would satisfy everyone, but because he thinks that people who disagree about the human good understand that they are disagreeing about the same thing. They are not talking about, say, architecture and tennis, in which the terms are so different that we would wonder how two people arguing about the relative merits of a good lobby and a good volley

got into the same conversation. An argument over the relative merits of artistic and athletic achievement in a complete human life, by contrast, does make sense, even if we are not certain that there is one and only one best solution to the problem.

For an (apparent) example of the slide from "an appreciation of the historical and socially constructed character of such categories [as "human nature"] to the "anti-essentialist" position that there is no human nature, see Fraser, note 1, at 106. There seems to be in Fraser's work a tension between her position on human nature and her position on needs. See note 5.

16. West, note 13, at 96–97. For a more elaborate statement, see West, "Relativism, Objectivity, and Law," 99 Yale L. J. 1473 (1990).

17. See note 11 and accompanying text.

18. C. Taylor, Sources of the Self: The Making of the Modern Identity 61 (1989). See also M. Perry, note 1, at 49.

19. C. Taylor, note 18, at 61–62.

20. In commenting on "that sort of impartiality that constitutes the moral point of view," James Griffin has written that "[w]e all agree that to look at things morally is to look at them, in some sense or other, impartially, granting every person some sort of equal status. Of course, we should have to make this notion of equal status more determinate—say through one interpretation or other of the Ideal Observer or Ideal Contractor. In any case, principles of equality can be principles of impartiality in this sense: they can express the spirit with which one will, if one is moral, consider the facts of the matter." J. Griffin, Well-Being 239 (1987).

21. J. Nickel, note 1, at 91.

22. See Scott, "Motive and Justification," 85 J. Philosophy 479, 499 (1988): "When he was deliberating about how to live, St. Augustine asked, 'What does anything matter, if it does not have to do with happiness?' His question requires explanation, because he is not advising selfishness nor the reduction of other people to utilities, and even qualification, because other things can have some weight. All the same, the answer he expects is obviously right: only a happy life matters conclusively. If I had a clear view of it, I could have no motive to decline it, I could regret nothing by accepting it, I would have nothing about which to deliberate further." Cf. Taylor, "Ancient Wisdom and Modern Folly," 13 Midwest Studies in Philosophy 54, 57, 58 (1988): "The Greek *eudaimonia* is always translated 'happiness,' which is unfortunate, for the meaning we attach to the word *happiness* is thin indeed compared to what the ancients meant by *eudaimonia*. *Fulfillment* might be a better term, though this, too, fails to capture the richness of the original term. . . . The concept of happiness in modern philosophy, as well as in popular thinking, is superficial indeed in comparison." For an extended discussion of the "Why be moral?" problem from a neo-Aristotelian perspective, see R. Bittner, What Reason Demands (1983; Eng. tr. 1989).

23. J. Nickel, note 1, at 91.

24. C. Taylor, note 18, at 87.

25. See B. Williams, Ethics and the Limits of Philosophy 103–4 (1985).

26. For my earlier reflections on such an approach, see M. Perry, note 1, at 82–90.

27. See, e.g., J. Nickel, note 1. For a compilation of human-rights documents,

transnational (e.g., European, African, Central American) as well as international, see R. Lillich, ed., International Human Rights Instruments (1986).

28. For example, section 1 of the Fourteenth Amendment to the United States Constitution provides, in relevant part: "[N]or shall any State deprive any person of life, liberty, or property, without due process of law; nor deny to any person within its jurisdiction the equal protection of the laws."

29. See Küng, "What Is True Religion?: Toward an Ecumenical Criteriology," in I.. Swidler, ed., Toward a Universal Theology of Religion 231, 239–43 (1987); Steinfels, "The Search for an Alternative," Commonweal, Nov. 30, 1981, at 660, 661 (commenting on the importance of the distinction "between the human and the 'truly human' "); Nussbaum, "Aristotle on Human Nature and the Foundations of Ethics" (forthcoming) (discussing the difference, for the Greeks, between, on the one hand, the life of a beastly anthropomorph, like the Cyclops, or of a godly anthropomorph, like Zeus, and, on the other, the truly human life).

30. H. Putnam, The Many Faces of Realism 60–61 (1987).

31. John 13:34. See also John 15:12. This translation, and all translations of the Jewish and Christian Bibles in this book, are those of The New Jerusalem Bible (1985).

32. In the Bible God—Ultimate Reality—is often imaged as "parent", sometimes as "father", sometimes as "mother". See R. Ruether, Sexism and God-Talk: Toward a Feminist Theology (1983).

33. Bokser & Bokser, "Introduction: The Spirituality of the Talmud," in The Talmud: Selected Writings 7, 30–31 (1989) (selected and translated by B. Bokser) (footnotes omitted).

34. Nussbaum, note 29.

35. Cf. Tinder, "Can We Be Good without God? The Political Meaning of Christianity," Atlantic, Dec. 1989, at 69, 80 (passages rearranged and emphasis added):

> Nietzsche's stature is owing to the courage and profundity that enabled him to make all this unmistakably clear. He delineated with overpowering eloquence the consequences of giving up Christianity, *and every like view of the universe and humanity.* His approval of those consequences and his hatred of Christianity give force to his argument. Many would like to think that there are no consequences—that we can continue treasuring the life and welfare, the civil rights and political authority, of every person without believing in a God who renders such attitudes and conduct compelling. Nietzsche shows that we cannot. We cannot give up the Christian God—*and the transcendence given other names in other faiths*—and go on as before. We must give up Christian morality too. If the God-man is nothing more than an illusion, the same thing is true of the idea that every individual possesses incalculable worth. The standard *agape* collapses. It becomes explicable only on Nietzsche's terms: as a device by which the weak and failing exact from the strong and distinguished a deference they do not deserve. Thus the spiritual center of Western politics fades and vanishes. If the principle of personal dignity disappears, the kind of political order we are used to—one structured by standards such as liberty for all human beings and equality under the law— becomes indefensible.

Cf. L. Kolakowski, Religion 191 (1982): "When Pierre Bayle argued that morality does not depend on religion, he was speaking mainly of psychological independence; he pointed out that atheists are capable of achieving the highest moral standards . . . and of putting to shame most of the faithful Christians. That is obviously true as far as it goes, but this matter-of-fact argument leaves the question of validity intact; neither does it solve the question of the effective sources of the moral strength and moral convictions of those 'virtuous pagans.' "

36. See chapter 4.

37. See, e.g., An-Na'im, "Human Rights in the Muslim World: Socio-Political Conditions and Scriptural Imperatives," 3 Harvard Human Rights L. J. 13 (1990); Nhlapo, "International Protection of Human Rights and the Family: African Variations on a Common Theme," 3 International J. L. & Family 1 (1989).

38. See L. Rouner, ed., Human Rights and the World's Religions (1988); A. Swidler, ed., Human Rights in Religious Traditions (1988); H. Küng & J. Moltmann, eds., The Ethics of World Religions and Human Rights (1990) (volume 2 of the 1990 Concilium); R. Traer, Faith in Human Rights: Support in Religious Traditions for a Global Struggle (1991); see also Rossi, "Moral Community, Imagination, and Human Rights: Philosophical Considerations on Uniting Traditions," in A. Hennelly & J. Langan, eds., Human Rights in the Americas: The Struggle for Consensus 167, 173 (1982) (noting convergence between Marxism and Catholicism).

39. See chapter 3, note 3.

Chapter 3

1. As I explained in chapter 1, the only truly neutral/impartial practice of political justification is one that lets everyone rely on her relevant convictions. Of course, such a practice often yields not neutral/impartial arguments but arguments that presuppose the authority of disputed convictions.

2. 5 OED 64 (1989).

3. See H. Coward, Pluralism: Challenge to World Religions 107 (1985): "[S]piritual growth arises not from religious isolationism or exclusivism but rather in the context of religious pluralism. . . . [This is] substantiated by the experience of those now seriously engaged in [interreligious] dialogue, namely, that the result is an enriching and deepening of one's own religious experience." See generally J. Dunne, The Way of All the Earth: Experiments in Truth and Religion (1972); L. Swidler, ed., Toward a Universal Theology of Religion (1987); J. Cobb, Jr., & C. Ives, eds., The Emptying God: A Buddhist-Jewish-Christian Conversation (1990). For an exemplary illustration of just how fruitful such a challenge can be, see Tracy, "Kenosis, Sunyata, and Trinity: A Dialogue with Masao Abe," in id., at 135.

4. The Williamsburg Charter: A National Celebration and Reaffirmation of the First Amendment Religious Liberty Clauses 8 (1988).

5. Id. at 19.

6. For a partly different and partly similar taxonomy of "reasons why persons who hold religious convictions bring the language of faith to bear on public choices", see Lovin, "Perry, Naturalism, and Religion in Public," 63 Tulane L. Rev.

1517, 1526–32 (1989) (identifying and illustrating *"proclamation, conversion,* and *articulation"*).

7. A person might not want to reveal her deepest reasons for supporting the choices she does.

8. See C. Perelman, Justice, Law, and Argument 132 (1980); C. Perelman, The Realm of Rhetoric 2–3, 31 (1982). What Rawls has said about justification is better said about persuasion: "[J]ustification is argument addressed to those who disagree with us, or to ourselves when we are of two minds. It presumes a clash of views between persons or within one person, and seeks to convince others, or ourselves, of the reasonableness of the principles upon which our claims and judgments are founded. Being designed to reconcile by reason, justification proceeds from what all parties to the discussion hold in common." J. Rawls, A Theory of Justice 580 (1971).

9. Cf. Nagel, "Moral Conflict and Political Legitimacy," 16 Philosophy & Public Affairs 215, 218 (1987): " 'Justification' here does not mean 'persuasion.' It is a normative concept: arguments that justify may fail to persuade, if addressed to an unreasonable audience; and arguments that persuade may fail to justify. Nonetheless, justifications hope to persuade the reasonable. . . ."

10. R. Beiner, Political Judgment 138–39 (1983).

11. J. Murray, We Hold These Truths 23 (1960).

12. D. Lochhead, The Dialogical Imperative: A Christian Reflection on Interfaith Encounter 93 (1988)

13. See C. Taylor, Philosophy and the Human Sciences 190–91 (1985):

> What has been argued in the different theories of the social nature of man is not just that men cannot physically survive alone, but much more that they could only develop their characteristically human capacities in society. The claim is that living in a society is a necessary condition of the development of rationality, in some sense of this property, or of becoming a moral agent in the full sense of the term, or of becoming a fully responsible, autonomous being. These variations and other similar ones represent the different forms in which a thesis about man as a social animal have been or could be couched. What they have in common is the view that outside society . . . our distinctively human capacities could not develop. From the standpoint of the thesis, . . . is it irrelvant whether an organism born from a human womb would go on living in the wilderness; what is important is that this organism could not realize its specifically human potential.

See also J. Segundo, Faith and Ideologies 307 (1982; Eng. tr. 1984). Cf. Wong, "On Flourishing and Finding One's Identity in Community," 13 Midwest Studies in Philosophy 324, 324–28 (1988) (commenting on "our flourishing as *social* beings").

14. Cf. Pitkin, "Justice: On Relating Public and Private," 9 Political Theory 327, 347–48 (1981): "Drawn into public life by personal need, fear, ambition or interest, we are there forced to acknowledge the power of others and appeal to their standards, even as we try to get them to acknowledge our power and standards. We are forced to find or create a common language of purposes and aspirations, not merely to clothe our private outlook in public disguise, but to become aware ourselves of

its public meaning. . . . Economic man becomes a citizen. . . . We discover connections to others and learn to care about those connections."

15. R. Beiner, note 10, at 152.

16. See G. Hallett, Christian Neighbor-Love: An Assessment of Six Rival Versions (1989).

17. D. Lochhead, note 12, at 81.

18. F. Dallmayr, Polis and Praxis: Exercises in Contemporary Political Theory 196 (1984) (quoting H.-G. Gadamer, Truth and Method 321, 323–25 [Eng. tr. 1975]).

Chapter 4

1. Consider, for example, Nagel's discussion of "the exercise of a common critical rationality" in Nagel, "Moral Conflict and Political Legitimacy," 16 Philosophy & Public Affairs 215 (1987).

2. On "rational acceptability", see H. Putnam, Reason, Truth and History (1981).

3. My concern in this chapter is with the rationality (rational acceptability) of beliefs (claims, propositions, etc.). We may say that a person's choice is rational— that the choice is a rational one *for him* to make—if, and to the extent, the beliefs presupposed by his choice are rational *for him*.

4. Cr. Hollenbach, "Remarks on Alasdair MacIntyre's *Whose Justice? Which Rationality?* [1988]," unpublished ms. (1989): "[C]ritical reasoning and enquiry can become necessary [within a tradition] for a number of reasons, chiefly three: either the received tradition finds itself subject to a number of interpretations that require adjudication; or the tradition encounters new questions which its mode of enquiry up to now has not prepared it to answer; or the tradition meets an alternative tradition that confronts it with an alternative but understandable account about the truth of how things are or with an account that simply cannot be understood."

5. A. MacIntyre, Whose Justice? Which Rationality? 359 (1988). For a careful discussion of revision of belief, see G. Harman, Change in View: Principles of Reasoning (1986).

6. See J. Meiland & M. Krausz, eds., Relativism: Cognitive and Moral 4 (1982): "[J]ust as our ordinary conception of truth allows a person to hold beliefs which are false, so too the notion of relative truth must allow an individual to hold beliefs which are false *for him* or *her*. If it were not possible for an individual to hold beliefs which were false for him or her, then the notion of relative truth would be superfluous; for then to say that a belief is true for Jones would only be a roundabout way of saying that it was one of Jones' beliefs. And we do not need a new way of saying *that*." See also Devine, "Relativism," 67 Monist 405, 406 (1984):

> [R]elativism is not individualistic subjectivism, for which anything goes intellectually; nor is it collective subjectivism, which would settle intellectual questions by voting. The analogy with law makes this point clear: while law is relative to a particular society, law and public opinion are not the same thing. Not anything goes by way of legal argument—the precedents and

statutes have to be taken into account. But one can say, so long as one does not do so too often, that the decision of the courts, even those of the last resort, are legally and not just morally or politically wrong. Likewise a moral relativist who finds his basic standards in the ethos of a given society can disagree with the majority of that society (though perhaps not the over-whelming majority) on some moral issue, so long as he is prepared to defend his disagreement on grounds whose relevance the majority is prepared to accept. In brief, while the standards we employ are (according to the relativist) grounded in the fact of their acceptance by a group to which we belong, the application of these standards is objective and not a matter of what people think.

7. See R. Geuss, The Idea of a Critical Theory 31 (1981); C. Perelman, Justice, Law, and Argument 150 (1980).

8. B. Williams, Ethics and the Limits of Philosophy 113 (1985). For a dissenting voice, see Audi, "The Architecture of Reason", unpublished ms. (1988) (Presidential Address, American Philosophical Association, Central Division, 1988). However, it is not clear to what extent, if any, there are real differences between Audi's carefully revised "epistemological foundationalism" and a sophisticated coherentist epistemology. In any event, the opposition between coherentism and foundationalism is misleading if not false: The coherentist conceptions of rationality/reasoning/justification does not presuppose that there are foundational beliefs ("some favored class of statements", in Williams' words). See note 9 and accompanying text. But neither does the coherentist account presuppose or entail that there are no such epistemically privileged premises. See text accompanying note 13. See generally Triplett, "Recent Work on Foundationalism," 27 American Philosophical Q. 93 (1990).

9. Stout, "Holism and Comparative Ethics," J. Religious Ethics 301, 312 (1983).

10. Devine, note 6, at 412.

11. See Baker, "On the Very Idea of a Form of Life," 27 Inquiry 277, 279 (1984):

[W]hen we think of forms of life as conventional, . . . "we are thinking of convention not as the arrangements a particular culture has found conve-nient, in terms of its history and geography, for effecting the necessities of human existence, but as those forms of life which are normal to any group of creatures we call human, any group about which we will say, for example, that they have a past to which they respond, or a geographical environment which they manipulate or exploit in certain ways for certain humanly compre-hensible motives. Here the array of 'conventions' are not patterns of life which differentiate human beings from one another, but those exigencies of conduct and feeling which all humans share." This passage makes it clear that—the amorphousness of life notwithstanding—most fundamentally, the human species is the locus of forms of life. For specific purposes, "form of life" is sometimes applied to practices that are not universal, as when writers take religion (or a particular religion) to be a form of life, or when writers speak of different societies as exhibiting different forms of life. Although I think that these narrower uses of "form of life" illustrate the elasticity of the idea, and suggest that forms of life, though not clearly demarcated, are thoroughly interwoven and even "nested", they do not tell against the point that Wittgenstein's first concern is with human practices, not with local options.

(Quoting S. Cavell, *The Claim of Reason: Wittgenstein, Skepticism, Morality and Tragedy* 111 [1979].) Cf. Sharrock & Anderson, "Criticizing Forms of Life," 60 *Philosophy* 394, 395, 398 (1985):

> Whether there are insuperable obstacles to mutual understanding (and, therefore, to external criticism) is not, then, something to be determined *a priori*, for the simple reason that the answer will depend on the nature of the differences and disagreements involved. . . .
>
> There is no basis in Wittgenstein's numerous comments on the nature of human beings and their lives for supposing that understanding between them must be either impossible or inevitable. He seems to try to maintain a perspicuous view of the balance of homogeneity and heterogeneity among human beings. He tries not to lose sight of the fact that human beings are, after all, human beings, members of the same species with their animal constitution (which has ramifying consequences for the lives they do lead) in common. At the same time he emphasized how much the practices which they create may diverge from one another. Human lives develop in very different directions from the common "starting points" provided by their species inheritance. It is the fact that human beings are the kinds of creatures that they are which lets them take to training, to learn language and other practices. The fact that a human being might, with equal case, have been inducted into either of two ways of life does not, however, mean that having been drawn into the one he can now adopt the other with the same facility as if he had been brought up to it—learning a second language is not the same as learning a first and, of course, a language like ours makes Chinese harder to learn than French. Two ways of life might, then, be organized in such ways that the grasp of one is inimical to the understanding of the other.

12. Rorty, "Science as Solidarity," in J. Nelson, A. Megill, & D. McCloskey, eds., The Rhetoric of the Human Sciences 38, 43 (1987). See also Matilal, "Ethical Relativism and Confrontation of Cultures," in M. Krausz, ed., Relativism: Interpretation and Confrontation 339, 352 (1989). Cf. B. Williams, note 8, at 158 ("A fully individuable culture [or moral community] is at best a rare thing. Cultures, subcultures, fragments of cultures, constantly meet one another and exchange or modify practices and attitudes."); Rorty, "Solidarity or Objectivity," in J. Rajchman & C. West, eds., Post-Analytic Philosophy 3, 8–9 (1985) ("[A]lternative cultures are not to be thought of on the model of alternative geometries. Alternative geometries are irreconcilable because they have axiomatic structures, and contradictory axioms. The are *designed* to be irreconcilable. Cultures are not so designed, and do not have axiomatic structures."); Matilal, this note, at 356; Stroud, "The Study of Human Nature and the Subjectivity of Value," in 10 Tanner Lectures on Human Values 211, 252–53 (1989) ("We cannot make sense of other people believing something we know to be obviously false unless we have some explanation in the particular case of

how they come to get it wrong. And that explanation will work only if we understand them to share in common with us other beliefs and attitudes in the midst of which their particular, localized error (as we see it) can be make intelligible.").

13. See note 8. There are many different versions of "foundationalist" epistemology. See Triplett, note 8.

14. A. McIntyre, note 5, at 351.

15. On the metaphor of the "web" of beliefs, see W. Quine & J. Ullian, The Web of Belief (2d ed. 1978).

16. M. Adler, Six Great Ideas 43, 44 (1981).

17. See O. Flanagan, The Science of the Mind (1984).

18. See J. Stout, The Flight from Authority 151, 152, 153–54 (1981):

> [Steven] Lukes argues that there are universal criteria of rationality as well as context-dependent ones, and that the former include . . . the notion of truth as correspondence to reality. . . . At times he seems to be insisting only that all language users "share a reality which is independent of how it is conceived," but he will have trouble finding live opponents for that thesis. . . . The issue [Thomas] Kuhn seems to be raising has to do with how "correspondence to reality" could ever function nontrivially as a criterion of rationality. Yet it is this question that Lukes begs. To say that something is a *criterion* of rationality or of truth is to imply that it is the kind of thing one could appeal to in a dispute over what should be counted as rational or as true, but to say that a theory corresponds to reality seems to add nothing to the notion that it is true and therefore ought to be accepted. What we want to be told is how to tell the true from the false, the justified from the unjustified. That is what we expect from criteria of truth and rational acceptance. For "correspondence" to become a criterion in this sense, we would have to characterize the "reality" to which correspondence is sought. But the characterization we choose will place within the logical space of one or another theory of the way things are. What Lukes seems to want, however, is a theory-independent criterion for judging which theory gets it right. The problem is that "reality" cannot be theory-independent without ceasing to be a criterion. We are perfectly free to use "reality" to signify "the purely vacuous notion of the ineffable cause of sense and goal of the intellect," but we would be foolish to suppose that any notion this vacuous could help us award the title of truth. A less vacuous notion of "reality," on the other hand, would be theory-dependent and therefore relative in a way that might encourage just the worries Lukes is trying to undercut.

(Citing S. Lukes, Essays in Social Theory [1977]). See also J. Meiland & M. Krausz, note 6, at 13–17 (discussing Nelson Goodman, Ways of Worldmaking [1978]).

19. Jackson, "The Theory and Practice of Discomfort: Richard Rorty and Pragmatism," 51 Thomist 270, 279 (1987).

20. See R. Rorty, Consequences of Pragmatism vi, xix (1982) (emphasis added):

> When the correspondence theorist offers that the truth about the world consists in a relation of "correspondence" between certain sentences (many of which, no doubt, have yet to be formulated) and the world itself[,] the

pragmatist can only fall back on saying, once again, that many centuries of attempts to explain what "correspondence" is have failed, especially when it comes to explaining how the final vocabulary of future physics will somehow be Nature's Own—the one which, at long last, lets us formulate sentences which lock on to Nature's own way of thinking of herself. . . . *It is the impossible attempt to step outside our skins—the traditions, linguistic and other, within which we do our thinkning and self-criticism—and compare ourselves with something absolute.*

See also H. Putnam, note 2, at ix, 49, 128, 130, 134 (emphasis added):

[T]he "copy" theory of truth . . . [is] the conception according to which a statement is true just in case it "corresponds to the (mind-independent) facts". . . . On this perspective, the world exists of some fixed totality of mind-independent objects. There is exactly one true and complete description of "the way the world is". Truth involves some sort of correspondence relation between words or thought-signs and external things and sets of things. I shall call this perspective the *externalist* perspective, because its favorite point of view is a God's Eye point of view. . . . The idea that truth is a passive copy of what is "really" (mind-independently, discourse-independently) "there" has collapsed under the critiques of Kant, Wittgenstein, and other philosophers even if it continues to have a deep hold on our thinking. . . . *[T]he notion of comparing our system of beliefs with unconceptualized reality to see if they match makes no sense. . . . [T]he notion of a transcendental match between our representation and the world in itself is nonsense.*

21. Timothy Jackson has warned against conflating "alethiology (theory of the nature of truth) with epistemology (theory of the test for truth). . . . [C]orrespondence to reality cannot be appealed to *in epistemology* as a criterion against which to measure knowledge claims. . . . In fact, the correspondence theory is an alethiological theory only and thus does not enter into the justification of claims to know." Jackson, note 19, at 279.

22. Wonnell, "Truth and the Marketplace of Ideas," 19 U. California/Davis L. Rev. 669, 678 n. 50 (1986) (quoting K. Popper, Conjectures and Refutations 225 [1968]).

23. H. Putnam, note 2, at 134. See note 20.

24. See Jackson, note 19, at 280: "[W]hen [Richard] Rorty explicitly *identifies* desirable or warranted belief with truth, he is contradicting his own best insights and drifting into nihilism."

25. H. Putnam, note 2, at 55, 56.

26. R. Rorty, note 20, at vi.

27. R. Rorty, Contingency, Irony and Solidarity 5 (1989). Rorty calls this statement a "platitude". Id.

28. See note 18.

29. R. Rorty, note 27. See id. at 4 et seq.

30. See id., ch. 1 ("The Contingency of Language").

31. See note 11.

32. See Ruth Anna Putnam, "Creating Facts and Values," 60 Philosophy 187 (1985).

33. For example, his views on human nature, which are pluralist but not nihilist. See chapter 2, note 6. See also M. Perry, Morality, Politics, and Law 45, 48, & 184 (1988) (discussing Putnam's "moderate", as distinct from Richard Rorty's "extreme", "anthropological relativism").

34. H. Putnam, note 2. at xi.

35. A. MacIntyre, note 5, at 357. See id. at 357–58:

> The commonest candidate . . . for that which corresponds to a judgment in this way is a fact. But facts, like telescopes and wigs for gentlemen, were a seventeenth-century invention. . . . It is of course and always was harmless, philosophically and otherwise, to use the word "fact" of what a judgment states. What is and was not harmless, but highly misleading, was to conceive of a realm of facts independent of judgment or of any other form of linguistic expression, so that judgments or statements or sentences could be paired off with facts, truth or falsity being the alleged relationship between such paired items. This kind of correspondence theory of truth arrived on the scene only comparatively recently and has been as conclusively refuted as any philosophical theory can be. . . .

36. Cf. Rorty, "Science as Solidarity," note 12, at 43–44: "From a pragmatist point of view, to say that what is rational for us now to believe may not be *true* is simply to say that somebody may come up with a better idea."

37. The conception does entail, however, that every instance of reasoning, including self-critical reasoning, "begins from the contingency and positively of some set of established beliefs". A. MacIntyre, note 5, at 360. MacIntyre calls this the "anti-Cartesian" position. Id.

38. Id. at 360.

39. See note 36 and accompanying text. See also D. Brink, Moral Realism and the Foundations of Ethics 31 (1989).

40. A. MacIntyre, note 5, at 360–61.

41. Id. at 361. See also MacIntyre, "Epistemological Crises, Dramatic Narratives, and the Philosophy of Science," 60 Monist 453, 455 (1977): "[W]e are never in a position to claim that now we possess the truth or now we are fully rational. The most we can claim is that this is the best account which anyone has been able to give so far, and that our beliefs about what the marks of 'a best account so far' are will themselves change in what are at present unpredictable ways."

42. McCarthy, "Contra Relativism: A Thought-Experiment," in M. Krausz, note 12 at 260. See id. at 258–60. See also McCarthy, "Philosophical and Social Practice: Avoiding the Ethnocentric Predicament," unpublished ms. (1988); McCarthy, "After the Linguistic Turn: Critical Theory versus the New Pragmatism," unpublished ms. (1988). (In both of these as-yet-unpublished papers McCarthy is highly critical of Richard Rorty's ignoring or discounting "final truth" as a regulative ideal—moreover, as one *our* regulative ideals.)

Here, then, is one way to mediate the difference between those who, following Hans-Georg Gadamer, insist on the contextualist (hermeneutic, interpretive) nature of rationality (as well as of understanding) and therefore of moral rationality and those who, following Jürgen Habermas, aspire to a universalist ethics: The former group can be understood to emphasize the coherentist nature of all rationality, including moral rationality, and the latter can be understood to emphasize the importance of self-critical rationality and the vulnerability of any contextually supported moral claim to critical, including self-critical, challenge. But the two emphases can be understood, as they have been here, in this chapter, as complementary rather than competitive. See M. Gibbons, ed., Interpreting Politics 16–20 (1987) (suggesting the possibility of such a mediation of Gadamer's and Habermas' contending views).

43. According to Michael Moore, the "ontology" of one who is a "realist about some class of entities . . . maintains both: (1) that the entities in question exist, and (2) that their existence is independent of any individual's mind or any community's conventions." Moore, The Interpretive Turn in Modern Theory: A Turn for the Worse?," 41 Stanford L. Rev. 871, 878 (1989). See id. at 880–81:

> Those who straighforwardly disagree with realists are often called antirealists. Corresponding to the two essential tenets of realist ontology are two kinds of antirealists: (1) those who deny the existence of some class of entities, . . . and (2) those who grant the existence of such entities but deny their independence from our minds or our conventions. The first kind of antirealist is a skeptic; the second is an idealist. The idealist can be either a subjectivist or a conventionalist. In either case, the idealist asserts that the entities in question exist only as ideas—either as the ideas of each of us (subjectivism), or as those shared ideas we call social conventions (conventionalism).

44. See H. Putnam, The Many Faces of Realism 17 (1987): "One can be *both* a realist *and* a conceptual relativist." See also Smith, "Plausible, If Not True," Times Literary Supp., Sept. 4, 1987, at 963. For an extended argument that "a coherentist epistemology is compatible with a realist metaphysics", and, in particular, with a moral-realist position, see D. Brink, note 39. (The quoted language appears at 143.) For an argument that one can consistently be a scientific realist and yet "readily deny the correspondence theory of truth", see Almeder, "Scientific Realism and Explanation," 26 American Philosophical Q. 173 (1989). (The quoted language appears at 173.) See also Moore, note 43, at 880 (explaining that a metaphysical realist can adhere either to a foundational or to a nonfoundational conception of rationality).

45. Consider, in that regard, that scientific practice does not presuppose scientific realism, though, of course, a scientist may happen to be a scientific realist. Scientific realism is a position in the philosophy of science, not in science itself. Moreover, scientific realism does not presuppose or entail a correspondence account either of rationality or of truth. For an elegant portrayal of scientific realism, see McMullin, "A Case for Scientific Realism," in J. Leplin, ed., Scientific Realism 8 (1984). See also Almeder, note 44.

46. Richard Rorty seems to embrace self-critical reflective practices without embracing realism. See Rorty, note 12.

47. R. Rorty, note 27, at 189.

48. Jackson, note 19, at 284–85. See id. at 289: "[O]ne may acknowledge the perpetual uncertainty and fallibility of any human judgment without letting go of a realist theory of truth. . . . Conversely, letting go of realism will in all probability leave a society without the wherewithal to found or sustain a commitment to liberty, equality, or fraternity—much less sorority. Such a society may live for a time on past cultural capital embodied in liberal institutions and traditions, but a purely conventional virtue will not last long. The issue is one of motivation and consistency." See also McShea, "Making Truth," London Rev. Books, Dec. 4, 1986.

49. Michael Moore's claim that "[a]ll realists will adhere to . . . [the] correspondence theory of truth" (Moore, note 43, at 279) is wrong. The correspondence theory it, as Putnam has said, an "externalist" theory of truth. One can, like Putnam, be a realist (see note 44), but, like Putnam, adhere to an "internalist" theory of truth. See note 25 and accompanying text.

50. Elgin, "The Relativity of Fact and the Objectivity of Value," in M. Krausz, note 12, at 86, 91.

51. See McCarthy, "Contra Relativism: A Thought-Experiment," note 42, at 260 et seq. See also MacIntyre, note 5, at 364. On the critique and revision of belief from the "inside", see note 6.

52. See pp. 130–31.

53. See pp. 84–98.

This chapter is addressed principally to the question "What is rationality?" I have discussed rationality mainly as a predicate of beliefs (claims, propositions, etc.) and, indirectly, of the choices persons make. See note 3. In another sense, however, "rationality" refers to a human capacity. See Honneth, "Enlightenment and Rationality," 84 J. Philosophy 692, 695 (1987): "[T]he position of rationality within the whole of human life . . . is now regarded as that form of reflexive interval which is necessary once a well-functioning form of action hitherto successful in practical terms is disturbed by problems. In this manner, the inclination of subjects capable of action to make use of fallible knowledge reflexively in the solution of problems of action posed in practice comes to be called 'rationality.' " Understood as a human capacity/ability for reflexive problem solving (in which some beliefs are accepted and others rejected—and, relatedly, some choices are accepted and others rejected—on the basis of what other beliefs are authoritative for the person), so-called "instrumental" rationality is but one aspect of rationality. See id. at 696–97:

> [I]f "rationality" describes the human capacity for a reflexive mastering of practical problems, then the mere fact that there are different classes of problems which human beings encounter in the course of everyday practice means that a certain compulsion exists to differentiate within the concept of rationality; thus, we claim to behave rationally not only when we encounter a technical problem, but also, for example, if we come into moral conflict with others. As soon as one can demonstrate that the course of human life entails different types of rational knowledge, however, this also highlights the fact that the model of rational relation to objects which has prevailed in modern Europe constitutes but a one-sided interpretation of the human capacity for reason. A purpose-directed knowledge of states of affairs, which is what the thesis on instrumentalism suggests is the predominant feature of

reason, comprises only one of the forms that the rational relation of a person to itself and its world can take. . . .

Chapter 5

1. D. Tracy, The Analogical Imagination 13 (1981). See also K. Greenawalt, Religious Convictions and Political Choice 6 (1988): "A good many professors and other intellectuals display a hostility or skeptical indifference to religion that amounts to a thinly disguised contempt for belief in any reality beyond that discoverable by scientific inquiry and ordinary human experience." One doesn't have to look too far, either in contemporary popular or intellectual culture, to find examples of explicit or implicit putdowns of religion. For example, in a recent article in the *New York Times*, the author described Harvard Law Dean Robert Clark as "[a former] candidate for the Catholic priesthood who lost his faith after reading too much philosophy." Emerson, "When Legal Titans Clash," New York Times Mag., Apr. 22, 1990, at 26, 28. The implicit point—that reading philosophy (and other sophisticated intellectual activity?) is subversive of religious faith—is just silly. (This is not to deny that reading philosophy, like reading much else, especially contemporary theology, can be subversive of particular religious beliefs. See pp. 73–74.) I doubt Dean Clark has read a fraction of the philosophy mastered by a theologian like the University of Chicago's David Tracy, himself a Catholic priest. (On Tracy, see Kennedy, "A Dissenting Voice: Catholic Theologian David Tracy," New York Times Mag., Nov. 9, 1986, at 20.) Cf. Kronman, "Precedent and Tradition," 99 Yale L. J. 1029, 1031 (1990): "Religion, . . . whether it be quietly pietistic or mystical in character, at some point always demands an 'intellectual sacrifice' that is incompatible with the uncompromising rationalism of philosophy." I wonder where one would locate the "intellectual sacrifice" in, for example, David Braine's *The Reality of Time and the Existence of God* (1988). Garry Wills has recently observed and commented critically on the condescending discomfort experienced by "the learned" and the mainstream media when confronted by religion. See G. Wills, Under God: Religion and American Politics 15–25 (1990).

2. See Lovin, "Perry, Naturalism, and Religion in Public," 63 Tulane L. Rev. 1517, 1538–39 (1989).

3. C. Taylor, Sources of the Self: The Making of the Modern Identity 18 (1989). Taylor also argues that "those whose spiritual agenda is mainly defined in this way are in a fundamentally different existential predicament from that which dominated most previous cultures and still defines the lives of other people today." Id. On the "notorious vagueness" of the question "What is the Meaning of Life?", see Joske, "Philosophy and the Meaning of Life," in E. Klemke, ed., The Meaning of Life 248, 248 et seq. (1981). See also Hepburn, "Questions about the Meaning of Life," in id. at 209.

4. Siddhartha was the prince who became the Buddha. Herman Hesse fictionalized the story in *Siddhartha* (1951).

5. For a (vicarious) encounter with exemplary evil, see Friedrich, "The Kingdom of Auschwitz," Atlantic, Sept. 1981, at 30.

6. A. Camus, The Myth of Sisyphus and Other Essays 5 (1944; Eng. tr. 1955). See L. Kolakowski, the Presence of Myth (1989), especially ch. 8: "The Phenomenon of the World's Indifference". Cf. B. Pascal, Pensees 95 (Penguin Books ed. 1966): "The eternal silence of these infinite spaces fills me with dread."

7. For Tolstoy's eloquent account of his struggle with the problem of meaning, see his *Confession* (1884; D. Patterson tr. 1983). See also Perrett, "Tolstoy, Death, and the Meaning of Life," 60 Philosophy 231 (1985). For a seriocomic account of one man's struggle with the problem of meaning, see Woody Allen's wonderful screenplay, *Hannah and Her Sisters* (1987), especially pp. 93–98, 108–10, 129–34, 144–45, & 168–73.

8. A. Heschel, Who Is Man? 75 (1965). See D. Tracy, Plurality and Ambiguity: Hermeneutics, Religion, Hope 87 (1987): "Like strictly metaphysical questions, religious questions must be questions on the nature of Ultimate Reality. Unlike metaphysical questions, religious questions deliberately ask the question of the meaning and truth of Ultimate Reality not only as it is in itself *but as it is existentially related to us.* The religious classics are testimonies to the responses of the religions to those questions." (Emphasis added.) Cf. F. Dostoevsky, The Brothers Karamazov 235 (Norton ed. 1976): "For the secret of man's being is not only to live but to have something to live for. Without a stable conception of the object of life, man would not consent to go on living, and would rather destroy himself than remain on earth, though he had bread in abundance." (This is one of the Grand Inquisitor's statements in chapter 5 of Book Five.)

9. See Joske, note 3, at 249 et seq.

10. See L. Kolakowski, note 6, at 69–70. Anyone tempted by reductionist arguments should consult David Tracy's *Plurality and Ambiguity: Hermeneutics, Religion, Hope*, note 8, especially chapter 5: "Resistance and Hope: The Question of Religion". See also H. Küng, Does God Exist?: An Answer for Today 189–339 (1978; Eng. tr. 1980) (discussing Feuerbach, Marx, and Freud); R. Coles, The Spiritual Life of Children, chapter 1: "Psychoanalysis and Religion" (1990). Cf. Boswell, "Quite Contrary," New Republic, June 15, 1987, at 37: "I regard psychoanalysis as a revealed religion. . . . [I]t is a self-referential and unfalsifiable system. . . . [I]t is based on insights from honored individuals about a non-observable world, rather than on a body of repeated experiments and proofs."

11. The Williamsburg Charter: A National Celebration and Reaffirmation of the First Amendment Religious Liberty Clauses 9 (1988).

12. Victor Frankl, in Man's Search for Meaning (1946; Eng. tr. 1959), quoted in E. Klemke, note 3, at vii. On the search for meaning and the deeply human character of the search, see L. Kolakowski, Metaphysical Horror (1988); see also L. Kolakowski, note 6.

13. See Joske, note 3, at 250: "If, as Kurt Vonnegut speculates in *The Sirens of Titan,* the ultimate end of human activity is the delivery of a small piece of steel to a wrecked space ship wanting to continue a journey of no importance whatsoever, the end would be too trivial to justify the means." See also R. Nozick, Philosophical Explanations 586 (1981): "If the cosmic role of human beings was to provide a negative lesson to some others ('don't act like them') or to provide needed food to passing intergalactic travelers who *were* important, this would not suit our

aspirations—not even if afterwards the intergalactic travelers smacked their lips and said that we tasted good."

14. Edwards, "Life, Meaning and Value of," 4 Encyclopedia of Philosophy 467, 470 (P. Edwards ed. 1967). Whether Clarence Darrow was in fact "one of the most compassionate men who ever lived" is open to serious question. See G. Wills, note 1, chapters 8–9.

15. Might it be said that Darrow was a man of faith but not belief? See note 39 and accompanying text.

16. Cf. L. Kolakowski, Religion 191 (1982) (quoted in chapter 2, note 35). On the issue of suicide, see Camus's "The Myth of Sisyphus" in A. Camus, note 6, at 1–102. Cf. P. Levi, quoted in Ozick, "The Suicide Note," New Republic, Mar. 21, 1987, at 32, 36: "Suicide is an act of man and not of the animal. It is a meditated act, a noninstinctive, an unnatural choice."

17. Several contributors to *The Meaning of Life,* note 3, offer such a position. That life is provisionally meaningful, at least, and that we should sit back and enjoy it—especially if there's a Marx Brothers movie nearby—is the position Mickey Sachs arrives at near the end of Woody Allen's *Hannah and Her Sisters.* See W. Allen, note 7, at 172.

18. A. Heschel, note 8, at 78. See also note 8 (Dostoevsky quote).

19. Cf. "Religion," 13 OED 568 (1989).

20. See notes 36 & 42 (Tracy quotes).

21. See Braybrooke, "Ideology," in 4 Encyclopedia of Philosophy 124 (P. Edwards ed. 1967).

22. Harvey Egan has written that "there is a sense in which all great religions are mystical at heart and that mysticism is the full-flowering of any religious tradition." H. Egan, What Are They Saying about Mysticism? 17 (1982). According to Wayne Proudfoot, the very ubiquity of mystical experience among the world religions suggests that mysticism may be regarded as "a *paradigm* of religious experience." W. Proudfoot, Religious Experience xviii (1985). Some commentators distinguish between two fundamental types of mystical experience, or two kinds of union with God or the Absolute the mystic achieves: (1) the experience of union but not identity with God (as attested to by mystics in theistic traditions such as Christianity, Judaism, and Islam), and (2) the experience of complete absorption into the divine. Cf. id. at 121: "The terms in which the subject understands what is happening to him are constitutive of the experience; consequently those in different traditions have different experiences. Jewish and Buddhist mystics [for example] bring entirely different doctrinal commitments, expectations, and rules for identifying their mental and bodily states to their experiences, and thus *devekuth* and *nirvana* cannot be the same."

23. According to William James, "transience" is a third mark of mystical experience. Commenting on James, Proudfoot writes:

> The two secondary marks by which James characterizes the mystical state, transience and passivity, are also related to the noetic quality of the experience. Passivity conveys the sense of being grasped and of being subject to some power beyond oneself. Both passivity and transience reflect the per-

ception that the experience is not under the subject's voluntary control. It cannot be manipulated or guaranteed by the subject's decision or by causes that he might set in motion. He can prepare himself for it, but the experience is finally not subject to his control. The rules for the identification of an experience as mystical include the condition that he judge it to be something other than an artifact of his own thought and actions.

Proudfoot, note 22, at 147–48.

24. M. Kundera, The Unbearable Lightness of Being 139 (1984) (emphasis added). See R. Coles, note 10, at 37: "The questions Tolstoy asked, and Gaugin in, say, his great Tahiti triptych, completed just before he died ('Where Do We Come From?, What Are We?, Where Are We Going?'), are the eternal questions children ask most intensely, unremittingly, and subtly than we sometimes imagine."

25. "Not the individual man nor a single generation by its own power, can erect the bridge that leads to God. Faith is the achievement of many generations, an effort accumulated over centuries. Many of its ideas are as the light of the star that left its source a long time ago. Many enigmatic songs, unfathomable today, are the resonance of voices of bygone times. There is a collective memory of God in the human spirit, and it is this memory which is the main source of our faith." From Abraham Heschel's two-part essay "Faith", first published in volume 10 of *The Reconstructionist,* Nov. 3 & 17, 1944. For a later statement on faith, incorporating some of the original essay, see A. Heschel, Man Is Not Alone 159–76 (1951). On community/tradition as a principal matrix of moral beliefs, see M. Perry, Morality, Politics, and Law 22–33 (1988). Cf. note 49 and accompanying text (Burtchaell quote).

26. See. D. Carmody & J. Carmody, Western Ways to the Center: An Introduction to Religions of the West 198–99 (1983): "All people by nature desire to know the mystery from which they come and to which they go." See also A. Heschel, note 8, at 28: "In an old rabbinic text three other questions are suggested: '*Whence* did you come?' '*Whither* are you going?' 'Before *whom* are you destined to give account?' "

27. D. Tracy, note 8, at 86.

28. D. Tracy, note 1, at 4.

29. See pp. 59–62.

30. See D. Tracy, note 8, at 92; Küng, "What Is True Religion?: Toward an Ecumenical Criteriology," in L. Swidler, ed., Toward a Universal Theology of Religion 231, 235 (1987).

31. See note 39 and accompanying text.

32. Unfortunately, secular intellectuals sometimes assume that bad theology is the only theology there is, and that "bad theology" is therefore redundant. For a discussion of the problem, see Clark, "With Rationality and Love," Times Literary Supp., Sept. 26, 1986, at 1047. Cf. Rushdie, "The Book Burning," New York Rev., Mar. 2, 1989, at 26: "[T]he forces of inhumanity are on the march. 'Battle lines are being drawn up in India today,' one of my characters [in Rushdie's *The Satanic Verses* (1988)] remarks, 'Secular versus religious, the light versus the dark. Better you choose which side you are on.' " (For a sensitive reflection on the Rushdie affair, see Walzer, "The Sins of Salman: The Do's and Don't's of Blasphemy," New Republic, Apr. 10, 1989, at 13.)

33. See note 36. Cf. T. Merton, New Seeds of Contemplation 24 (1961).
34. Deuteronomy 5:8–9. See also Exodus 20:4–5.
35. A. Heschel, I Asked for Wonder: A Spiritual Anthology of Abraham Joshua Heschel 49 (S. Dresner ed. 1984).
36. This is the first of the eighty-one entries that constitute the *Tao Te Ching*, attributed to the ancient Chinese sage Lao Tsu. I have relied principally on the new translation by Stephen Mitchell (1988).

David Tracy's comments about the richness, the variety, but, finally, the problematic character—the limits—of all talk about Ultimate Reality, and especially of God-talk (talk about God, "theo-logizing"), are compelling:

> In and through even the best speech for Ultimate Reality, greater obscurity eventually emerges to manifest a religious sense of that Reality as ultimate mystery. Silence may be the most appropriate kind of speech for evoking this necessary sense of the radical mystery—as mystics insist when they say, "Those who know do not speak; those who speak do not know." The most refined theological discourse of the classic theologians ranges widely but returns at last to a deepened sense of the same ultimate mystery: the amazing freedom with all traditional doctrinal formulations in Meister Eckhart; the confident portrayals of God in Genesis and Exodus become the passionate outbursts of the prophets and the painful reflections of Job, Ecclesiastes, and Lamentations; the disturbing light cast by the biblical metaphors for the "wrath of God" on all temptations to sentimentalize what love means when the believer says, "God is love"; the proclamation of the hidden and revealed God in Luther and Calvin; the *deus otiosus* vision of God in the Gnostic traditions; the repressed discourse of the witches; the startling female imagery for Ultimate Reality in both the great matriarchal traditions and the great Wisdom traditions of both Greeks and Jews; the power of the sacred dialectically divorcing itself from the profane manifested in all religions; the extraordinary subtleties of rabbinic writing on God become the uncanny paradoxes of Kabbalistic thought on God's existence in the very materiality of letters and texts; the subtle debates in Hindu philosophical reflections on monism and polytheism; the many faces of the Divine in the stories of Shiva and Krishna; the puzzling sense that, despite all appearances to the contrary, there is "nothing here that is not Zeus" in Aeschylus and Sophocles; the terror caused by Dionysius in Euripedes' *Bacchae;* the refusal to cling even to concepts of "God" in order to become free to experience Ultimate Reality as Emptiness in much Buddhist thought; the moving declaration of that wondrous clarifier Thomas Aquinas, "All that I have written is straw; I shall write no more"; Karl Rahner's insistence on the radical incomprehensibility of both God and ourselves understood through and in our most comprehensible philosophical and theological speech; . . . the "God beyond God" language of Paul Tillich and all theologians who acknowledge how deadening traditional God-language can easily become; the refusal to speak God's name in classical Judaism; the insistence on speaking that name in classical Islam; the hesitant musings on the present-absent God in Buber become the courageous attempts to forge new languages for a new covenant

with God in the post-*tremendum* theologies of Cohen, Fackenheim, and Greenberg. There is no classic discourse on Ultimate Reality that can be understood as mastering its own speech. If any human discourse gives true testimony to Ultimate Reality, it must necessarily prove uncontrollable and unmasterable.

D. Tracy, note 8, at 108–9. Cf. M. Buber, quoted in H. Küng, note 10, at 508:

["God"] is the most loaded of all words used by men. None has been so soiled, so mauled. But that is the very reason I cannot give it up. Generations of men have blamed this word for the burdens of their troubled lives and crushed it to the ground; it lies in the dust, bearing all their burdens. Generations of men with their religious divisions have torn the word apart; they have killed for it and died for it; it bears all their fingerprints and is stained with all their blood. Where would I find a word to equal it, to describe supreme reality? If I were to take the purest, most sparkling term from the innermost treasury of the philosophers, I could capture in it no more than a noncommittal idea, not the presence of what I mean, of what generations of men in the vastness of their living and dying have venerated and degraded. . . . We must respect those who taboo it, since they revolt against the wrong and mischief that were so readily claimed to be authorized in the name of God; but we cannot relinquish it. It is easy to understand why there are some who propose a period of silence about the "last things," so that the misused words may be redeemed. But this is not the way to redeem them. We cannot clean up the term "God" and we cannot make it whole; but, stained and mauled as it is, we can raise it from the ground and set it above an hour of great sorrow.

For a feminist-theological reflection on God-talk, see R. Ruether, Sexism and God-Talk: Toward a Feminist Theology (1983); J. Plaskow and C. Christ, eds., Weaving the Visions: New Patterns in Feminist Spirituality, part 2: "Naming the Sacred" (1989).

37. On trust in the ultimate meaningfulness of life as the basic religious response, see H. Küng, note 10. See also note 39 and accompanying text. Cf. Ruether, "Infallibility Fundamental Antithesis of Faith," National Catholic Reporter, Apr. 21, 1989, at 18: "[F]aith is, finally, trust in God's faithfulness to us."

38. Heschel, note 25.

39. Davis, "Religion and the Making of Society," 81 Northwestern U. L. Rev. 718, 728–29 (1987). See also D. Tracy, note 1, at 47; Küng, note 30, at 235; Heschel, "Faith," note 25:

Faith is sensitiveness to what transcends nature, knowledge and will, awareness of the ultimate, alertness to the holy dimension of all reality. Faith is a force in man, lying deeper than the stratum of reason and its nature cannot be defined in abstract, static terms. To have faith is not to infer the beyond from the wretched here, but to perceive the wonder that is here and to be stirred by the desire to integrate the self into the holy order of living. It is not a deduction but an intuition, not a form of knowledge, of being convinced without proof, but the attitude of mind towards ideas whose scope is wider than its own capacity to grasp. . . .

Faith as the act of believing should be distinguished from creed as the content, as that in which we believe. Faith, itself as little rational as love of beauty or motherly affection, becomes a dogma or a doctrine when pressed into an opinion. Our creed is, like music, a translation of the unutterable into sounds, thoughts, words, deeds. The original is known to God alone. And what is expressed and taught as a creed is but the adaptation of the uncommon spirit to the common sense. Yet it is the creed that keeps the flame when our thoughts go out and we lose the sight of our beloved dreams. For the words of our great sages, full of never aging grace, are to us like a mother that never forgets, that is not impatient of folly or failing.

There are many creeds but only one faith. Creeds may change, develop and grow flat, while the substance of faith remains the same in all ages. The overgrowth of creed may bring about the disintegration of that substance. The proper relation is a minimum of creed and a maximum of faith. . . .

Faith is something that comes out of the soul. It is not an information that is absorbed but an attitude, existing prior to the formulation of any creed.

Cf. Panikkar, "Religious Pluralism: The Metaphysical Challenge," in L. Rouner, ed., *Religious Pluralism* 97, 108 (1984) (explaining that although "[o]ne should not identify a religion with its doctrinal aspect, . . . one should not minimize it either").

40. H. Kuitert, *Everything Is Politics but Politics Is Not Everything* 58 (1986).
41. Davis, note 39, at 729.
42. David Tracy has elaborated the point, which is crucial:

As reflection on Ultimate Reality, and thereby on the limit questions of our existence, theological interpretations, like all such interpretations, must always be a highly precarious mode of inquiry. Theologians can never claim certainty but, at best, highly tentative relative adequacy. Theologians cannot escape the same plurality and ambiguity that affect all discourse. . . .

. . . [R]eligions do claim . . . that Ultimate Reality has revealed itself and that there is a way of liberation for any human being. But even this startling possibility can only be understood by us if we will risk interpreting it. It is possible that some interpreters may have encountered the power of Ultimate Reality. They may have experienced, therefore, religious enlightenment and emancipation. But these claims can be interpreted only by the same kinds of human beings as before: finite and contingent members of particular societies and cultures. They demand our best efforts at rigorous, critical, and genuine conversation. They demand retrieval, critique, and suspicion. . . .

Theologians should not pretend that they understand any religion without intrepreting it with the full demands that we have seen that word to impose on all interpretations. Nor should they hope that understanding-as-interpretation will be free from their own finitude, contingency, and faults. Karl Barth spoke for all theologians in all traditions when he stated, "The angels will laugh when they read my theology." Nor should theologicans expect to be free of the unconscious systemic distortions that inevitably pervade all discourse. As

Reinhold Niebuhr insisted, our best acts of creation are, at the same time, the best examples of our ambiguity. In principle, theologians should be open to every hermeneutic that can illuminate their demanding task. At their best, they are alert to any hermeneutic of retrieval that can interpret the religious event rightly, whether that event be the higher consciousness promoted and practiced in Yoga, in Zen, and in all the great mystical traditions or the gift and power of God's judgment and healing proclaimed in Judaism, Christianity, and Islam. Theologians should be alert as well to the need for any hermeneutic suspicion that can further instruct their own religious suspicions of the endemic, unconscious reality of either sin, avidya, or dishonor. They should be open to any explanatory method—historical-critical methods, social-scientific methods, semiotics and structuralist methods, post-structuralist methods, hermeneutical discourse analysis—that can help to assess errors in traditional religious interpretations. They should use any form of argument that enhances the critical conversation with the classic religious texts and symbols. They should be open to any form of critical theory that helps spot the distortions suspected in the religious classics themselves. . . .

These strategies of both retrieval and suspicion, and often retrieval through suspicion, should also free religious persons and traditions to open themselves to other hermeneutics of critique and suspicion, whatever their source. For believers to be unable to learn from secular feminists on the patriarchal nature of most religions or to be unwilling to be challenged by Feuerbach, Darwin, Marx, Freud, or Nietzsche is to refuse to take seriously the religion's own suspicions on the existence of those fundamental distortions named sin, ignorance, or illusion. The interpretations of believers will, of course, be grounded in some fundamental trust in, and loyalty to, the Ultimate Reality both disclosed and concealed in one's own religious tradition. But fundamental trust, as any experience of friendship can teach, is not immune to either criticism or suspicion. A religious person will ordinarily fashion some hermeneutics of trust, even one of friendship and love, for the religious classics of her or his tradition. But, as any genuine understanding of friendship shows, friendship often demands both critique and suspicion. A belief in a pure and innocent love is one of the less happy inventions of the romantics. A friendship that never includes critique and even, when appropriate, suspicion is a friendship barely removed from the polite and wary communication of strangers. As Buber showed, in every I-Thou encounter, however transient, we encounter some new dimension of reality. But if that encounter is to prove more than transitory, the difficult ways of friendship need a trust powerful enough to risk itself in critique and suspicion. To claim that this may be true of all our other loves but not true of our love for, and trust in, our religious tradition makes very little sense either hermeneutically or religiously.

D. Tracy, note 8, at 84–85, 86, 97–98, 112. Clearly, the Vatican's theological bureaucracy, headed by Cardinal Joseph Ratzinger, has not heeded the spirit of Tracy's comments. See [Vatican] Congregation for the Doctrine of the Faith, "Instruction on the Ecclesial Vocation of the Theologian," 20 Origins 117 (1990). (The document was signed for the Congregation by Cardinal Ratzinger.) For one (typical) reaction to the Vatican's effort to silence public dissent by Catholic theologians, see Steinfels, "The Vatican Warns Catholic Theologians over Public Dissent," New York Times, June 27, 1990, at A1, A6: "The Rev. Richard A. McCormick, a professor of theology at the University of Notre Dame, said, 'The first reaction of many if not most theologians will be to dissent from that document on dissent. I think that Vatican officials have the attitude that the ability to dissent is somehow a grant from ecclesial authority when in fact it is rooted very deeply in the contingency and imperfection of human knowing,' Father McCormick said." For another such reaction, see Ostling, "Drawing the Line on Dissent," Time, July 9, 1990, at 62: "Snapped the Rev. Richard McBrien, outspoken chairman of theology at the University of Notre Dame: 'This is redolent of another era. It's like an outbreak of polio; we thought we had it conquered. This document comes out the church of the 1940s and 1950s. The document is not a surprise; it's an embarrassment.' " Of course, the Vatican should not be confused with the Catholic Church itself—a confusion to which the Vatican sometimes seems to fall prey. Cf. J. Segundo, Theology and the Church: A Response to Cardinal Ratzinger and a Warning to the Whole Church (1985); L. Swidler, ed., Consensus in Theology? A Dialogue with Hans Küng and Edward Schillebeeckx (1980).

Tracy's insistent admonitions about theological interpretation/discourse have an obvious and powerful relevance to moral discourse generally, including—especially?—political-moral discourse. No such discourse is immune to the severely corrosive influence either of individual or of group self-interest.

43. Quoted in R. Brown, Spirituality and Liberation: Overcoming the Great Fallacy 5 (1988).

44. [Vatican] Congregation for the Doctrine of the Faith, note 42, at 120.

45. On the meaning of "moral", see C. Taylor, note 3, at 3: "Much contemporary moral philosophy, particularly but not only in the English-speaking world, has given such a narrow focus to morality. . . . This moral philosophy has tended to focus on what it is right to do rather than on what it is good to be, on defining the content of obligation rather than the nature of the good life. . . . This philosophy has accredited a cramped and truncated view of morality in a narrow sense, as well as of the whole range of issues involved in the attempt to live the best possible life, and this not only among professional philosophers, but with a wider public." See also id. at 4, 14–15, 63–64, 79, 87. Taylor's book (note 3) is, among other things, a powerful argument for a different, larger understanding of "moral", an Aristotelian rather than a Kantian understanding. Taylor's project has an obvious affinity with Alasdair MacIntyre's and Martha Nussbaum's respective projects. See A. MacIntyre, After Virtue (2d ed. 1984); A. MacIntyre, Whose Justice? Which Rationality? (1988); A. MacIntyre, Three Rival Versions of Moral Enquiry: Encyclopedia, Genealogy, and Tradition (1990); Nussbaum, "Non-Relative Virtues: An Aristotelian Approach," 13 Midwest Studies in Philosophy 32 (1988); Nussbaum, "Aristotle on Human Nature and the Foundations of Ethics" (forthcoming).

46. See pp. 23–27.

47. See p. 39 and note 29.

48. E. Schillebeeckx, The Schillebeeckx Reader 262 (R. Schreiter ed. 1984).

49. Burtchaell, "The Sources of Conscience," 13 Notre Dame Mag. 20, 20–21 (Winter 1984–85). (On our neighbor's always turning out to be the most unlikely person, see Luke 10:29–37 ["Parable of the Good Samaritan"].) Burtchaell continues:

> Nothing is specifically Christian about this method of making judgments about human experience. That is why it is strange to call any of our moral convictions "religious," let alone sectarian, since they arise from a dialogue that ranges through so many communities and draws from so many sources. And when debate and dialogue and testimony do fructify into conviction, and conviction into consensus, nothing could be more absurd than to expect that consensus to be confined within a person's privacy or a church's walls. Convictions are what we live by. Do we have anything better to share with one another?

Burtchaell, this note, at 21. (For a revised version of Burtchaell's essay, and for several other illuminating essays by Father Burtchaell, see J. Burtchaell, The Giving and Taking of Life [1989].) See also Küng, note 30, at 239–43; J. Fuchs, Christian Ethics in a Secular Arena (1984); chapter 2, note 29. Not all contemporary Catholic theologians are an enlightened as Father Burtchaell as to the nature of moral-theological development (though many are, like Küng and Fuchs). Even the post–Vatican II Catholic Church has its share—more that its share?—of authoritarian and even "fundamentalist" theological types. See Coleman, "Who Are the Catholic 'Fundamentalists'?," Commonweal, Jan. 27, 1989, at 42; Haring, "Does God Condemn Contraception?: A Question for the Whole Church," Commonweal, Feb., 1989, at 69.

Modern secular moral philosophy has, in the main, ignored the problem of meaning—much to its detriment. (See Wiggins, "Truth, Invention, and the Meaning of Life," 1976 Proceedings of British Academy 331.) How can the question of the good or right way to live or act, especially the question of what way (or ways) of life befits/fulfills us as human beings, be answered independently of the question of the meaningfulness (or absurdity) of human existence? Consider the claim, often made (see, e.g., P. Singer, Practical Ethics 10–12 [1979]), that in deciding what one ought, as a moral matter, to do one should adopt an "impartial" or "universal" point of view, that in making a moral choice one should attend to the relevant interests of others no less than to one's own, that one should count them equally with one's own. Is there any justification for that (or similar) claim or claims, much less any justification for a radically altruistic ethic of human solidarity of the sort portrayed in the Gospel (see notes 52–71 and accompanying text), independent of a conception, a vision, of the meaningfulness of life, in particular, of the meaningfulness of the life of the person to whom the claim is addressed? (For an extended negative response, see R. Bittner, What Reason Demands [1983; Eng. tr. 1989]. See also G. Tinder, The Political Meaning of Christianity [1990]. On the neo-Kantian effort "to defend Kant's account of moral motivation", see Thomas, "Moral Motivation: Kantians versus Humeans (and Evolution)," 13 Midwest Studies in Philosophy 367 [1988].) Insisting that to choose "morally" or "ethically" simply *means* to choose from a "universal point of view"—sometimes called "the moral point of view"—is unavailing, for then the question becomes: "Why should anyone care about choosing 'morally', or, indeed, about being 'moral', in *that* sense?" (For a discussion of the problem, see M. Perry, note 25, at 21–23 & 223–27. See also R. Bittner, supra this note; Goldsworthy, "God or Mackie? The Dilemma of Secular Moral Philosophy," 1985 American J. Jurisprudence 43; Scott, "Motive and Justification," 85 J. Philosophy 479 [1988].) "[U]nless we really want to think of moral philosophy as the casuistry of emergencies," wrote the British philosopher David Wiggins, "the question of meaning is a better focus for ethics and metaethics than the textbook problem 'What shall I do?' " Wiggins, supra this note, at 331. Wiggins added: "[P]hilosophy has put *happiness* in the place which should have been occupied in moral philosophy by *meaning*." Id. at 332. In bracketing the problem of meaning, secular moral philosophy has ended up a largely barren source of insight—or, at best, a profoundly incomplete source (see Gibbard, "Reasonably Reciprocal," Times Literary Supp., Feb. 20, 1987, at 177 [reviewing D. Gauthier, Morals by Agreement (1986)]—into the question of how it makes sense for us human beings, individually or collectively, to live our lives. "It would be interesting and fruitful to pick over the wreckage of defunct and discredited ethical theories and see what their negligence of the problem of life's having a meaning contributed to their ruin." Wiggins, supra this note, at 375.

50. See Panikkar, "Religion or Politics: The Western Dilemma," in P. Merkl & N. Smart, eds., Religion and Politics in the Modern World 44, 58 (1983): "Politics is always more—or other—than just 'politics,' . . . [involving] that which men have always called religion. Religion is always less—or other—than 'religion:' it contains within itself that which men have called politics." Panikkar's essay challenges the too-easy distinction between "religion" and "politics".

51. Swidler, "Interreligious and Interideological Dialogue: The Matrix for All Systematic Reflection Today," in L. Swidler, note 30, at 5, 16.

52. H. Putnam, The Many Faces of Realism 60 (1987).

52. See Introduction to N. Biggar, J. Scott, & W. Schweiker, eds., Cities of Gods: Faith, Politics, and Pluralism in Judaism, Christianity and Islam 1, 2 (1986): "[A]s long as certain sets of moral beliefs make moral claims upon those who hold them, religious faith is bound to move faithful Jews, Christians and Muslims through political judgments to political actions with political consequences. Nor is this only so when those judgments lead to the self-conscious commission of political acts; for even if a particular kind of religious self-understanding compels a member of the faithful to withdraw from the political process, such an act of omission constitutes a political statement and carries political consequences all its own." See also G. Tinder, note 49; Roelofs, "Liberation Theology: The Recovery of Biblical Radicalism," 82 American Political Science Rev. 549 (1988); Roelofs, "Hebraic-Biblical Political Thinking," 20 Polity 572 (1988).

54. See text accompanying note 60.

55. See A. Heschel, The Prophets (1962).

56. See. L. Boff & C. Boff, Introducing Liberation Theology (1986; Eng. tr. 1987); R. Brown, Theology in a New Key: Responding to Liberation Themes (1978); R. Brown, Unexpected News: Reading the Bible with Third World Eyes (1984); R. Brown, note 43; D. Cohn-Sherbok, On Earth as It Is in Heaven: Jews, Christians, and Liberation Theology (1987); M. Ellis, Toward a Jewish Theology of

Liberation (1984; rev. ed. 1989); A. McGovern, Liberation Theology and Its Critics: Toward an Assessment (1989); Roelofs, "Liberation Theology: The Recovery of Biblical Radicalism," note 53.

57. E. Schillebeeckx, note 48, at 274.

58. John 13:34. See also John 15:12.

59. Matthew 25:33–45. See also Luke 10:29–37 ("Parable of the Good Samaritan"). Richard McBrien, chair of the Theology Department at Notre Dame, has reported that

> [t]he letter entitled Political Responsibility, issued by the Administrative Board of the United States Catholic Conference in March 1984 [13 Origins 732 (1984)], grounded political involvement in love of neighbor, which goes beyond individual relationships to embrace the entire human community, and in Christ's specific call to reach out and help those in need, which also goes beyond individual relationships to embrace the institutions and structures of society, the economy, and politics. The purpose of such involvement is to promote human rights and to denounce violations of such rights; to call attention to the moral and religious dimensions of secular issues; to keep alive the values of the Gospel as a norm of social and political life; and to point out the demands of Christian faith for a just transformation of society.

McBrien, "The Church and Politics," 1 J. L., Ethics & Public Policy 57, 61 (1984).

60. Roelofs, "Church and State in America: Toward a Biblically Derived Reformulation of Their Relationship," 50 Rev. Politics 561, 175 (1988). Although Roelofs refers, where I have put the ellipsis, to the passage accompanying this note (and to Luke 6:20), his principal reference is to Luke 4:18–19 (which he quotes), in which Jesus proclaims (quoting Isaiah 61:1–2): "The Spirit of the Lord is upon me / because he has annointed me to preach good news to the poor. / He has sent me to proclaim release to the captives / and recovering of sight to the blind / to set at liberty those who are oppressed, / to proclaim the acceptable year of the Lord."

61. K. Rahner, 6 Theological Investigations 231, 236 (1969).

62. Id. at 247.

63. 1 John 4:20. See also Luke 10:29–37 ("Parable of the Good Samaritan").

64. See K. Rahner, note 61, at 232.

65. See id. at 238–39.

66. Tracy prefers the (equivalent, in my view) term "mystical-prophetic". See Tracy, "The Uneasy Alliance Reconceived: Catholic Theological Method, Modernity, and Postmodernity," 50 Theological Studies 548, 561 (1989) ("mystical-prophetic"); Tracy, "On Naming the Present," 1 Concilium 66, 80–84 (1990) (on "mystical-prophetic resistance and hope").

67. R. Brown, note 43, at 116. Brown adds: "Today we would also feel it important to help the man find a job. But Meister Eckhart is pointing in the right direction." Id.

68. Id. at 131.

69. Quoted in id. at 131–32. See also K. Rahner, Visions and Prophecies 14 n. 12 (1964): "It must be realized that in earthly man this emptying of self [characteristic of mystical experience] will not be accomplished by practicing pure inwardness, but by

real activity which is called humility, service, love of our neighbor, the cross and death. One must descend into hell together with Christ; lose one's soul, not directly to the God who is above all names but in the service of one's brethren." Cf. R. Brown, note 43, at 134: " 'Mystical language' (as [Peruvian liberation theologian Gustavo] Gutierrez . . . calls it) 'expresses the gratuitousness of God's love; prophetic language expresses the demands this love makes' . . . As Guiterrez writes . . . : 'We need a language that is both contemplative [mystical] and prophetic; contemplative because it ponders a God who is love; prophetic because it talks about a liberator God who rejects the situation of injustice in which the poor live, and also the structural causes of that situation.' "

70. Hauerwas, "A Christian Critique of Christian America," in J. Pennock & J. Chapman, eds., Religion, Morality, and the Law 110, 113 (1988).

71. See G. Tinder, note 49; Panikkar, note 39, at 106; "Religions are the least private human phenomena that we know. Cultures, wars, politics, and human relations of all sorts are influenced by the religious convictions of people."

72. See chapter 3, note 3. See also J. Cobb, Beyond Dialogue: Toward a Mutual Transformation of Christianity and Buddhism (1982); Cobb, "The Meaning of Pluralism for Christian Self-Understanding," in L. Rouner, note 39, at 161, 173–79.

73. See R. Habito, Total Liberation: Zen Spiritualty and the Social Dimension (1989); A. Pieris, An Asian Theology of Liberation (1988). Compare, to the passage from Matthew's Gospel quoted above (text accompanying note 59), this passage by Shantideva, "a poet-saint who has been called the Thomas à Kempis of Buddhism" (H. Smith, The Religions of Man 183–84 [1986]):

> May I be a balm to the sick, their healer and
>   servitor until sickness come never again;
> May I quench with rains of food and drink the
>   anguish of hunger and thirst;
> May I be in the famine of the age's end their
>   drink and meat;
> May I become an unfailing store for the poor, and
>   serve them with manifold things for their need;
> My own being and my pleasures, all my
>   righteousness in the past, present and future,
>   I surrender indifferently,
> That all creatures may win through to their end.

Quoted in id. at 121.

74. See, e.g., J. Eusden, Zen and Christian (1981); A. Graham, Conversations: Christian and Buddhist (1968); B. Griffiths, The Marriage of East and West (1982); T. Merton, Zen and the Birds of Appetite (1968); A. Pieris, Love Meets Wisdom: A Christian Experience of Buddhism (1988). Cf. R. Panikkar, The Silence of God: The Answer of the Buddha (1970; Eng. tr. 1989).

75. Quoted in H. Küng, Does God Exist? 490 (1978; Eng. tr. 1980). See also Panikkar, note 50, at 55: "A politics that is really concerned with the human *polis* and desires to be something more than a technocracy at the service of an ideology (of whatever sort) can not only not ignore the religious roots of the problems presented,

but must take into its reckoning that human happiness is not exclusively a matter of intake of calories, that peace does not automatically result from a balance of power, that distribution of wealth is not purely economic problem, nor questions of demography simply of a technical, medical or even moral sort, and so on."

76. E. Schillebeeckx, note 48 at 274. See R. Neuhaus, The Naked Public Square: Religion and Democracy in America (1984), especially ch. 5: "The Vulnerability of the Naked Square".

77. See K. Wald, Religion and Politics in the United States 284–85 (1987).

78. See J. Murray, We Hold These Truths 23–24 (1960).

79. Cf. Hollenbach, "The Growing End of an Argument," America, Nov. 30, 1985, at 363, 365: "The chief point in the argument today is not *whether* the voice of the [Catholic] bishops, for example, should be raised, but rather *what* should be said when it is."

Chapter 6

1. John Courtney Murray, We Hold These Truths 6, 14 (1960). The statement Murray quotes is from T. Gilby, *Between Community and Society* (1923). (The statement as quoted by Murray says "by men"; I have substituted "by persons".)

2. R. Beiner, Political Judgment 142–43 (1983) (passages rearranged). See id. at 129–52; MacIntyre, "Moral Arguments and Social Contexts," 80 J. Philosophy 590 (1983).

3. Cf. Devine, "Relativism," 67 Monist 405, 412 (1984): "[O]ne can maintain that truth is framework-relative, while conceding for a large range of propositions nearly all frameworks coincide."

4. Rorty, "Science as Solidarity," in J. Nelson, A. Megill, & D. McCloskey, eds., The Rhetoric of the Human Sciences 38, 43 (1987). See also, Matilal, "Ethical Relativism and Confrontation of Cultures," M. Krausz, ed., Relativism: Interpretation and Confrontation 339, 352 (1989).

5. B. Williams, Ethics and the Limits of Philosophy 158 (1985). Cf. Rorty, "Solidarity or Objectivity," in J. Rajchman & C. West, eds., Post-Analytic Philosophy 3, 8–9 (1985) ("[A]lternative cultures are not to be thought of on the model of alternative geometries. Alternative geometries are irreconcilable because they have axiomatic structures, and contradictory axioms. They are *designed* to be irreconcilable. Cultures are not so designed, and do not have axiomatic structures."); Matilal, note 4, at 356.

6. See chapter 3, note 3.

7. S. Toulmin, R. Rieke, & A. Janik, An Introduction to Reasoning 165 (2d ed. 1984).

8. See A. MacIntyre, After Virtue 6 et seq. (1981).

9. See D. Tracy, Plurality and Ambiguity: Hermeneutics, Religion, Hope 112 (1987):

> The interpretations of [religious] believers will, of course, be grounded in some fundamental trust in, and loyalty to, the Ultimate Reality both disclosed and concealed in one's own religious tradition. But fundamental trust,

as any experience of friendship can teach, is not immune to either criticism or suspicion. A religious person will ordinarily fashion some hermeneutics of trust, even one of friendship and love, for the religious classics of her or his tradition. But, as any genuine understanding of friendship shows, friendship often demands both critique and suspicion. A belief in a pure and innocent love is one of the less happy inventions of the romantics. A friendship that never includes critique and even, when appropriate, suspicion is a friendship barely removed from the polite and wary communication of strangers. As Buber showed, in every I-Thou encounter, however transient, we encounter some new dimension of reality. But if that encounter is to prove more than transitory, the difficult ways of friendship need a trust powerful enough to risk itself in critique and suspicion. To claim that this may be true of all our other loves but not true of our love for, and trust in, our religious tradition makes very little sense either hermeneutically or religiously.

10. See p. 41.

11. But cf. section IV of this chapter, in which I discuss the establishment clause of the First Amendment.

12. See M. Stackhouse, Creeds, Society, and Human Rights: A Study in Three Cultures, chs. 2–4 (1984).

13. 20 Origins 133, 135 (1990).

14. J. Coleman, An American Strategic Theology 186 (1982).

15. For Coleman's critical comments on "the tradition of classic republican theory", see Coleman, "A Possible Role for Biblical Religion in Public Life," in Hollenbach, eds., "Theology and Philosophy in Public: A Symposium on John Courtney's Murray's Unfinished Agenda," 40 Theological Studies 701, 702–3 (1979); J. Coleman, note 14, at 186–87.

16. Id. at 192–93. Coleman first presented his argument in the context of a 1979 symposium devoted to "re-examining one of [John Courtney] Murray's central methodological convictions: that the [Catholic] Church's contribution to public ethical discourse in America will be most responsible and persuasive if it is formulated in the categories of philosophical reason rather than expressed in the symbols of religious belief." Hollenbach, note 15, at 700. Coleman's contribution to the symposium—"A Possible Role for Biblical Religion in Public Life", in id. at 701—was the basis for his later, more elaborate argument in J. Coleman, note 14, ch. 9: "American Culture and Religious Ethics". This was the general question, more or less, debated in the Murray symposium:

> When a member or representative of a religious community—or simply someone with religious convictions, even if he is not a member of a religious community—enters the public square to address a controversial political issue, what "language" should he speak: the language of his own religious-moral convictions or, instead, some less sectarian, more secular language?

The problem of what language to speak—religious or secular—is a problem for any religious community that would speak in the public square, or for any religious person who would. The related challenge of developing a mediating language—a language that mediates between the sectarian language of a religious community and the secular language of the larger, pluralistic society—is a challenge for any religious community (or person) that would speak in the public square.

Catholic moral theology has traditionally sought to speak a language—the language of "natural law"—that it claimed to be accessible to and valid for human reason generally, as distinct from a language accessible only to members of a particular community of faith, somehow graced by revelation. Protestant moral theology has traditionally preferred to speak the language of scripture. See Coleman, note 15, at 704:

> American Catholic social thought in general and [John Courtney] Murray in particular appealed generously to the American liberal tradition of public philosophy and the classic understanding of republican virtue embedded in the medieval synthesis. Curiously, however, they were very sparing in invoking biblical religion and the prophetic tradition in their efforts to address issues of public policy.
>
> There are two reasons for this Catholic reluctance to evoke biblical imagery in public discourse. Much of the public religious rhetoric for American self-understanding was couched in a particularist Protestant form which excluded a more generously pluralistic understanding of America. Perhaps one reason why American Catholics and Jews have never conceived of the American proposition as a covenant—even a broken one—was because Protestant covenant thought tended in practice to exclude the new immigrants. Hence, for American Catholics as for Jews, more "secular" Enlightenment forms and traditions promised inclusion and legitimacy in ways Protestant evangelical imagery foreclosed. As Murray states it, the Protestant identification with America led to "Nativism in all its manifold forms, ugly and refined, popular and academic, fanatic and liberal. The neo-Nativist as well as the paleo-Nativist addresses to the Catholic substantially the same charge: 'You are among us but not of us.' "
>
> . . . [Murray] made no religious claims for the founding act of America as such. Catholics, decidedly, were not here in force when the Puritans and their God made a covenant with the land. Nor were they ever conspicuously invited to join the covenant. They preferred, therefore, a less religious, more civil understanding of America.
>
> The second reason for Catholic predilection for the two traditions of republican theory and liberal philosophy is the Catholic recognition of the need for secular warrant for social claims in a pluralist society. This penchant is rooted in Catholic natural-law thought.

For a variety of reasons, in the period since the Second Vatican Council (1962–65) Catholic moral theology has been more willing to speak the language of scripture (as well as the language of natural law). In the United States this change has perhaps been most dramatically evident in the two letters issued by the National Conference of Catholic Bishops on, respectively, nuclear deterrence (1983) and the U.S. economy (1986). See National Conference of Catholic Bishops, Challenge of Peace: God's Promise and Our Response (1983); National Conference of Catholic Bishops, Economic Justice for All: Catholic Social Teaching and the U.S. Economy

(1986). The issue joined in the Murray symposium was whether the language of scripture, and other religious language, belongs in the public square—and, if so, to what extent and in what ways. As the editor of the symposium framed the question: "How particularistic or how universalistic should the Christian contribution to American social thought be?" Hollenbach, note 15, at 713.

17. J. Coleman, note 14, at 193–94. Coleman adds: "I am further strongly convinced that the Enlightenment desire for an unmediated universal fraternity and language (resting as it did on unreflected allegiance to *very particular* communities and language, conditioned by time and culture) was destructive of the lesser, real 'fraternities'—in [Wilson Carey] McWilliams' sense—in American life." Id. at 194.

18. Id. For those who mistakenly think that "religious" = "sectarian", see Baer, "The Supreme Court's Discriminatory Use of the Term 'Sectarian'," 6 J. L. & Politics 449 (1990).

19. J. Coleman, note 14, at 194–95.

20. Id. at 195, 197. Cf. U.S. Catholic Conference Administrative Board, "Political Responsibility: Choices for the Future," 17 Origins 370, 372 (1987): "The application of Gospel values to real situations is an essential work of the Christian community. Christians believe the Gospel is the measure of human realities. However, specific political proposals do not in themselves constitute the Gospel."

21. Cf. J. Cobb, Jr., & C. Ives, eds., The Emptying God: A Buddhist-Jewish-Christian Conversation (1990); H. Coward, ed., Hindu-Christian Dialogue: Perspectives and Encounters (1989); E. Tooker, ed., Native North American Spirituality of the Eastern Woodlands (1979).

22. See pp. 41, 81.

23. Cf. Kymlicka, "Liberal Individualism and Liberal Neutrality," 99 Ethics 883, 899–905 (1989). I will discuss elsewhere the relation of the institution/practice of judicial review in constitutional cases to dialogic politics. See M. Perry, The Constitution in the Courts (forthcoming).

24. R. Beiner, note 2, at 152.

25. See pp. 39–41.

26. See Rabkin, "Disestablished Religion in America," 86 Public Interest 124, 124–25 (Winter 1987):

> Religion may help people to develop the self-restraint required by a constitutional democracy. "Our Constitution was designed for a religious and moral people and for no other" was how John Adams put it. But such formulations, gratifying as they may be to the American self-image, tend to obscure an important fact about "religion": Not every kind of religion is compatible with a liberal constitutional order. The stability of our constitutional order owes much to the fact that the dominant religious tendencies through most of American history have, in fact, been quite compatible with liberal democracy and religious tolerance and have not, by and large, forced people to make wrenching choices between religious and civil obligations.

For an argument that "[t]here is . . . a deep connection between Christianity and liberalism", see Siedentop, "Liberalism: The Christian Connection," Times Literary Supp., Mar. 24–30, 1989, at 308. "The former provides, historically and normatively, the foundation for the latter. It is unfortunate, even dangerous, that the West is so little conscious of this connection. For it cuts Western culture off from its roots, and weakens both its ability and inclincation to defend its own values." Id. See also G. Tinder, The Political Meaning of Christianity (1990). Cf. Mayer, "The Trouble with the ACLU," Progressive, Feb. 1980, at 48, 50: "This habitual association [of the ACLU] with the unloved and forgotten of the world suggests to me, and to my amazement, a profoundly religious, and profoundly Christian, well-spring in a rigorously secular institution. After all these decades of unrelenting struggle to maintain the separation of church and state, what a shock it would be to the ACLU to discover it itself is a church, moved to care for the uncared-for by a power which exceeds its nature and ours."

27. See chapter 5, note 56.

28. See Roelofs, "Liberation Theology: The Recovery of Biblical Radicalism," 82 American Political Science Rev. 549 (1988).

29. R. Beiner, note 2, at 142–143, 146 (passages rearranged).

30. John Rawls has recently suggested the possibility of a "political conception of justice" supported by "an overlapping consensus". See p. 27. My suggestion that various values or premises are authoritative for us as Americans—constitutional premises about the proper relation between human beings and their government and religious premises about, for example, our responsibility for one another's basic well-being—has an obvious affinity with a Rawlsian strategy of identifying normative materials, concerning political morality, supported by a wide consensus. I'm not suggesting, however, that the constitutional and religious premises can support a full-blown, systematically elaborated "political conception of justice"— or, if they can, that they can support only one such conception. (I'm not denying it either.)

31. See Solum, "On the Indeterminacy Crisis: Critiquing Critical Dogma," 54 U. Chicago L. Rev. 462 (1987).

32. See note 20 and accompanying text.

33. MacIntyre, "Does Applied Ethics Rest on a Mistake?," 67 Monist 498, 510 (1984). See H. McCloskey & A. Brill, Dimensions of Tolerance: What Americans Believe about Civil Liberties 48–58 (1983); Prothro & Grigg, "Fundamental Principles of Democracy: Bases of Agreement and Disagreement," 22 J. Politics 276 (1960).

34. R. Beiner, note 2, at 141. See also J. Murray, note 1, at 11: "The whole premise of the public argument, if it is to be civilized and civilizing, is that the consensus is real, that among the people everything is not in doubt, but that there is a core of agreement, concurrence, acquiescence. We hold certain truths; therefore we can argue about them. . . . There can be no argument, except on the premise, and within a context, of agreement. *Mutatis mutandi,* this is true of scientific, philosophical, and theological argument. It is no less true of political argument." Cf. Beiner, note 2, at 138–44.

35. See M. Perry, Morality, Politics, and Law 33–36 (1988).

36. See R. Dworkin, Law's Empire 72–73 (1986).

37. See S. Hauerwas, A Community of Character 60 (1981): "A community is a group of persons who share a history and whose common set of interpretations

about that history provides the basis for common actions. These interpretations may be quite diverse and controversial even within the community, but are sufficient to provide individual members with the sense that they are more alike than unalike."

38. D. Levine, The Flight from Ambiguity 42–43 (1985).

39. Id. at 43. See id. at 41–43.

40. Pitkin, "Justice: On Relating Public and Private," 9 Political Theory 327, 344. See id. at 344–45 (1981):

> Kant suggests something analogous in his concept of moral autonomy: that we are not mature as moral actors until we have become self-governing, have learned to take responsibility not only for our actions but also for the norms and principles according to which we act. As long as we live only by habit or tradition, unaware that they mask an implicit choice, there is something about ourselves as actors in the world that we are not seeing and for which we are not acknowledging our responsibility. . . . Kant even speaks of 'law-making' here, but he is speaking metaphorically. . . . Aristotelian citizenship goes beyond Kant's concept of moral autonomy: it is concerned not merely with metaphorical legislation enacted by the individual, but with the actual experience of making, applying, and changing the norms by which the community lives through public deliberation, debate, and action.

41. See pp. 9–10.

42. I'm not suggesting that such indeterminacy doesn't serve other, less salutary functions. For example, the indeterminacy of shared norms tends to obscure the extent to which, and thus facilitates denial or repression of the fact that, dissensus permeates a society.

43. See note 5 and accompanying text.

44. Hinman, "Can a Form of Life Be Wrong?," 58 Philosophy 339, 349–51 (1983).

45. D. Lochhead, The Dialogical Imperative: A Christian Reflection on Interfaith Encounter 67 (1988).

46. Perhaps the cognitive/affective distinction is misleading; perhaps it is better to understand our cognitive capacities as including our affective capacities. A rational/affective distinction seems similarly problematic (is it the same distinction?). Whatever terms we use to mark it, the difference in question is between our analytic capacities and our affective capacities.

47. The traits I discuss in this section are virtues *relative to the practice of ecumenical political dialogue.*

48. See Hehir, "Responsibilities and Temptations of Power: A Catholic View," unpublished ms. (1988). Cf. H. Coward, Pluralism: Challenge to World Religions 107 (1985).

49. Hehir, note 48. Cf. Swidler, "Interreligious and Interideologocal Dialogue: The Matrix for All Systematic Reflection Today," in L. Swidler, ed., Toward a Universal Theology of Religion 5, 15–16 (1987).

50. Cf. Swidler, note 49, at 16: "Each participant . . . must attempt to experience the [conversation] partner's religion or ideology 'from within.' A religion or

ideology is not merely something of the head, but also of the spirit, heart, and 'whole being,' individual and communal."

51. Lovin, "Empiricism and Christian Social Thought," Annual of Society of Christian Ethics 25, 41 (1982).

52. See B. Barber, Strong Democracy: Participatory Politics for a New Age 174, 175–76 (1984):

> [T]alk as communication obviously involves receiving as well as expressing, hearing as well as speaking, and empathizing as well as uttering. The liberal reduction of talk to speech has unfortunately inspired political institutions that foster the articulation of interests but that slight the difficult art of listening. . . .
>
> "I will listen" means to the strong democrat not that I will scan my adversary's position for weakness and potential trade-offs. . . . It means, rather, "I will put myself in his place, I will try to understand, I will strain to hear what makes us alike, I will listen for a common rhetoric evocative of a common purpose or a common good." . . .
>
> The empathetic listener becomes more like his interlocutor as the two bridge the differences between them by conversation and mutual understanding. Indeed, one measure of healthy political talk is the amount of *silence* it permits and encourages, for silence is the precious medium in which reflection is nurtured and empathy can grow. Without it, there is only the babble of raucous interests and interests vying for the deaf ears of impatient adversaries. . . . The Quaker meeting carries a message for . . . [liberals], but they are often too busy articulating their interests to hear it.

53. See Swidler, note 49, at 14.

54. D. Tracy, note 9, at 19 (quoting B. Lonergan, Method in Theology 231 [1972]). Cf. D. Tracy, this note, at 26–27: "[A]rguments on ideal-speech conditions are transcendental in the sense that they claim to provide the necessary conditions for a contingent situation, namely, the implicit claim to validity in all communication. This is a claim to contingent, not absolute, necessity. By contrast, transcendental arguments on the existence or nonexistence of the universe or God are strictly transcendental arguments. Communication could be other than it is, but in fact is not. We reason discursively. We inquire. We converse. We argue. We are human beings, not angels."

55. See H. Putnam, The Many Faces of Realism 77 (1987).

56. See Swidler, note 49, at 15–16. On self-critical rationality, see pp. 59–62.

57. See chapter 3, note 3 (Coward quote). Cf. Hick, "Religious Pluralism and Absolute Claims," in L. Rouner, ed., Religious Pluralism 193, 194 (1984). A principal participant in contemporary interreligious dialogue, Raimundo Panikkar (a Catholic priest immersed in both Hinduism and Buddhism), has written that "the very nature of truth is pluralistic." Panikkar, "Religious Pluralism: The Metaphysical Challenge," in L. Rouner, this note, at 97, 98.

58. R. Geuss, The Idea of a Critical Theory 53–54 (1981).

59. Davis, "Religion and the Making of Society," 81 Northwestern U. L. Rev. 718, 728 (1987).

60. Id. at 729–30. See also D. Tracy, note 9, at 83–84: "Despite their own sin and ignorance, the religions, at their best, always bear extraordinary powers of resistance. When not domesticated as sacred canopies for the status quo nor wasted by their own self-contradictory grasps at power, the religions live by resisting. The chief resistance of religions is to more of the same."

61. Cf. Cobb, "The Meaning of Pluralism for Christian Self-Understanding," in L. Rouner, note 57, at 161, 174–75:

> In faithfulness to Christ I must be open to others. When I recognize in those others something of worth and importance that I have not derived from my own tradition, I must be ready to learn even if that threatens my present beliefs. I cannot predetermine what the content of that learning will be or preestablish categories within which to appropriate it. I cannot predetermine how radical the effects of that learning will be. I cannot predetermine that there are some beliefs or habits of mind which I will safeguard at all costs. I cannot even know that, when I have learned what I have to learn here and been transformed by it, I will still see faithfulness to Christ as my calling. I cannot predetermine that I will be a Christian at all. That is what I mean by full openness. In faithfulness to Christ I must be prepared to give up even faithfulness to Christ. If that is where I am led, to remain a Christian would be to become an idolater in the name of Christ. That would be blasphemy.

See also Swidler, note 49, at 6.

62. Hehir, "The Perennial Need for Philosophic Discourse," in Hollenbach, note 15, at 710, 710. Hehir, with Coleman, David Hollenbach, and Robin Lovin, was a participant in the Murray symposium discussed in note 16.

63. Id. at 711 (emphasis added). See id. at 711–12: "The pluralism . . . is radically complicated when the debate about human rights and human needs is cast in a global framework. Correlatively, the need for a systemic theory of justice, encompassing the range of human rights contained in both U.N. covenants, poses problems for articulating such a theory in theological terms. If the theory must create a common ground of discourse, it is difficult to see how the effort will be advanced by retaining in an explicit way those images which are derived from the specific insights of faith."

64. See note 16. Hehir's focus in the Murray symposium (see note 16), however, was not moral-theological discourse either generally or even in the Church itself, but the Church's political-moral discourse in the public square.

65. Recall, in that regard, David Tracy's compelling reflection on the fundamental importance to theology of a "hermeneutic of suspicion". See chapter 5, note 42.

66. U.S. Catholic Conference Administrative Board, note 20, at 371 (emphasis added).

67. Lovin, "Why the Church Needs the World: Faith, Realism, and the Public Life," unpublished ms. (1988 Sorenson Lecture, Yale Divinity School). Lovin's essay is an elegantly thoughtful argument in support of what I am here calling external deliberation.

68. Cf. Hollenbach, note 15, at 714: "[T]he degree to which the received religious tradition of the Church needs correction or revision in light of secular

knowledge and contemporary social experience is . . . a question for fundamental theology."

69. Davis, note 59, at 729. See id.: "[Religious people] must refrain from using any weapons to advance their beliefs other than the force of the better argument."

70. Id.

71. D. Hollenbach, Justice, Peace, and Human Rights 6 (1988). Referring to "a crisis of moral reason", Hollenbach warns that "[i]t has become increasingly difficult to sustain the natural-law tradition's robust confidence that intelligent exercise of reason by persons in different social locations, from diverse cultures, and with differing intellectual backgrounds will lead to identical conclusions about the way society should be organized." Id.

72. See Gedicks, "Some Political Implications of Religious Belief," 4 Notre Dame J. L., Ethics, & Public Policy 419, 441 & n. 95 (1990).

73. J. Murray, note 1, at 14.

74. See, e.g., Macedo, "The Politics of Justification," 18 Political Theory 280, 281 (1990): "The [justificatory] reasons must be *public* in the sense of being widely and openly accessible; appeals to inner convictions or faith, special insight, secret information, or very difficult forms of reasoning are ruled out."

75. For a defense of "the requirement of public reason" on the basis of "the argument for the need for stability", see Solum, "Faith and Justice," 39 DePaul U. L. Rev. 1083, 1095–97 (1990).

76. Id. at 1096. Solum is stating the argument, not endorsing it. Indeed, Solum is wary of the argument. See id. at 1096–97. Solum cites, as an instance of the argument, Carter, "The Religiously Devout Judge," 64 Notre Dame L. Rev. 932, 939 (1989). Cf. J. Murray, note 1, at 23–24 (counseling wariness about "project[ing] into the future of the Republic the nightmares, real or fancied, of the past.").

77. For such an argument, see Solum, note 75, at 1092–95.

78. For development of the point, see W. Galston, Liberal Purposes: Goods, Virtues, and Diversity in the Liberal State, ch. 5 (forthcoming, 1991); see also J. Finnis, Natural Law and Natural Rights 221–22 (1980); G. Dworkin, "Equal Respect and the Enforcement of Morality," 7 Social Philosophy & Policy 180 (1990). Solum acknowledges the point, but in my view fails to rebut it, in Solum, note 75, at 1093, n. 32.

79. E Schillebeeckx, The Schillebeeckx Reader 263 (R. Schreiter ed. 1984).

80. See note 16.

81. Hehir, note 48. (Hehir is obviously more sympathetic here than he was in the Murray symposium to the sort of position John Coleman has espoused, in which "religious insight and argument" are central rather than marginal to, even excluded from, public political argument.) The drafters of *The Williamsburg Charter* articulated a similar contention: "Arguments for public policy should be more than private convictions shouted out loud. For persuasion to be principled, private convictions should be translated into publicly accessible claims. Such public claims should be made publicly accessible for two reasons: first, because they must engage those who do not share the same private convictions, and second, because they should be directed toward the common good." The Williamsburg Charter: A National Celebration and Reaffirmation of the First Amendment Religious Liberty

Clauses 22 (1988). See also Neuhhaus, "Nihilism without the Abyss: Law, Rights, and Transcendent Good," 5 J. L. & Religion 53, 62 (1987): "[P]ublicly assertive religious forces will have to learn that the remedy for the naked public square is not naked religion in public. They will have to develop a mediating language by which ultimate truths can be related to the penultimate and prepenultimate questions of political and legal contest." In quoting this passage, Stanley Hauerwas writes that "[r]ather than condemning the Moral Majority, Neuhaus seeks to help them enter the public debate by basing their appeals on principles that are accessible to the public." Hauerwas, "A Christian Critique of Christian America," in J. Pennock & J. Chapman, eds., Religion, Morality, and the Law 110, 118 (1988). But, as I have tried to suggest in this section of the chapter, there is more—much more—to participating in ecumenical political dialogue than simply making one's (dogmatic?) claims more accessible to the public.

82. Indeed, "there may be more disagreement. But at least we would know what we are disagreeing about, namely, different accounts of the transcendent good by which we might order our life together." Neuhaus, note 81, at 62.

83. Cf. D. Hollenbach, note 71, at 9 (commenting on the dangers of "religious imperialism or theological triumphalism"), 11: "[T]he fact that the [Catholic C]hurch's social mission has become more immediately grounded in biblical and theological perspectives since the [Second Vatican C]ouncil may intensify the temptation to move in this direction. In order to avoid this danger it is important to note how the council sought to counter the privatization of Christian faith without falling into the ecclesiastical triumphalism of the integralist theology."

84. Bernardin, "The Consistent Ethic of Life after *Webster*," 19 Origins 741, 748 (1990).

85. Cf. Baer, note 18.

86. J. Coleman, note 14, at 196. See Marty, "When My Virtue Doesn't Match Your Virtue," 105 Christian Century 1094, 1096 (1988): "[R]eligionists who do not invoke the privileged insights of their revelation or magisterium can enhance and qualify rationality with community experience, intuition, attention to symbol, ritual, and narrative. Of course, these communities and their spokespersons argue with one another. But so do philosophical rationalists."

87. Cf. Mitchell, "Should Law Be Christian?," Law & Justice, no. 96/97 (1988), at 12, 21:

> But, the objection may be pressed, can a religious body argue its case in a secular forum (i.e., one that is not already antecedently committed to the religion in question)? Either, it may be said, it will rely on Christian premises, which *ex hypothesi* opponents will not accept; or it will employ purely secular premises, in which case the ensuing law will not be Christian. In neither case will any genuine debate have taken place between Christians and non-Christians. The dichotomy, however, is altogether too neat to be convincing. It presupposes that there is and always must be a complete discontinuity between Christian and secular reasoning. Certainly this can occur—if, for example, the Christian is an extreme fundamentalist and the secular thinker regards individual preferences as the sole basis for morality.

But in the sort of Western society we have in mind, the moral intuitions of those who are not religiously committed have been influenced by centuries of Christianity, and the mainline Christian churches have for some time been at pains to take account of developments in the human sciences and in the humanities which bear upon the interpretation of Christian doctrine. In a period during which the narrowness of the official churches has often driven genuinely Christian developments into other channels, it is not in fact all that easy to determine which ideas are of purely secular origin. But, these cultural reflections apart, Christians would presumably want to argue (at least, many of them would) that the Christian revelation does not require us to interpret the nature of man in ways for which there is otherwise no warrant but rather affords a deeper understanding of man as he essentially is. If that is so, there is room for a genuine exchange of ideas.

88. From a transcript of a panel discussion, published in 5 J. L. & Religion 95, 103 (1988). For a profound essay on appropriating traditions, or aspects of traditions, not one's own, see J. Dunne, The Way of All the Earth: Experiments in Truth and Religion (1972).

89. Cf. D. Hollenbach, note 71, at 9 (on the importance of distinguishing the Church's "social mission from religious imperialism or theological triumphalism").

90. D. Tracy, note 9, at 88.

91. Id. at 88–89.

92. See note 19 and accompanying text. Cf. Robinson, "Religious Discourse and the Reinvigoration of American Political Life," 4 Notre Dame J. L., Ethics & Society 385, 392 (1990):

> Lincoln [in the Gettysburg Address] does not require his hearers to believe that Jesus rose from the dead, or even that the dead shall themselves rise. This is the domain of religious belief, and, being not responsive to volition, the state should not (because it cannot) require it of anyone. What Lincoln does do, however, is to invite his hearers to integrate their faith with their political experience, to illuminate the latter by reference to the former, and to invigorate the former by way of its contact with the latter. For Lincoln, the whole universe of religious discourse was admissible in political speech. We should be as free to convey political convictions in religious imagery as Lincoln was.

93. Burtchaell, "The Source of Conscience," 13 Notre Dame Mag. 20, 20–21 (Winter 1984–85). For a fuller excerpt of Burtchaell's comments, see chapter 5, note 49 and accompanying text.

94. See Audi, "Religion and the Ethics of Political Participation," 100 Ethics 386, 396 (1990): "[C]itizens are to do their best to resolve public policy questions, especially when they concern what coercive laws to have, by seeking adequate secular reasons for a solution; and while religious or any other kinds of factors can enter into the discussion, final resolution to adopt a policy should be warranted by secular considerations and set forth as so justified."

Given that public accessibility is a constitutive virtue of ecumenical political dialogue, it seems that my position on the proper place of religious premises about the human in American public life and the position espoused by David Richards (in his review of Kent Greenawalt's *Religious Convictions and Political Choice* [1988]) are quite close. See Richards, Book Review, 23 Georgia L. Rev. 1189, 1198–1200 (1989).

95. See pp. 17–18.

96. Cf. Greenawalt, "Religious Convictions and Political Choice: Some Further Thoughts," 39 DePaul L. Rev. 1019, 1043 n. 65.

97. The establishment clause is a part of the First Amendment to the United States Constitution; it is, indeed, the first clause of the First Amendment and, therefore, of the Bill of Rights. The second clause of the First Amendment/Bill of Rights forbids government to make any law "prohibiting the free exercise" of religion. The establishment clause and the free exercise clause, as it is called, constitute what has been termed "the first liberty": religious liberty. See W. Miller, The First Liberty: Religion and the American Republic (1985).

The First Amendment applies, by itself, only to the federal government. However, the religion clauses of the First Amendment, like the rest of the First Amendment, including the clauses protecting freedom of speech and freedom of the press, do apply to the governments of the fifty states, because, according to the Supreme Court, those clauses were made applicable to the states by section one of the Fourteenth Amendment, which by its very terms applies to state government. Although that interpretation of section one of the Fourteenth Amendment has been controversial, the interpretation is now a securely established feature of American constitutional law.

98. See generally J. Nowak, R. Rotunda, & J. Young, Constitutional Law, ch. 17 (3d ed. 1986); L. Tribe, American Constitutional Law, ch. 14 (2d ed. 1988); Note, "Developments in the Law—Religion and the State," 100 Harvard L. Rev. 1606 (1987).

99. For a different view, see the dissenting opinion of Chief Justice Rehnquist in *Wallace v. Jaffree,* 472 U.S. 38, 91 (1985).

100. See chapter 5, note 8 and accompanying text.

101. See Smith, "Separation and the 'Secular': Reconstructing the Disestablishment Decision," 67 Texas L. Rev. 955 (1989). Cf. Catholic Bishops of Ohio, "Statement on Abortion and Political Life," 19 Origins 499, 500 (1989): "In an earlier day, religious and moral principles led us to confront the issues of slavery and civil rights for minorities. In our day, are they to be excluded as we confront such issues as housing for the poor, access to health care and equal treatment for the handicapped?"

102. See chapter 5, note 49 and accompanying text.

103. Lemon v. Kurtzman, 403 U.S. 602, 612 (1971). For an impressive critique of the "secularist" (v. "separationist") understanding of the establishment clause, see Smith, note 101.

104. K. Greenawalt, Religious Convictions and Political Choice 94 (1988).

105. See id., ch. 5: "Inappropriate Grounds of Restriction: Consenting Sexual Acts as Sins".

106. Id. at 94–95.

107. See Smith, note 101, at 1003: "Nearly all religious beliefs and practices have temporal consequences that attract favor for earthly reasons."

108. Mitchell, note 87, at 21.

109. See Roe v. Wade, 410 U.S. 113 (1973). The due process clause of the Fourteenth Amendment forbids state government to "deprive any person of life, liberty, or property, without due process of law".

110. I have myself made such an argument: M. Perry, note 35, at 172–78. The equal protection clause forbids state government to "deny to any person within its jurisdiction the equal protection of the laws".

111. See Harris v. McRae, 448 U.S. 297, 319–20 (1980). After finishing this book I encountered a provocative argument that abortions before the end of the twentieth week of pregnancy are constitutionally privileged under the establishment clause. See P. Wenz, Abortion Rights as Religious Freedom (forthcoming, 1991). Though I do not agree with Professor Wenz's establishment clause argument, his thoughtful book is well worth reading. See also Dow, "The Establishment Clause Argument for Choice," 20 Golden Gate U. L. Rev. 479 (1990).

112. See Tribe, "A Nation Held Hostage," New York Times, July 2, 1990, at A13 (op-ed page): "[T]he fetus is alive. It belongs to the human species. It elicits sympathy and even love, in part because it is so dependent and helpless."

113. Catholic Bishops of the United States, "Resolution on Abortion," 19 Origins 395 (1989). See also McHugh, "Political Responsibility and Respect for Life," 19 Origins 460 (1989).

114. Catholic Bishops of Wisconsin, "A Consistent Ethic of Life," 19 Origins 461, 462 (1989).

115. May, "Faith and Moral Teaching in a Democratic Nation," 19 Origins 385, 388 (1989).

116. Bernardin, note 84, at 746. See also Myers, "Obligations of Catholics and Rights of Unborn Children," 20 Origins 65, 68 (1990); O'Connor, "Abortion: Questions and Answers," 20 Origins 97 (1990). Cf. Roach, "War of Words on Abortion," 20 Origins 88, 89 (1990) (responding to the accusation that a call for restrictive abortion legislation is a call to "legislate morality"): "That's not a new argument. In the heat of the civil rights debate, Martin Luther King Jr. was accused on wanting to legislate morality. He replied that the law could not make people love their neighbors, but it could stop their lynching them."

117. See Simmons, "Religious Liberty and the Abortions Debate," 32 J. Church & State 567–572 (1990).

118. See chapter 5, note 8 and accompanying text.

119. See p. 9.

120. See chapter 5, note 49 and accompanying text.

121. See Karen G. Gervais, "Reply to Professor Greenawalt" (unpublished paper delivered to Third Annual Conference on Law, Religion, and Ethics, October 25–26, 1990, Hamline University School of Law). Cf. Wiggins, "Truth, Invention, and the Meaning of Life," 1976 Proceedings of British Academy 331.

122. See. T. Nagel, What Does It All Mean? ch. 10 "The Meaning of Life"). Cf. B. Ackerman, Social Justice in the Liberal State 368 (1980): "There is no meaning in the bowels of the universe."

123. Greenawalt, note 96, at 1032 (emphasis added).

124. See p. 9.

125. See chapter 5, note 000 and accompanying text. Cf. Clark, "With Rationality and Love," Times Literary Supp., Sept, 26, 1986, at 1047, (review of R. Dawkins, The Blind Watchmaker [1985]): "[A]theists and unthinking media-managers are unconsciously conspiring with naive 'fundamentalists' to paint a ridiculous picture of theism that all great Doctors of the Church would have spurned as idolatry."

126. Id.

127. On religious fundamentalism, see T. O'Meara, Fundamentalism: A Catholic Perspective (1990). Cf. R. Brown, The Critical Meaning of the Bible (1981).

128. See notes 15 and 16 and accompanying text.

129. See note 16. For an example of dialogue precipitated by the bishops' letter on the economy, see C. Strain, ed., Prophetic Visions and Economic Realities: Protestants, Jews, and Catholics Confront the Bishops's Letter on the Economy (1989).

130. In *Cruzan* a majority of the United States Supreme Court ruled that a person's right to refuse life-sustaining medical treatment (e.g., intravenous nutrition and hydration) is a part of the "liberty" protected against deprivation "without due process of law" by section one of the Fourteenth Amendment. (A majority of the Court also ruled that in acting as it did, Missouri had not deprived Nancy Cruzan of her right in violation of the due process clause.) Briefs (some supporting Nancy Cruzan, some supporting Missouri) were submitted by the Evangelical Lutheran Church in America, the United States Catholic Conference, Agudath Israel of America, and the United Methodist Church.

It is one thing for legislators, and the citizens they represent, to rely on religious-moral premises in deliberating about, making, and justifying political choices. But what about judges: To what extent and in what way, if any, is it ever appropriate for judges to rely on religious-moral premises in deliberating about, deciding, and justifying their decisions in the cases before them? See Carter, note 76, esp. at 943–44. Professor Carter's answer, which I find congenial, is based on a view of the proper relation of religion to politics much like the one I elaborate and defend in this book. For a different answer, based on an ideal of political justification much like the one I criticize in chapter 1, see Solum, note 75.

131. Murray and Bernardin are quoted in Unsworth, "Seamless Garment Shredded," National Catholic Reporter, Dec. 20, 1985, at 8.

132. Foot, "Moral Relativism," in J. Meiland & M. Krausz, eds., Relativism: Cognitive and Moral 152, 164 (1982). For Foot's perceptive explanation why "relativists, and subjectivists generally," are not able to take the whole journey, see id. at 165–66.

133. R. Beiner, note 2, at 186 n. 17.

134. H. Arendt, The Human Condition 9 (1959). See Canovan, "Friendship, Truth, and Politics: Hannah Arendt and Toleration," in S. Mendus, ed., Justifying Toleration: Conceptual and Historical Perspectives 177, 177 (1988); Canovan, "Arendt, Rousseau, and Human Plurality in Politics," 45 J. Politics 286 (1983).

135. See Walzer, "A Critique of Philosophical Conversation," 21 Philosophical Forum 182 (1989–90).

136. See p. 100.

137. J. Murray, note 1, at 24. (Where Murray wrote "informed men" I have substituted "informed persons".)

138. Canovan, "Friendship, Truth, and Politics: Hannah Arendt and Toleration," in S. Mendus, note 134, at 198.

139. Id. (Where Canovan says "debate" I have substituted "dialogue".)

140. D. Lochhead, note 45, at 79.

141. See pp. 47–51.

142. D. Lochhead, note 45, at 79.

143. On self-critical rationality, see pp. 59–62.

144. See M. Walzer, Interpretation and Social Criticism (1987). For a discussion of the revision of tradition on the basis of tradition (and, analogously, the revision of self on the basis of self), see M. Perry, note 35, at 28–33.

145. M. Walzer, note 144, at 64. See also id. at 64 n. 19. As Roberto Unger has written, "The more a structure of thought or relationship provides for the occasions and instruments of its own revision, the less you must choose between maintaining it and abandoning it for the sake of the things it exludes. You can just remake or reimagine it. . . . Society improves by laying its practical and imaginative order ever more open to correction." R. Unger, Passion: An Essay on Personality 10, 264 (1984).

146. See chapter 1, note 1 and accompanying text.

Chapter 7

1. D. Lochhead, The Dialogical Imperative: A Christian Reflection on Interfaith Encounter 75 (1988). Noting that "not all conversations are dialogue", Lochhead adds: "We might choose to converse with the Klu Klux Klan, for example. [But o]ur conversation would not be dialogue." Id. See also Swidler, "Interreligious and Interideological Dialogue: The Matrix for All Systematic Reflection Today," in L. Swidler, ed., Toward a Universal Theology of Religion 5, 28 (1987). Lochhead develops the distinction between (mere) conversation and dialogue ("dialogue as relationship") in chapter 13 of his book.

2. Smith, "The Restoration of Tolerance," 78 California L. Rev. 305, 306 (1990). For a discussion of the point, which is conceptual, see Mendus, "Introduction," in S. Mendus, ed., Justifying Toleration: Conceptual and Historical Perspectives 3–5 (1988); Warnock, "The Limits of Toleration," in S. Mendus & D. Edwards, eds., On Toleration 123, 126–27 (1987). See also Hampton, "Should Political Philosophy Be Done without Metaphysics?," 99 Ethics 791, 810–11 (1989) (arguing that "there is a difference between tolerance of another's ideas and tolerance of another's holding of these ideas. . . . [T]he principle of toleration requires only the second kind of tolerance, not the first kind."). For a discussion of "false" or "debased tolerance", as distinct from "genuine tolerance", see The Williamsburg Charter: A National Celebration and Reaffirmation of the First Amendment Religious Liberty Clauses 21 (1988).

3. See Smith, note 2, at 334: "Tolerance may seem to be an unstable and perhaps even internally contradictory attitude. Tolerance entails permitting others

to hold and disseminate erroneous beliefs, but since they are . . . wrong, these beliefs represent an evil that individuals and, it would seem, governments should want to combat. If one is convinced that a particular idea is false, practical reason suggests that one should repress that idea. This is the logic of intolerance, which a tolerant regime must overcome."

4. Much of what follows in this and the next section is drawn from M. Perry, Morality, Politics, and Law, ch. 4 (1988).

5. H. Putnam, Reason, Truth and History 148–49 (1981). See id. at 161–62.

6. See generally Harrison, "Relativism and Tolerance," in J. Meiland & M. Krausz, eds., Relativism: Cognitive and Moral 229 (1982). See also J. Raz, The Authority of Law 271 (1979); Scheffler, "Moral Scepticism and Ideals of the Person," 62 Monist 288, 300–301 (1979); Blackburn, "Rule-Following and Moral Realism," in Wittgenstein: To Follow a Rule 163, 176 (S. Holtzman & C. Leich eds. 1981). Cf. Harman, "Human Flourishing, Ethics, and Liberty," 12 Philosophy & Public Affairs 307, 321 (1983): "[We can] condemn other people as evil, bad, or dangerous by our lights, or take them to be our enemies. Nothing prevents us from using our values to judge other people and other moralities. But we only fool ourselves if we think our values give *reasons* to others who do not accept those values." For an example of the second misconception, see Warnock, note 2, at 135.

7. See C. Taylor, Sources of the Self: The Making of the Modern Identity 67–68 (1989).

8. Rorty, "Postmodernist Bourgeois Liberalism," 80 J. Philosophy 583, 589 (1983). See H. Putnam, note 5, at 161–62.

9. There may be, and in the United States there are, constitutional norms governing the decision whether to pursue a coercive political strategy. For example, the First Amendment protects freedom of speech, freedom of the press, and the free exercise of religion.

10. See Popper, "Toleration and Intellectual Responsibility," in S. Mendus & D. Edwards, note 2, at 17, 18.

11. J. S. Mill, On Liberty 74 (E. Rapaport ed. 1978).

12. See p. 100.

13. Cf. chapter 2, note 6 (Putnam quote).

14. Cuomo, "Religious Belief and Public Morality: A Catholic Governor's Perspective," 1 Notre Dame J. L., Ethics & Public Policy 13, 16 (1984).

15. Although to coerce someone to make a choice she does not want to make is to cause her to suffer, it might be to prevent her from suffering, too. To prevent someone from crossing a bridge she believes to be safe but that is in fact unsafe is to prevent her from suffering, even though, at least initially, she suffers the frustration of being stopped from crossing the bridge. Bear in mind that the considerations I am now sketching are *not* being offered as conclusive reasons against coercing someone to make a choice she does not want to make, but merely as reasons. In a given situation, there may well be better reasons for pursuing a coercive strategy, as the unsafe-bridge example suggests.

16. See Canovan, "Friendship, Truth, and Politics: Hannah Arendt and Toleration," in S. Mendus, note 2, at 177, 197–98.

17. Sibley, "Religion and the Law: Some Thoughts on Their Intersections," 2 J.

L. & Religion 41, 53 (1984). See Cranston, in S. Mendus & D. Edwards, note 2, at 101, 104: "[John Locke] insisted that magistrates had 'nothing to do with the good of men's souls'. It was not the magistrate's duty to 'punish every vice'. His only duty was to keep the peace."

18. J. Noonan, Persons and Masks of the Law xii (1976). (Noonan added: "We can often apply force to those we do not see, but we cannot, I think, love them. Only in the response of person to person can Augustine's sublime fusion be achieved, in which justice is defined as 'love serving only the one loved.' " Id.) Cf. McBrien, "The Church and Politics," 1 J. L., Ethics & Public Policy 57, 61 (1984):

> The letter entitled Political Responsibility, issued by the Administrative Board of the United States Catholic Conference in March 1984 [13 Origins 732 (1984)], grounded political involvement in love of neighbor, which goes beyond individual relationships to embrace the entire human community, and in Christ's specific call to reach out and help those in need, which also goes beyond individual relationships to embrace the institutions and structures of society, the economy, and politics. The purpose of such involvement is to promote human rights and to denounce violations of such rights; to call attention to the moral and religious dimensions of secular issues; to keep alive the values of the Gospel as a norm of social and political life; and to point out the demands of Christian faith for a just transformation of society.

19. Boyle, "A Catholic Perspective on Morality and the Law," 1 J. L. & Religion 227, 235, 236 (1983). See id. at 235:

> Given this conception of morality the question arises as to what the purpose might be for seeking to legally proscribe actions which one judges to be immoral. For, surely it is doubtful that such legal proscription can in any efficient way contribute to the moral goal of a person's choosing to do what is right because he or she sees it to be right. Legal enforcement of a prohibition can guarantee only behavioral compliance; it cannot guarantee—and can in many cases do little to promote—the person's making the right choices or making them for the morally appropriate reasons. Fear of punishment might cause a person to comply with a norm—it might even be a motive for choosing to comply with the norm; but it does not contribute and, in fact, may hinder a person's making the choice to conform to the norm precisely because this is judged to be the right thing to do. In fact, even if one judges that obeying the law is the right thing to do—because it is obeying the law—this morally relevant ground for choosing in accord with the law is not the initial moral reason for judging that the action in question should not be done. So, even if there is morally significant compliance with the law the reason could be quite different from the reason the act was morally proscribed in the first place.

As Michael Walzer has recently reminded us, John Locke, too, based his brief for religious tolerance on his (Protestant) theology. See M. Walzer, Interpretation and Social Criticism 52–56 (1987). For a comment on Locke, and a generalization of Locke's point, see Smith, note 2, at 336–38.

20. J. Murray, We Hold These Truths 164 (Image Books ed. 1964).

21. See Smith, note 2, at 342. See also Mitchell, "Should Law Be Christian?." Law & Justice, no. 96/97 (1988), at 12, 17: "No legal system can operate effectively without requiring some people sometimes to act against their consciences or refrain from acting according to them. The most that can be claimed is that lawmakers should avoid, so far as possible, legislating in such a way as to do violence to people's consciences."

22. See Matthew 25:34–40.

23. Boyle, "Positivism, Natural Law, and Disestablishment: Some Questions Raised by MacCormick's Moralistic Amoralism," 20 Valparaiso U. L. Rev. 55, 59 (1985) (quoting T. Aquinas, Summa Theologiae at First Part of the Second Part, Question 96, Article 2). See Mendus, note 2, at 5: "[T]oleration is a good in so far as it is required by the principle of respect for persons. It is, however, also limited by the principle. . . ." For a demonstrative refutation of an extreme conception of tolerance—the libertarian conception—see Raz, "Autonomy, Toleration, and the Harm Principle," in S. Mendus, note 2, at 155.

24. Roach, "War of Words on Abortion," 20 Origins 88, 89 (1990) (responding to the accusation that a call for restrictive abortion legislation is a call to "legislate morality").

25. See B. Mitchell, Law, Morality, and Religion 134 (1967): "The function of the law is not only to protect individuals from harm, but to protect the essential institutions of a society. These functions overlap, since the sorts of harm an individual may suffer are to some extent determined by the institutions he lives under."

26. Cf. Warnock, note 2, at 125 (commenting on John Stuart Mill's failure to address, *inter alia,* the question "Who is to count as a possible object of harm?").

27. The considerations relevant to the issue of tolerance are also relevant to the issue of conscientious disobedience. Put another way, the considerations relevant to the issue of tolerance on the part of those who must decide whether to make, or to maintain, a particular coercive law are also relevant to the issue of tolerance on the part of those must decide whether to obey a particular law, especially a law that requires a person either (a) to do what she believes she morally ought not to do or (b) to refrain from doing what she believes she morally ought to do. Why should we obey laws—what considerations should inform our judgment whether to obey laws—that, in our view, require us to do what is wrong? I have addressed the issue of conscientious disobedience elsewhere: M. Perry, note 4, ch. 5.

28. See pp. 39–41.

29. See p. 92.

30. Of course, some of these values can support a coercive political strategy as well as oppose it. For example, the values of compassion and community support a law criminalizing behavior that causes suffering and destroys community. Consider, in that regard, a law banning racial descrimination. Implicit, I think, in the principal consideration supporting a coercive political strategy (which I am about to discuss) are the values of compassion and community.

31. B. Mitchell, note 25, at 135.

32. See pp. 100–11.

33. Query what significant differences there are, if any, between the value of

"autonomy", which figures so prominently in contemporary political-philosophical literature, and the value articulated by Boyle (note 19 and accompanying text): "making choices that conform to one's [informed] conscience". On autonomy, see generally G. Dworkin, The Theory and Practice of Autonomy (1988).

34. Smith, note 2, at 356.

35. On "deontological" (or Right-prior-to-Good) liberalism, see M. Sandel, Liberalism and the Limits of Justice, esp. 3–4 (1982). Deontological liberalism is neo-Kantian rather than Kantian in character because it "differs from Kant among other things in making no demands on a theory of noumenal freedom, and also, importantly, in admitting considerations of a general empirical kind in determining fundamental moral demands, which Kant at least supposed himself not to be doing." Williams, "Persons, Character, and Morality," in B. Williams, Moral Luck 1, 1 (1981). See also M. Sandel, this note, at 39. The Kantian dimension of such liberalism resides partly in its abstraction from—its annihilation of?—the identities of persons. Kant's view (according to Roger Scruton, a sympathetic interpreter) was that

> [i]f we are to find an imperative that recommends itself on the basis of reason alone, then we must abstract from all the distinctions between rational agents, discounting their interests, desires and ambitions, and all the "empirical conditions" which circumscribe their actions. Only then will we base our law in practical reason alone, since we will have abstracted from any other ground. By this process of abstraction I arrive at the "point of view of a member of the intelligible world." This is a point of view outside my own experience, which could therefore be adopted by any rational being, whatever his circumstances. The law that I formulate will then be an imperative that applies universally, to all rational beings.

R. Scruton, Kant 69 (1982).

The affinity between Kant's view and the view of liberal thinkers like John Rawls (in his early work; see p. 23) is apparent. For them,

> the moral point of view is basically different from a non-moral, and in particular self-interested, point of view, and by a difference of kind; . . . the moral point of view is specially characterized by its impartiality and its indifference to any particular relations to particular persons, and . . . moral thought requires abstraction from particular characteristics of the parties, including the agent, except in so far as these can be treated as universal features of any morally similar situation; and . . . the motivations of a moral agent, correspondingly, involve a rational application of impartial principle and are thus different in kind from the sorts of motivations that he might have for treating some particular persons (for instance, though not exclusively, himself) differently because he happened to have some particular interest towards them.

Williams, this note, at 2.

The Kantian perspective is problematic, as Ronald Beiner, among others, has noted:

Because the rational subject, for Kant, may be viewed from two perspectives, empirical and transcendental, it is always problematical how the transcendental perspective that guides Kant in the three Critiques can be related back to the actual human concerns of knowing, acting, and judging subjects in the phenomenal world. Here we are presented with problems that apply generally within transcendental idealism. If the transcendental subject is a universal subject and if the only way for it to win a rationally compelling basis for its principles of judgment is by ascending to a universal standpoint detached from all contingent empirical conditions, what is it that gives the deliberations of this subject enough determinacy to have any content at all? In the ascent to universality, at what point is one sufficiently distanced from the particular and the contingent to satisfy the transcendental requirement, and what particularities of human experience can be tolerated without this requirement being violated? And if it is through shedding all particularity and contingency that the Kantian subject secures transcendental validity for its judgments, doesn't the standpoint of the transcendental subject turn into no standpoint at all, and isn't the universal self in danger of becoming selfless? How far can the 'enlarged mentality' expand without ceasing to be the possession of an individuated subject retaining its own identity?

R. Beiner, Political Judgment 33–34 (1983). See also R. Scruton, Sexual Desire: A Moral Philosophy of the Erotic 324–25 (1986).

36. On the "teleological" or "naturalist" conception of morality, see M. Perry, note 4, ch. 1; see also chapter 5 of this book, notes 45 & 49.

37. For an elaboration and defense of neo-Aristotelian liberalism (and a critique of neo-Kantian liberalism), see Beiner, "The Moral Vocabulary of Liberalism, Nomos (forthcoming) (arguing "that the moral self-understanding of liberalism would be notably strengthened, both theoretically and practically, if it were to shift from a Kantian discourse of rights and individual autonomy to an Aristotelian discourse of virtues and character formation"). See also Raz, "Liberalism, Skepticism, and Democracy," 74 Iowa L. Rev. 761 (1989). A neo-Aristotelian liberalism does *not* necessarily subscribe to any of Aristotle's particular convictions about human good. See (in addition to Beiner, this note) Nussbaum, "Non-Relative Virtues: An Aristotelian Approach," 13 Midwest Studies in Philosophy 32 (1988).

38. The distinction between neo-Kantian and neo-Aristotelian conceptions of (liberal) politics ought not to be confused with the different distinction between neo-Kantian and neo-Aristotelian conceptions of morality. While a neo-Aristotelian conception of politics would seem to presuppose a neo-Aristotelian conception of morality, a neo-Kantian conception of politics need not be based on a neo-Kantian conception of morality. One could be both neo-Kantian with respect to politics—in particular, with respect to political justification—and neo-Aristotelian with respect to morality: One could believe that morality is fundamentally about human good or well-being (which is the neo-Aristotelian understanding of the subject matter of moral inquiry) but believe as well that conceptions of human good should play no or little role in political justification. See C. Taylor, note 7, at 531–32 n. 60.

Conclusion

1. As I write, Professor Smolin teaches at the Cumberland School of Law of Samford University.

2. I do not want to dispute, in this conclusion, Professor Smolin's understanding of the relevant positions of the various religious groups he lists.

3. See chapter 5, note 2 and accompanying text.

4. Contending, in the course of ecumenical political dialogue, for a fallibilist and/or pluralist attitude or position (when it fits the disputed question to do so) might sometimes require theological deliberation and argument. That would depend on the relevant beliefs of the particular participants in the dialogue. Such argument, like deliberation and argument of other kinds in the course of ecumenical political dialogue, is governed by the criterion of public accessibility, to which I am about to recur.

5. For a provocative argument that under the establishment clause of the First Amendment, infallibilist religious participation in politics should be disfavored relative to fallibilist religious participation, see Conkle, "Religious Purpose, Inerrancy, and the Establishment Clause: Questioning the Principle of Religious Equality," 67 Indiana Law Journal (forthcoming 1991).

6. See pp. 108–9.

7. See p. 106.

8. See Garry Wills, Under God: Religion and American Politics (1990). The introduction and chapter 7 of Wills' book are especially relevant.

9. R. Coles, The Spiritual Life of Children (1990). Aspects of Dr. Coles' book, which was published after I had finished this book, are especially relevant to my discussion of religion in chapter 5.

10. Glendon, "Notes on the Culture Struggle: Dr. [Martin Luther] King in the Law Schools," First Things, Nov. 1990, at 9.

11. Id. 10.

12. A friend, Ruth Colker, who teaches law at Tulane, asked me in a letter:

> Do you assume that introducing religious arguments into American politics would necessarily improve the quality of our present deliberations? If so, don't you need to situate that argument historically and geographically? In Louisana, there is no shortage of religion in politics. We supposedly value life and therefore keep trying to criminalize abortion . . . while we also offer no prenatal care, no sex education, very little welfare benefits, and a high rate of capital punishment. Poor people kill each other over disputes concerning change for a six pack of beer, indicating, to me, their enormous sense of hopelessness about their condition in a state that purports to value life and religion. If I want to talk about social issues in Louisiana, I *must* describe them in religious terms if I want to be heard. I *happen* also to consider most issues in religious terms. But, for me, there is very little connection between my religious values and the publicly held religious values. The religious nature of the conversation rarely serves as a connection.

13. See Schneiders, "Does The Bible Have a Postmodern Message?," in F. Burnham, ed., Postmodern Theology: Christian Faith in a Pluralist World 56, 64–65 (1989):

> [There are] two problems: the ideological *use* of Scripture, which is, if you will, an exterior problem; and the ideological *content* of Scripture, which is intrinsic to the text.
>
> The question of the *use* of Scripture for purposes of oppression is being focused in the third-world struggle of the poor for liberation from domination by the rich and for participation in the societies and cultures which have been, for so long, controlled by the economically powerful for their own advantage. The struggle involves wresting the sacred text from those who have used it to legitimate their oppressive regimes and strategies and delivering it into the hands of the oppressed as a resource for liberation. . . . The problem of the ideological use of Scripture is soluble and is slowly being solved.
>
> The second problem . . . , that of the ideological *content* of Scripture, is much more complicated. It is being focused in the struggle of women for liberation from patriarchal oppression in family, society, and church, and in the struggle of feminists, both men and women, to destroy the patriarchal ideology which grounds not only sexism but racism, classism, clericalism, and all the other forms of dualistic hierarchy in which the powerful dominate the weak in the name of God. Here the problem is not that Scripture has been *used* to legitimate oppression (although this is a continuing problem) but that the Bible itself is both a product and a producer of oppression, that some of its *content* is oppressive.

Schneiders' elaboration of the problem and her overview of the various responses of women (especially feminist theologians) and others to it (id. at 63–71) is excellent. (Schneiders is a feminist Christian theologian.) For a rich collection of feminist spiritual writings, see J. Plaskow & C. Christ, ed., Weaving the Visions: New Patterns in Feminist Spirituality (1989). Another good collection is A. Loades, ed., Feminist Theology: A Reader (1990). For a sensitive discussion of why feminist thought and (some) theological/spiritual thought can enrich one another, see Colker, "Feminism, Theology, and Abortion: Toward Love, Compassion, and Wisdom," 77 California L. Rev. 1011 (1989).

14. See chapter 7, note 27.

15. H. Putnam, The Many Faces of Realism 60–61 (1987).

16. See chapter 5, note 57 and accompanying text.

17. See M. Perry, Morality, Politics and Law, ch. 5: "Breaking Law: The Problem of Conscientious Disobedience" (1988).

18. To forestall misunderstanding, let me emphasize:

1. *Agape* does not romanticize the Other. To the contrary, *agape* sees the Other—in all her fallenness and even perversity—very clearly indeed. See G. Tinder, The Political Meaning of Christianity 43–44 (1990).

2. *Agape* does not deny one's Self. See G. Hallett, Christian Neighbor-Love (1989).

3. An act of love can be fundamentally misguided (premised on a mistake, etc.). Therefore, even though it may be an act of love, an exercise of political power can be fundamentally misguided—which is one reason why love should inhibit as well as inspire the exercise of political power.

Index